WE CAN BE
HEROES

ALSO BY PAUL BURSTON

Fiction

The Closer I Get
The Black Path
The Gay Divorcee
Lovers & Losers
Star People
Shameless

Non-Fiction

Queen's Country
A Queer Romance
Gutterheart
What Are You Looking At?

WE CAN BE HEROES

A SURVIVOR'S STORY

PAUL BURSTON

Little
a

Published by Little A, Seattle

www.apub.com

Amazon, the Amazon logo, and Little A are trademarks of Amazon.com, Inc.,
or its affiliates.

ISBN-13: 9781662501050
ISBN-10: 1662501056

Cover design by James Jones

Cover photography and photos on page 151 by Gordon Rainsford

Printed in the United States of America

*In loving memory of Vaughan Michael Williams,
Brian Kennedy, Michael Griffiths, Georg
Osterman, Derek Jarman and Spud Jones – not
forgetting Robin, Martyn, Colin, Hugo, John and
all the others who died far too soon. Rest in power.
And to survivors everywhere. I see you.*

'Every story needs a hero' – advice traditionally given to writers

Prologue:
Heaven Loves Ya

The first time I went to Heaven I never made it through the hallowed doors. I stood outside, chain-smoking furiously, furtively watching the men queuing to get in, looking for someone, anyone, who looked vaguely like me.

It was March 1985. I was nineteen years old, new to London, and a stranger to the gay world I'd only ever glimpsed in pop videos or read about in newspapers. I'd never been to a gay club or even a gay bar before. I didn't have any gay friends. I had no idea there were such things as gay helplines or gay youth groups. So I stood outside Heaven feeling much as I'd felt for most of my young life – isolated and alone.

Years of emotional insecurity, internalised homophobia and sexual repression had brought me to this point. I'd survived a childhood marred by abuse and school bullying. I'd entertained thoughts of suicide and had very nearly drowned. But none of that mattered any more. I'd escaped. I'd left my small town in South Wales and moved to London. Now, finally, I was on the cusp of a new life, a new beginning. A world of possibilities waited for me beyond those doors. All I had to do was step across the threshold.

I couldn't do it. I was still a teenager, and a tribal one at that. I'd been a Bowie boy, a post-punk, a New Romantic and an almost-goth. What I hadn't been, at least until now, was an out gay man. I'd come to Heaven looking for my tribe, and so far I was failing miserably. On that night in March 1985, I wore heavy eye make-up and had spiky, backcombed hair. I looked like the love child of Robert Smith of The Cure and Ian McCulloch of Echo & the Bunnymen. Everyone else queuing for the club looked more like members of the Village People – or so it seemed to me at the time. I desperately wanted to belong but these were not my people. I stood there for over an hour before finally admitting defeat, hot-footing it across Hungerford Bridge to Waterloo and catching the last train home.

Fast-forward a few weeks. Here I am again, hovering on the corner of Villiers Street with a cigarette pinched between my fingers, watching the boys go by. I'm about to venture underneath the arches and approach the familiar neon sign marking the entrance to the most famous gay club in Europe, if not the world. It's another Saturday night – my third in a row. My previous two visits ended before they even began, and I'm determined that this time I won't bottle it at the last minute. Steeling myself, I stub out my cigarette, join the queue and descend the stairs. As I pay the entrance fee and take my first step into this brave new world, a man swishes past screaming, 'So many men, so little time!' – the title of a popular gay dance track at the time. Saturday nights are men-only and there really are so many of them – hundreds of sweaty men, all on the pull. My eyes are drawn to the fan dancers with their bare chests, porn-star moustaches, and bandanas. My nose prickles at the unfamiliar, overwhelming smell of amyl nitrate. This world is like nothing I've ever experienced before. It's exhilarating and intimidating in equal measure. I'm terrified that someone might talk to me – and equally terrified that nobody will.

Standing at the edge of the dance floor with my back pressed firmly against the wall, the teenage taunts echo in my ears: 'Backs to the wall, boys!' 'Burston, you fucking poof!'

This is nothing like the nightclubs I frequented during my misspent youth in South Wales, where DJs talked over Top 40 tunes and my friends and I took our lives in our hands by wearing eyeliner. There are no cheesy DJs here and few hints of androgyny. The Heaven look is hyper-masculine and all-American. Tight white vests cling to gym-honed torsos. Perfect teeth glow under ultra-violet lights. Muscular arms reach towards the ceiling, hit by the laser beams mentioned on 'Relax' by Frankie Goes To Hollywood, the video for which was filmed in this very club. High above me is the iron walkway where David Bowie and Catherine Deneuve stalk their prey in the opening scene of Tony Scott's glossy vampire thriller *The Hunger*, while below them the goth band Bauhaus perform 'Bela Lugosi's Dead'.

There are no goth anthems playing tonight. The music is unfamiliar but undeniably infectious – that genre of American gay disco known as Hi-NRG, which will soon mutate into Eurodisco and influence everyone from New Order and Pet Shop Boys to Stock Aitken Waterman. One of the few tracks I recognise is the current Number One single in the UK, a song that cuts across all sexual boundaries and fills dance floors across the country – 'You Spin Me Round (Like A Record)' by Dead Or Alive.

Nobody spins me round. I feel like one of the girls at the school disco, waiting to be asked to dance, waiting to be chosen. But nobody asks me to dance. Nobody chooses me. I stand rooted to the same spot for hours, afraid to make eye contact with anyone, only vacating my space in order to venture to the bar or go to the toilet, where the groans of pleasure from the stalls fuel my already feverish imagination. I leave the club exactly as I arrived – friendless and alone.

But as I wait for the night bus in Trafalgar Square, I feel something I haven't felt before. It isn't just pride in myself for having finally conquered my fears and taken the first step on a journey of self-discovery. It's a sense of belonging. I know I'll be back – and next time, I won't just stand on the sidelines. I'll throw myself right into the thick of things.

Chapter 1:
Smalltown Boy

I was born five weeks premature to a woman who wasn't ready to be a mother.

I don't blame her. My parents' marriage wasn't a happy one. She was only nineteen when they first met, and training to be a nurse. Even before the wedding, the warning signs were there. My father had been engaged once before. His previous fiancée had broken off the engagement.

Bridgend in South Wales is a small town, so it's hardly surprising that one night the two young women crossed paths. My father's ex warned my mother, 'You don't know what you're marrying!'

It didn't take her long to find out.

There are gaps in my knowledge of my family history. My mother has never been one for dwelling on the past. What were those first few years of marriage like for her? Was there a particular incident that finally tipped her over the edge? I don't know. But considering the societal pressures of the time, it can't have been easy for her to do what she did next.

Still relatively newly wed, my mother packed her bags, left the marital home and fled to York, where her father lived when he wasn't serving at sea with the merchant navy. She began divorce proceedings. Then she discovered she was pregnant. My mother doesn't talk much about the circumstances surrounding my birth. I do know that she considered having an abortion. This was revealed to me one Christmas when we'd all had too much to drink. I also know that it would have been extremely difficult for her to have had an abortion in 1965. The Abortion Act wasn't passed until 1967.

In any case, she changed her mind, gave birth to me and found it difficult to bond. These days she would probably be diagnosed as suffering from postnatal depression, though for many years any mention of mental illness was met with a derisory snort. 'Depressed?' she'd say, rolling her eyes. 'I wish I had time to be depressed!'

Joking aside, my mother didn't have much time for anything, least of all herself. She was a single mother now.

Mum's father, my grandad, was an infrequent but much-loved presence in my life – and made me dream of a world of possibilities beyond the small town where I grew up. He'd stowed away at the age of sixteen, and was eventually awarded a medal for his military service. When he wasn't in uniform, he was a snappy dresser, favouring sharp suits, hats and silk ties. Mum often says I remind her of him. He died when I was in my mid-twenties. His funeral was held in Yorkshire, and later we scattered his ashes in the sea at Barry Docks. It was a blustery day, and a sudden gust of wind blew his remains back into the faces of his grieving relatives. Someone joked, 'We've all got a bit of Grandad in us now.' I like to think I do.

I never met my grandmother. Growing up, whenever I asked about her, I was told she'd died before I was born. The reality is that she walked out on her family when my mother was still a child, though I only discovered this fairly recently. For my mum, the emotional wounds inflicted during childhood were hard to bear and best avoided. This is one of the many lessons I learned from her – and am still unlearning.

I never really stopped to question why I was born in York but raised in South Wales, until I was sixteen and applied for my first passport. There it was, handwritten in black ink on my birth certificate. Place of birth – York. When I asked my mum, she got upset. Any mention of my father was a trigger for her. Over the years, I've heard varying accounts of what happened immediately after I was born. In one version of events, she wrote to tell him he had a son. In another, someone tipped him off and he drove to York to bring her home. His name appears on my birth certificate, along with his occupation at the time – a steel mill operator. There's no mention of my mother's occupation. Together, they decided to give the marriage another go – 'for the good of the child', as people told themselves back then.

But it wasn't good for the child. It wasn't good at all. As far as I was concerned, it was the worst decision she could have made.

In 1965, the year I was born, *Round The Horne* was first broadcast on BBC Radio, and listeners were introduced to Hugh Paddick and Kenneth Williams as Julian and Sandy, a couple of camp characters who spoke in the gay slang known as Polari. Male homosexuality was still illegal, and punishable with a prison sentence. I was approaching my second birthday when the Sexual Offences Act of 1967 partially decriminalised sex between consenting adult males over the age of twenty-one. I was five years old when the Gay Liberation Front was founded in the UK; six when London held its first Gay Pride march and David Bowie first appeared as Ziggy Stardust on *Top Of The Pops*, dressed in a multicoloured jumpsuit, plastered in make-up and singing 'Starman'.

I say all this because I knew I was different from a very young age. The other boys did, too. In my first year at junior school, I became attached to a boy called Andrew. Too attached, some people thought. My parents were summoned to the school; a complaint had been made. Nothing was ever explained to me, but suddenly Andrew and I were no longer seated together in class. He avoided me in the playground and started hanging around with other boys.

I started hanging around with girls. They found me amusing, and didn't mind that I wasn't good at rugby and didn't display the macho aggression boys in Bridgend were encouraged to develop from a young age. At junior school I was called a poof and a sissy long before I knew what those words meant – though I knew they weren't something to aspire to. And it didn't stop there.

'Can you beat him up?' a local lad asked my friend Mark one day when we were playing together by the river.

'Anyone can beat him up,' my so-called friend replied.

I remember feeling deeply betrayed by this, but Mark was right. Anyone could beat me up – and frequently did. Whenever someone punched me, I froze. I was the boy who didn't fight back. Not then. Not like that.

I was bullied a lot at school. But I was just as fearful at home.

'I'll say one thing for your father,' my mother used to tell me. 'He never came home drunk.'

This may well be true. But it's hardly a glowing endorsement of his qualities as a father that the only accolade she could think of was his sobriety.

In 1971, Philip Larkin published his famous poem about the ways in which your mum and dad fuck you up. But in my case, my father fucked me up far more. I always knew my mother loved me. My father was ambivalent at best – and he was rarely at his best where I was concerned. There are no photos of me smiling as a small child – no moments of unguarded joy captured for posterity in picture frames or family albums. In each one I look sullen, wary, wounded.

Children are innately egocentric and have a tendency to blame themselves for what goes on around them. Did I do something wrong? Was it something I said? Or was I just not lovable enough? I never understood why my father treated me the way he did. I wasn't a difficult child. I never caused any trouble. I kept my head down and did well at school.

Sometimes my mother would accuse me of 'acting up' – something I always vigorously denied, though in years to come those words would take on a whole new meaning. Looking back, I think I was probably 'acting out' – but we didn't have the vocabulary for this then, at least not in working-class South Wales. Nobody ever questioned why I behaved the way I did – possibly because they didn't want to know. Some things were better left unsaid.

My mother's friend and former neighbour 'Auntie' Alma remembers me as a tongue-tied, nervous little boy who played with her son Phillip, always said 'please' and 'thank you', and shook with fear whenever my father came to collect me. Whenever there was trouble at home, it was Alma I ran to for help. There was never any love lost between Alma and my father. I think this is one reason why I've always felt so close to her.

My sister Debbie was born when I was two. By the time I was seven, my mother had returned to work part-time as a night nurse at the local hospital. She found her calling on what was then called the prem unit, caring for premature babies. While she worked, my younger sister and I would be left alone in the house with my father. These were the nights I dreaded the most.

I should say now that my sister's memories of this period are very different to mine. As she once told me, she was the child our parents planned in order to try to save their marriage. I was the child who wasn't planned and came along when they were on the verge of getting divorced. Our experiences were bound to be different. According to her, he was a stern but ultimately loving father. In my case, he was anything but.

My mother used to tell me, 'You were a nervous wreck until your father left.' For years, I wanted him gone from my life so desperately that I regularly wished him dead. But then my father bestowed upon me the one act of kindness he has ever shown me in my entire life. He walked out and moved in with another woman. It wasn't easy for my poor mum, though I was far too young to appreciate this at the time. All that mattered to me was that he'd gone.

Word soon spread around school that Paul Burston came from a broken home. Nothing could have been further from the truth. The day my father left was the day my home was fixed.

I've always loved reading and I've always written stories. At junior school I wrote adventure stories about a boy called Jim, heavily influenced by whatever I watched on TV that week – *Bonanza*, *Star Trek*, *Doctor Who*. On more than one occasion, my intrepid hero came face-to-face with a Dalek! It was life, Jim, but not as I knew it. My friend Caroline would illustrate the stories and our proud headmaster would insist that I read them aloud during morning assembly. At break time, boys would corner me in the playground and beat me up for showing off. But they didn't beat it out of me.

At home I was obsessed with marionettes, and would stage elaborate puppet shows in which Pinky and Perky would be abducted by a wicked witch and rescued by the unlikely duo of Disney's Goofy and Ermintrude the cow from *The Magic Roundabout*. Looking back, I think this was the start of my love of theatre – though typically I liked to be in complete control. I was the puppetmaster, after all. People who feel powerless in certain situations tend to make up for it in other ways.

To this day I can't picture my childhood bedroom. There aren't any photos in existence – or if there are, I've never seen them. I know there must have been marionettes hanging from a shelf. My mother tells me there were posters of birds and dinosaurs – childhood obsessions I now share with my youngest nephew. I remember the bed sheets, which were scratchy and made of nylon. But I can't recall the colour of the walls or the layout of the room at all. I don't know where the bed was positioned, though I do remember hiding under it.

For a long time, my memories of this period were always fractured. It would be decades before I understood why, and was able to find the missing pieces and fit them together.

Chapter 2:
Teenage Wildlife

I was nine years old when *The Naked Civil Servant* was first shown on British television. Based on the cult memoir by Quentin Crisp, the film starred John Hurt as the flamboyant, effeminate homosexual who braved the streets of London, 'blind with mascara and dumb with lipstick', searching for his Great Dark Man.

My mother was working that night and I watched the film with my stepfather. I'd only known him for a year or so at this point, but long enough to know that he was nothing like my father. My stepdad is kind, caring, likes a drink (he's Irish and very fond of whiskey) but rarely loses his temper. He's never hit me, hurt me or given me any reason to fear him.

We sat watching the film – him in his armchair, me perched on the sofa but wishing I could hide behind it. Afterwards, he turned to me and said, 'Your mother's worried you'll turn out like that.'

She wasn't the only one. These days I admire Crisp for the trailblazer he was. This was a man who grew up in the wake of the Wilde trial, when public displays of male homosexuality carried a prison sentence. But at the tender age of nine, I was far too young to appreciate this. He represented everything I was terrified of becoming. It wasn't just the flagrant effeminacy but the constant rejection – by his family, by his peers, by the people he encountered on the street. The man who stamped on his foot in the bus queue. The gangs who hounded him at night.

There are plenty of gay men alive today who fear rejection from their parents (and from each other – anti-femme sentiment still runs high within the gay male community). The difference back then was that we had such little visibility, so few people to look up to, so few stories to call our own. Crisp's was the first gay life story I was ever aware of, and it wasn't a very happy one.

I've often wondered how different my adolescence might have been, had I known of the existence of other gay lives, other gay stories. I grew up at a time when gay men only ever appeared as figures of fun on TV or as the subject of scandal in the tabloids my stepdad read at the breakfast table. There were no YA novels aimed at younger gay readers when I was a boy. There were no gay characters on television soap operas, no *Beautiful Thing*, no *Queer As Folk*, no *Glee*. We were never the heroes of our own stories.

Stories are important. They help shape who we are and how we see ourselves. With no positive gay influence to guide me, I turned inwards. When I was bullied at school, I kept it to myself. I didn't dare tell my parents. I was afraid they'd reject me. The sense of shame grew. The feeling of isolation was overwhelming. I became a stranger to myself and to those closest to me. I think many gay children know this feeling all too well.

By the time I reached my early teens I had a few friends who were misfits like me, but whose friendship wouldn't have stood the test of my disclosure – or at least that's how it felt to me at the time. Rafik joined my junior school when he and his Ugandan Asian parents were expelled by Idi Amin and resettled in South Wales. The same kids who called me 'poof' called him 'Sambo', but Rafik was made of sterner stuff and could take care of himself. I loved going to his house after school and eating food I'd never tried before – spicy curries that set my taste buds on fire. We're still in touch today.

I also became friendly with two brothers who lived just up the road. Jinan and Mazin had a Welsh mother called Jenny and an Iraqi father called Kamal. Their parents were university-educated, left-wing and the first activists I ever met. They took me on CND marches, much to the amusement of my Tory-voting parents.

Jinan and I were in the same year at school and would often walk home together – either down the dual carriageway or through the centre of town with its multitude of shoe shops, an indoor market, and the shopping arcade known as The Rhiw, which housed the local branches of Boots and WHSmith. Jinan was far sportier than me and could handle himself in a fight. But we were both susceptible to peer pressure, which is what led to us getting caught shoplifting from Boots. We only did it for a dare – I stole a tube of glue.

I thought I'd got away with it until a female store detective in horn-rimmed spectacles grabbed me firmly by the shoulder on the pavement outside. 'You run, sonny, and I'll pull your bloody arm off!'

The police arrived and asked if we were glue sniffers. I didn't know what they meant. They phoned our parents and put us in the police cells.

When my mum came to collect me, I laughed nervously.

'It's not funny, Paul!' she snapped. 'I've never felt so ashamed!'

Jinan was remarkably handsome and I'd be lying if I said I never fancied him. But my biggest teenage crush was on a boy called Billy. Unlike me, Jinan played rugby and football. He was a member of the local recreation centre and introduced me to the wonders of weight training. Billy was a regular at the gym. He also did ridiculous things like running for miles with a bin liner under his sweatshirt to help burn off body fat. Had it existed back then, he'd have been a contender for the cover of *Men's Health* magazine. He had the kind of lean, muscular physique I could only dream of – and frequently did.

At fourteen, I joined a local cycling team known as the Ogmore Valley Wheelers. Pretty soon, the changes in my body started to draw attention.

'Haven't you got big legs, Paul?' my stepdad's friend Tom would say, squeezing my thigh through the thin fabric of my school uniform trousers.

As soon as he left, my mum would nudge my stepdad, roll her eyes and laugh. 'I think he fancies you, Paul!'

Tom wasn't his real name. He was a local businessman who put a lot of work my stepdad's way. He was married and lived in a large, detached house in a posh part of town. I've changed his name because one day his wife came home and found him hanging in the hallway. The death was recorded as a suicide.

'Why would he do that?' my mother asked, aghast.

I had a pretty good idea, but said nothing.

I'd already given suicide a lot of thought. By the age of fourteen, I knew for certain that I was gay – and desperately didn't want to be. By this point the bullying had got so bad that there were days when I was afraid to go to school. I skipped classes and improvised homemade explosive devices from pieces of scrap steel drilled out at metalwork class, packed with gunpowder from the shotgun cartridges my stepdad kept hidden away in his gun box. I built bonfires and waited for the intense heat to ignite the powder and cause the metal to explode. To this day I have a small scar on my right hand from a flying piece of shrapnel. In my darker moments, I fantasised that these makeshift explosives could somehow be deployed against the boys who bullied me. I'd build a bonfire, lure them to it and *bang!* Job done.

But mostly I thought about killing myself. I toyed with the idea of slitting my wrists. I stole one of my stepdad's razorblades and had everything all planned out. There are certain skills you acquire as a horny teenage boy, certain discoveries you learn to put to good use. One of these is that, if you're right-handed, using your left hand to pleasure yourself can intensify the experience. The hand feels less like your own. So it was my left hand I used to hold the razor blade and press it against my right wrist, hoping the sense of disassociation would somehow make the task easier.

But it was no use. I couldn't go through with it. The thought of all that blood put me off. I had the knowledge but not the courage. My mother always said I had a low pain threshold. She didn't know the half of it.

I'd heard that painkillers could offer an easier way out, if taken in sufficient quantities. My mum kept packets of paracetamol in the kitchen cupboard, so I'd help myself to two or three at a time and stockpile them in my bedside drawer.

I'd already discovered the numbing effects of alcohol. The first time I got seriously drunk was at morning assembly. I was twelve years old and had arrived at school with an innocent-looking pop bottle filled with a cocktail made from the contents of my parents' drinks cabinet – Harveys Bristol Cream, Teacher's Whisky, Gordon's Gin and Schweppes Bitter Lemon. I remember swaying in time to 'The Lord's My Shepherd' before falling over. My friend Karen covered for me, telling a concerned teacher I had a stomach bug. I was sent home, and spent the day hiding out in the local playing fields.

By the time I was fourteen, my taste in alcohol was a little more refined. I planned to wash the paracetamol down with neat vodka. I'd also discovered pop music, the importance of which can't be overstated. Because, when I was fourteen, David Bowie saved my life.

Years earlier, I'd had a friend at junior school called Richard who often invited me back to his house for tea. Richard had a teenage brother who wore crotch-hugging purple flares and played us songs about astronauts, aliens and the all-important question of whether there was life on Mars. I was probably too fixated on Richard's brother's crotch to pay much attention to the music, so when I first saw David Bowie's video for 'Boys Keep Swinging' on *Top Of The Pops*, I didn't associate him with the songs I'd listened to all those years ago.

In a subversive send-up of gender roles, the video showed Bowie performing in a swaggering, alpha-male style, with three female backing singers – each played by him in drag. To drive the point home, at the end of the song two of the backing singers sashayed down the catwalk, tore off their wig and smeared their lipstick with the back of their hand. The third looked like an ageing Marlene Dietrich and simply blew a kiss to the camera.

Watching from my parents' sofa, I was freaked out – and strangely fascinated.

Not everyone was as impressed as me. Usually when an artist appeared on *Top Of The Pops*, the exposure sent their single racing up the charts. After the video for 'Boys Keep Swinging' was shown, the song dropped four places.

1979 was the year I discovered Blondie and pinned an enormous poster of Debbie Harry on my bedroom wall – much to the relief of my mother, who chose to see this as a sign of burgeoning heterosexual yearnings. By the end of that year I'd turned fourteen, and the poster of Debbie Harry was replaced with one of David Bowie during his Thin White Duke phase – hollow-cheeked, pasty-skinned, orange hair slicked back, cigarette dangling from his lips.

'I don't know what you see in him,' my mother remarked. 'He looks ill!'

In retrospect, he did – and he was. The photo was taken at the height of Bowie's cocaine addiction. But what I saw in him was an image of queerness I'd never seen before. Famously bisexual, often androgynous, and so hip it hurt, Bowie didn't just say that being queer was okay. He said it was something to aspire to. To a self-loathing, deeply closeted fourteen-year-old, that was a powerful statement. Here, finally, was the role model I'd been searching for all my life.

I bought every Bowie album I could find, pored over every lyric. I listened to the Ziggy Stardust album 'at maximum volume', as instructed on the record sleeve. At the end of 'Rock 'n' Roll Suicide', when the song builds to a crescendo and he assures his listeners that they're not alone, it was as if he were throwing me a lifeline. I read every book and magazine article, studied every photograph for inspiration. Here he was in the famous 'man dress' designed by Mr Fish, his long locks styled like Lauren Bacall. Here he was as Ziggy Stardust, telling *Melody Maker* he was gay and always had been, even when he was plain old David Jones. Here he was as the Thin White Duke in a crisp white shirt and black waistcoat, his hair swept back like a silent film star's. Each reinvention told me that I could be anything or anyone I wanted to be. I became a Bowie fan, a tacky thing, one of the New Wave boys he sang about on 'Teenage Wildlife', pushing my luck in plastic pegged trousers and suede winklepickers. I grew my hair and wore silver bracelets, prompting my friend Dean's mum to ask me, 'Are you a boy or a girl?'

This rapid onset of sexual ambiguity put my mother in a whirl.

'If you pierce your ears, I'll throw you out,' she warned me.

I pierced my ears.

'If you dye your hair, I'll throw you out,' she said.

I dyed my hair jet black. It took her a week to notice.

I wasn't the only Bowie fan living under my parents' roof. My sister Jac was born when I was twelve. By the time I was fifteen, she'd already shown herself to be a force to be reckoned with. When Jac was only three years old, the family health visitor had come to the house to test her communication skills. She was surprised that my little sister didn't seem to know any nursery rhymes.

'She's not very responsive, is she?' the woman said.

'Ask her to sing you a song instead,' Mum replied. 'She likes listening to pop music.'

Moments later, Jac recited the chorus to 'Ashes To Ashes', the one where David Bowie announces that Major Tom is a junky.

My mother didn't know where to look. I'm surprised she didn't receive a visit from social services. But I knew then that I had a friend for life.

From the age of sixteen onwards, I changed my hair colour regularly – blond, brunette, the inevitable flaming Bowie orange.

Then I began experimenting with make-up – eyeliner, eyeshadow, a bit of blush. I drew the line at lipstick, but to all intents and purposes I didn't look so very different to the flamboyant image of Quentin Crisp that had so disturbed me at the age of nine.

With one notable exception. I still vigorously denied the fact that I was homosexual.

I'd always had girlfriends. At twelve I was madly in love with a girl called Lorraine. At sixteen I went on a school trip to Cambridge and lost my virginity to a girl called Nicola. The sex wasn't terrible, but it wasn't what I wanted, either. To be honest, I didn't know what I wanted – or what gay men actually did. For years I thought that 'bumming' was when two men rubbed their backsides together.

I had devastating crushes on boys – Billy, mostly, but also a teenage surfer with a curly mullet and a nickname so ridiculous it doesn't bear repeating. One night at a house party he dared me and my girlfriend to join him and his girlfriend in a kissing game.

First he kissed my girlfriend. Then I kissed his. Then the two girls kissed each other. Then he kissed me.

I still recall the charge of electricity when I felt his mouth on mine. It was like nothing I'd ever experienced before.

'I've been dying to do that for ages,' he said with a grin.

I have a photo of us, taken a few weeks later at a local nightclub. I'm dressed in a Marilyn Monroe T-shirt and peaked cap, with an orange quiff and panda eye make-up. He's wearing a checked shirt and has his head resting on my shoulder.

Shortly afterwards, at another house party, I made a drunken pass at him and he recoiled in horror. 'Don't be disgusting!'

And that was the extent of my homosexual experience for the next three years. I repressed my sexuality and channelled all my energy into my escape plan. I needed to get as far away from home as possible. The only way to do that was through higher education, which meant staying on for A levels and applying to go to university. Only then would I have the opportunity to be myself.

Then, in 1983, an extraordinary thing happened – David Bowie announced a world tour, his first in five years. It didn't matter to me that *Let's Dance* wasn't a patch on previous albums. This was a chance to see my personal saviour live on stage! I applied for tickets, and in July my friend Robin drove us all the way from Bridgend to Milton Keynes Bowl for the Serious Moonlight tour. I wore an Aladdin Sane kimono-style outfit and matching orange mullet, a mere ten years out of date. Bowie sported a selection of pastel suits and a scrambled-egg hairdo. Most of the audience wouldn't have looked out of place at a Phil Collins concert. I remember feeling distinctly underwhelmed. This wasn't the Bowie I'd worshipped from afar. But by the end of the night, his sheer showmanship had won me over.

Driving home on the motorway afterwards, Robin fell asleep at the wheel and we very nearly crashed. Imagine the irony if we had. David Bowie saved my life – and seeing him live killed me. Instead he remained a guiding light, just as he was for so many of the pop artists who dominated the charts during my late teens – everyone from Boy George and Annie Lennox to The Smiths and Echo & the Bunnymen. When Boy George first appeared with Culture Club on *Top Of The Pops*, the reaction was similar to the time Bowie sang 'Starman'. Alienated teenage outsiders loved every second. Their parents were bemused, bothered or bewildered.

'I suppose that's a man as well, is it?' my stepdad said, gesturing at the TV.

'Of course not!' I replied, with the absolute confidence in one's beliefs only a teenager can muster. 'Nobody goes that far!' Shows you how much I knew.

George was always quick to acknowledge Bowie's influence. Others were keen to distance themselves from his current, less arty, more mainstream incarnation. When lead singer Ian McCulloch of Echo & the Bunnymen slated our hero's latest album, tour and hairstyle in the pages of teen music magazine *Smash Hits*, there was such an outcry from devoted Bowie fans that he was forced to defend himself by reaffirming his love of earlier albums and naming his favourite track.

The song he chose was 'Fantastic Voyage'. The opener to Bowie's often underrated *Lodger* album, the track is considered his first down-to-earth, socially conscious protest song – a precursor to his collaboration with Queen on the hit single 'Under Pressure'. On 'Fantastic Voyage', Bowie sings about the threat of nuclear war and the challenges of living in a world full of violence and jingoism. He also sings repeatedly about depression. Simply by being there, he helped lift me out of mine.

Chapter 3:
Nowhere Fast

In my final year at school, I was elected pupil governor. This was no indication of my popularity. It simply meant that I was deemed to be the person most likely to irritate our headmaster. I've often had problems with male authority figures. It doesn't take a genius to work out why.

The role of pupil governor was to represent the student body at meetings of the school board, voting on issues affecting the day-to-day running of the school. I was hardly representative. I may have been academic but my effeminate appearance was unusual, to say the least.

The school wasn't pleased and insisted on a second vote. The student body voted again – and I won by an even greater margin.

Brynteg was what some would call a bog-standard comprehensive. The headmaster had other ideas, insisting that senior staff wear academic gowns for morning assembly and strut around the quadrangle looking like characters from *Tom Brown's School Days*. It was all very in keeping with the return to Victorian values espoused by Margaret Thatcher, whom I've no doubt the headmaster voted for in the previous year's general election. And now he had to sit on the board of governors with a teenage boy who dyed his hair bright orange and wore make-up and earrings. We agreed that I'd tone it down a bit for the board, though I refused to let my hair go back to its natural colour.

Being pupil governor gave me my first taste of power, and a perverse kind of pleasure. I wasn't yet out but my appearance alone was queerly disruptive. It certainly rubbed some people up the wrong way. I had a teacher – I'll call him Mr Wheeler – who never tired of reminding us of how intellectually superior he was. He boasted endlessly about his MA, as if he were the first man in the history of the world to ever earn such a distinction. He had his clear favourites and I certainly wasn't one of them.

Mr Wheeler, of course, wasted no opportunity to get his academic drag on. He also liked to stand at the blackboard, playing pocket billiards or stroking his pointy beard and quoting Shakespeare.

'A rose by any other name,' he declared once, apropos of nothing.

I knew my Shakespeare and rose to the challenge. 'Would smell as sweet, so Romeo would were he not Romeo called.'

Mr Wheeler wasn't best pleased. 'Thank you, Mr Burston, for that pointless interruption.'

'I thought you were testing us on our Shakespeare,' I replied, innocently. 'Though I'm not sure what it has to do with today's lesson.'

Yes, I was a gobby teenager. According to my mother, this was nothing new. I'd been answering back since I was a small boy. 'You always had to ask why. Why this. Why that. Because I say so, that's why!'

'But that isn't logical,' I'd reply, and she'd fly into a temper.

'Why does everything have to be logical with you?'

'Because I'm a rational human being. Logic and reason are the bedrock of a civilised society. To deny them is a form of madness.'

Like many alienated outsiders, I was already a fan of The Smiths. The song titles seemed to sum up my life – 'Barbarism Begins at Home', 'Suffer Little Children', 'Nowhere Fast', 'Heaven Knows I'm Miserable Now'. I used humour as a defence weapon and adopted Morrissey's withering tone whenever possible, particularly when talking down to my mother.

Frankly, Mr Shankly, I'd have slapped me.

For my remaining A levels I took English Literature, Use of English and Religious Studies. No, I hadn't experienced a sudden Pauline conversion on the road to Damascus. I simply liked the teacher. Moira Jones was Brynteg's answer to Debbie Harry. She had blonde hair with black roots and wore smoky eye make-up. She had a cat named Owl, because her husband once asked for an owl for his birthday and she bought him a cat instead. That's the kind of woman Mrs Jones was – free-spirited and full of mischief.

She had an equally irreverent approach to her chosen subject. One afternoon we were studying John's Gospel and reached the verse where Jesus says that a prophet has no honour in his own country.

'Just like Shirley Bassey,' said Mrs Jones. 'Her name's dirt in Tiger Bay.'

Much as I'd always loved English, and was encouraged by my teachers Miss Price and Mr Archard, it was Religious Studies I enjoyed the most. I became obsessed with Christianity, though I didn't always excel at the subject. On one of my essays, Mrs Jones wrote, 'You haven't read sufficiently widely for this and have missed out some key points. On the other hand, you write well, clearly and in a concise manner. You will go far, my lad!'

I prayed that she was right. The further, the better.

I wasn't bullied as much in the sixth from, mainly because most of the bullies weren't particularly bright and had left school at sixteen. The few who stayed on for A levels became quite protective of me. I may have been a 'fucking tog' (that's local parlance for 'poof' or 'pansy') but I was their fucking tog, and they seemed to enjoy the fact that I irritated certain teachers as much as they did.

The highlight of my year as pupil governor was when Mr Wheeler applied for the post of head of middle school. Usually I sat in on job interviews. In this case I didn't think it would be appropriate, so I asked to see the headmaster and told him so.

Shortly afterwards, Mr Wheeler went to the headmaster's office to lodge a formal complaint about me being on the interview panel.

The headmaster informed him that I'd already shown great maturity by offering to withdraw. The interview went ahead without me. Mr Wheeler didn't get the job.

Years later, I revisited Brynteg to write a piece about teenage boys falling behind at school, for the *Sunday Times Magazine*. I was shown to the staffroom. Mr Wheeler was there. He still hadn't been promoted.

'Writing for the *Sunday Times*?' he sniffed. 'I suppose someone has to.'

'Still here?' I replied. 'I suppose someone has to be.'

For my eighteenth birthday, my friends David, Jon and Steven took me out, got me drunk, held me down and shaved off my eyebrows with a disposable razor. This wasn't in honour of David Bowie, who shaved off his eyebrows for Aladdin Sane in 1973, went to America and didn't grow them back again until he returned as the Thin White Duke in 1976. It was just a silly ritual we had. Someone turned eighteen, you shaved off their eyebrows – and sometimes their eyelashes. Looking back, I'm amazed we all escaped without being blinded – or at least suffering an eye injury.

That last year in school was very boozy. I'd been getting served in pubs since I was fifteen. Alcohol gave me confidence – and you needed a certain amount of Dutch courage to run around a small town in South Wales looking the way I did. But now my drinking was getting heavier and more self-destructive. Several times I passed out at parties and had to be taken home in a taxi, often vomiting in the back seat. My mother was furious and would leave my sick-splattered clothes in a heap on the kitchen floor for me to hand-wash the next day.

Clearly, these were not the actions of a happy, well-adjusted teenager. I didn't drink to be sociable. I drank until I had blackouts. To this day, I don't know what I said or did one drunken night to make a close friend of several years cut off all contact. Did I insult him? Did I make a drunken pass? I've no idea. When I turned up at his house the following morning, he refused to speak to me. I never saw him again.

I tried telling myself that my drinking wasn't unusual. Everyone did it. But they didn't – at least, not to the extent I did. I drank like someone with a death wish.

In time I would discover just how perilously thin the line between life and death can be. But for now I had to rein myself in and focus on my A levels. I had an offer to study English at Loughborough, though why I chose a university with such a heavy emphasis on sport I have no idea. I was trying to escape the land of rugby culture, not rediscover it. Besides, whoever heard of young gay men flocking to Loughborough? London was where it was at – whatever 'it' actually meant. My impression of London was largely drawn from Soft Cell songs, which suggested a city of neon lights and endless sexual opportunity. Naturally, this held a certain appeal.

The school careers adviser, Mr Daniels, recommended that we also apply to a higher-education college or polytechnic, in case we didn't get the grades required for university. So I duly applied to a college in Strawberry Hill on the outskirts of London, which was part of the University of Surrey. This way, I could get in with lower grades and still leave with a university degree.

Maybe it was a result of all the drinking, or maybe I was subconsciously self-sabotaging to avoid becoming the only gay in Loughborough, but I barely scraped through my A levels. I failed to achieve anything like my expected grades, scoring a B and two Es. Not enough to confirm my place at Loughborough. But enough to get me to London.

I nearly didn't get there at all.

I'd been working part-time since my early teens. I had a paper round, and later worked at the newsagent for two hours each morning before school. I also helped my stepdad on various construction jobs, including laying a patio and building an extension for my mum's friend Alma.

That summer I applied for a position as a playgroup leader with the local council. The children I was responsible for were aged between eight and ten. The playgroup was based at another school in the area, which had its own swimming pool. There were plenty of physical activities to keep the kids busy, so they could be returned to their parents at the end of the day, worn out and ready for an early night. I've always enjoyed being around children – I totally dote on my youngest nephew – and these kids were no exception. There was one boy in particular – I'll call him Matthew – who reminded me a lot of myself when I was his age. He was a bit of a loner, quite timid and easily scared. I suspected that he might have had childhood experiences similar to my own.

One day we took the kids swimming. Matthew couldn't swim but desperately wanted to join in with the others, so I volunteered to carry him on my shoulders across the pool. What I didn't know was that the gradient from the shallow end of the pool to the deep end was far steeper than usual – almost a complete drop-off. What I also didn't know was that I was walking dangerously close to the edge. One wrong move and I'd be out of my depth.

I've always been a pretty strong swimmer. As a teenager, it was one of the few forms of physical exercise I actually enjoyed. But it's hard to swim with a weight around your neck. Halfway across the pool, my foot slipped and I went under, swallowing mouthfuls of chlorinated water. Matthew panicked and clung tightly to my head. Thinking this was some kind of game, another child jumped on, and then another, pushing me further under. I could hear their screams as the water pressed against me.

Everything seemed to slow down and speed up at the same time. Then survival instinct kicked in and I lashed out, no longer thinking about anything but my need to breathe. I grappled with the tiny hands locked around my neck and tried to force my way to the surface, but it was impossible. There were too many flailing limbs in the way.

I tried to cry for help and swallowed more water. I remember the sting of chlorine in my nose and throat, the pressure building in my lungs, the panic setting in, the suffocating certainty that I was drowning.

I began to lose consciousness. And it was just like in the movies. My life literally flashed before my eyes. All eighteen years of it.

I can't recall the exact sequence of events that went through my mind that day. But I'm sure they included some of the following:

* The time my Auntie Elsie gave me a puff of her Woodbine cigarette 'so you'll never smoke again'. I was eight years old and not so easily dissuaded.

* My first kiss – with Lorraine, in the back seat of the Embassy cinema, while John Travolta made out with Olivia Newton-John in *Grease*.

* The time I went fishing for minnows in the local river and found a sack containing the body of a dead dog.

* The time I watched my stepsister's fiancé wash the coal dust off his naked body in a tin bath in front of the fire, and knew that the feelings he aroused in me weren't normal.

At some point I blacked out. When I regained consciousness, I was lying by the side of the pool and a young male lifeguard was giving me mouth-to-mouth resuscitation. I responded by coughing up water and a small puddle of vomit.

Technically speaking, it was my second gay kiss – or at least the second time another boy put his lips to mine. And the lifeguard, whose name I never even asked, wasn't disgusted by me but simply smiled and patted me gently on the back.

'You'll be okay,' he said – and somehow I knew I would be.

He'd saved my life and given me hope that, somewhere, there was a place for me. I just had to stay alive long enough to get there.

Chapter 4:
This Charming Man

In September 1984, this smalltown boy left Bridgend with everything he owned in a battered grey suitcase. As teenage adventures go, it wasn't nearly as romantic as my grandad running away to sea. But it was the best I could do. I was on my way to St Mary's College in Strawberry Hill, ostensibly to study English, Drama and Religious Studies, though in reality I was far more interested in exploring my sexuality. I thought I'd chosen well. Strawberry Hill was built by Horace Walpole – politician, writer and man of letters, whose reputation rested on his Gothic novel *The Castle of Otranto* and his fondness for wearing lavender suits. He never married.

With its neo-Gothic architecture and rolling green playing fields, the college could almost be a setting for *Another Country* – the 1984 period drama written by Julian Mitchell, which traded in the same soft-focus homoeroticism as *Brideshead Revisited* and had recently made a star of Rupert Everett. I had quite a crush on Everett, and imagined myself meeting a boy who'd fall for me the way he fell for Cary Elwes in the film.

But my mock-Gothic surroundings only served to mock me. There were no lovelorn, floppy-haired homosexuals at St Mary's

– or, if there were, they hadn't made themselves known to me. I'd planned to come out the moment I arrived, but despite the relative safety of the Drama department, the college as a whole didn't feel all that gay-friendly.

This was partly on account of it being a Catholic college – something I hadn't really considered until I turned up for my first Religious Studies lecture and was greeted by a man in a dog collar – but it was largely due to the abundance of young men studying what was laughingly called Sport Science, who were every bit as boorish as the rugby boys I'd escaped from in South Wales.

The irony of this wasn't lost on me. In fact, it was unavoidable. My room in the Old House hall of residence was on a corridor shared with dozens of rugby boys. They'd arrive back late at night drunk, on one occasion smashing the glass panel above my door and pushing the fire hose through, soaking me in my single bed and laughing like hyenas. Sometimes, they'd drag one of their number into the shower room, strip him naked and attempt to squeeze toothpaste under his foreskin or shave off his pubic hair. And they had the nerve to call me queer.

Amid the general misery of my first term, there was one glimmer of hope. During an English lecture one morning I made a friend called James. He was a fellow Smiths fan and slipped me a note which read, 'Eat me up, you handsome devil.'

James had pillow lips and wore his hair in a quiff like a young Elvis. He lived at home with his parents in New Malden and drove to college each day in his Mini. Though I often stayed over at his house, I never did eat him up. Nothing remotely sexual ever happened between us – and when I finally came out to him months later, he didn't take it too well at first. But for several months we had what would now be called a bromance. All we really shared was a taste in music, though it's fair to say that his taste in music was somewhat homoerotic in nature. James made me mixtapes with titles like *A Gay Assortment of All the Hits and More*, filled with swooning ballads by Marc Almond, David Bowie, Prefab Sprout and The Blow Monkeys.

One night he drove us to the Brixton Academy to see The Smiths' Meat Is Murder tour. The atmosphere was electric. As Morrissey sang 'This Charming Man', James and I were separated in the mosh pit. Struggling to fight my way back to him, I was parted from one of my suede winklepickers. I went one way and my left shoe went the other, never to be seen again. This might well have been a metaphor for our friendship. But for now his flirtatious behaviour fuelled my sexual frustration and made me determined to find a man who'd charm the pants off me.

Some people think that coming out is an event. 'What's your coming-out story?' they ask, as if there can only ever be one.

They're wrong. Ask any LGBTQ+ person and they'll tell you. Coming out isn't a single solitary event but an ongoing process. I don't have one coming-out story but a multitude of them. I've come out many times and in various different contexts – at work, in social settings, each time I book a double room in a hotel or weigh up the risk and decide whether or not to hold my partner's hand in public. I'm still coming out now.

But we all remember the first time we came out – when, where and who to. For me, it was in February 1985, on a frozen beach in South Wales, to a girl named Tracey Hope. It was half-term. I'd gone home to visit my parents and I'd taken Tracey along to show them I was settling in at college and making new friends. She was a little older than me, a second-year drama student, and reminded me of Meryl Streep in *The French Lieutenant's Woman*

– all Pre-Raphaelite locks, soulful eyes and cheekbones like wing mirrors. My parents kept referring to her as my girlfriend and I kept correcting them.

On Sunday morning we were walking on the beach at Southerndown, where I'd spent the previous few summers lusting over various boys while still dating girls and maintaining that I was straight. Now it was the depths of winter and the beach was barely recognisable. The surrounding cliffs were hung with icicles. It looked like a scene from an early '80s album cover – *Porcupine* by Echo & the Bunnymen.

Tracey and I took it in turns posing for photos – her crouching under the ice formations or staring wistfully out to sea; me camping it up with my arms outstretched.

Suddenly she turned to me and asked, 'Paul, are you gay?'

Caught off guard, I replied, 'No! Yes. Maybe.'

Of course I knew the answer, but knowing it and saying it were two very different things. I thought my world would end, when really it was just beginning. I burst into tears and Tracey told me it was going to be okay.

Years later I incorporated this scene into a novel called *The Gay Divorcee*. In the novel, Phil and Hazel aren't friends but lovers. And for Phil, it's a definite 'maybe'. Soon afterwards, he and Hazel are getting married.

Maybe if I'd stayed in Bridgend, my life would have taken a similar turn. Maybe I'd have ended up like my stepdad's friend Tom. But I'd already moved to London – city of endless possibilities. A few days after my Sunday morning confessional on Southerndown, I came out to my personal tutor, Gerard. In the absence of my parents, he was a father figure to me.

He asked me if I was certain I was gay and whether I'd done anything about it.

33

I told him I was and I hadn't.

He smiled and said, 'Well, maybe you should.'

Which is how I ended up outside Heaven. I'm sure there were smaller, less intimidating gay venues I could have gone to. In fact, I know there were. I'd seen them listed in a copy of *Time Out*. But I've never been one for doing things by halves. Having finally admitted to myself and two other people that I was gay, I was ready to jump feet first into the biggest gay club in London – or so I thought until I got there.

Perhaps if I hadn't gone alone, my introduction to the London gay scene would have been easier. But I didn't have any gay male friends I could call on, only a flirty straight boy who made me mixtapes with songs like 'How Soon Is Now' by The Smiths. So I went and I stood on my own, and I left on my own and I went home but I didn't cry or want to die. We weren't all as melodramatic as Morrissey.

It was on my second visit to Heaven that I had my first gay sexual encounter – if you can call it that. A man I'd had my eye on suddenly walked up to me and, without saying a word, shoved his hand down the front of my trousers. He frowned, withdrew his hand and disappeared. I'd never been judged on the size of my flaccid and frightened penis before. Nor did it cross my mind that his behaviour was in any way questionable. I simply assumed that this was how courtship was conducted in gay clubland.

Finally, after a further two visits, I was chatted up and taken home by a man called Tito who came from Spain and lived in Walthamstow. We didn't talk much at the club. I was too nervous. He pursued me around the venue's labyrinthian layout of bars, dance floors, walkways and staircases for over an hour, positioning himself directly in my line of vision and staring at me in that casual yet meaningful way gay men refer to as 'cruising'.

This was an art I hadn't mastered yet, but eventually I cracked a smile and he came over and introduced himself. He thought I was playing hard to get. I was too full of teenage bravado to tell him otherwise.

We took a cab back to his flat and were barely through the door before we started tearing each other's clothes off. I remember thinking, 'I'm going to do it! I'm finally going to do it!' I didn't know exactly what 'it' would entail and was too tongue-tied to ask. I remember climbing into bed, and the thrill of feeling a man's naked, hairy body next to mine. There was very little foreplay. I remember him reaching into the bedside drawer for a bottle of body lotion. Then, before I knew what was happening, he was inside me. It hurt like hell, but I didn't dare complain. I'd wanted this for so long. I didn't want to spoil the moment.

Afterwards, Tito seemed surprised and inordinately proud to learn that it was my first time. Personally, I wasn't sure that this was something I ever wanted to do again. But I arrived back in college the next day a changed man. I'd had sex with another man and the world hadn't ended.

The second time we met, Tito presented me with a photo of himself to carry in my wallet. As far as I was concerned, this meant that we were dating. I quickly got over my discomfort around sex and convinced myself that we had a future together. What I didn't know was that the man I now thought of as my boyfriend hadn't been entirely honest with me. I discovered this during the Easter holidays. The college halls of residence were closed and I'd gone home to my family. Tito rang and suggested I return to London early and help him flat-sit for a friend of his. Of course, I was desperate to see him. But I didn't have any money and I couldn't ask my mother or she might question me. So I took a load of my LPs to the local record and tape exchange, and scraped together the coach fare. I told my parents I'd been invited to stay with a friend from college and off I went.

Tito met me at Victoria coach station and took me back to a flat in Leytonstone. The first couple of days were bliss. We barely got out of bed. I was nineteen and making up for lost time. I was insatiable.

Then, on the third night, we went out for a drink and Tito introduced me to a man called Ron.

'This is Paul,' he said. 'He's a friend of mine.'

Personally, I thought we were rather more than just friends, but I didn't say anything.

'Really?' Ron said, and turned to me. 'And how exactly did you two meet?'

I didn't know how to respond, but it must have shown on my face because suddenly he and Tito were having a blazing row. Only Ron didn't call him Tito but Hector – and it turned out that they weren't just friends, either. Ron was Tito/Hector's long-term partner and had been away on business. He was every bit as surprised to learn of my existence as I was to learn of his.

The night ended abruptly with me bursting into tears, Ron storming off and Tito/Hector escorting me back to the flat, where I promised myself I absolutely, definitely wouldn't have sex with him.

I'm afraid I let myself down rather badly.

The remainder of the week felt like an eternity. I had nowhere else to turn. All my college friends were at home with their families. I couldn't face calling my parents and having to explain myself. I'd made my bed and now I had to lie in it – even if it meant sleeping alone.

My only source of comfort was a copy of *De Profundis* by Oscar Wilde. A letter written to Lord Alfred Douglas during Wilde's imprisonment in Reading Gaol, *De Profundis* recounts the tempestuous and toxic relationship that led to the writer's conviction for gross indecency. This isn't the witty, waspish Wilde of the popular imagination. *De Profundis* is filled with hurt and has been described as one of the greatest and most complex love letters ever written. It begins 'Dear Bosie' and ends 'Your Affectionate Friend' – but before Oscar can bring himself to sign off with such affection he lays out each of Bosie's character flaws in painstaking detail, recalling examples of his arrogance, greed, selfishness and vanity. The love that dare not speak its name is revealed to be a pretty one-sided form of love – an idea that certainly struck a chord.

Prior to this, my knowledge of Wilde was limited to *The Picture Of Dorian Gray* and a school production of *The Importance Of Being Earnest*, in which I played a manservant called Merriman and had hardly any lines. I think I spent more time in make-up than I did onstage.

Reading *De Profundis* for the first time, it felt as if every line had been written especially for me. I still have that dog-eared Penguin edition, complete with notes scribbled in pencil in the margins and key passages underlined. 'I don't write this letter to put bitterness into your heart,' Wilde writes in one passage, 'but to pluck it out of mine. For my own sake I must forgive you.'

I don't think I ever truly forgave Tito – though I did seduce him one last time, just to prove to myself that I could. As my week of solitary confinement drew to a close, he arranged to visit the flat to do some gardening. I greeted him in a borrowed bathrobe and lured him into bed. Afterwards, I told him it didn't mean anything and took satisfaction in the wounded look on his face.

Many years later, I was at a house party hosted by a friend of a friend. On the wall was a framed photo of our host with the first man I ever slept with.

'I see you know Tito,' I said.

'Tito?' the host replied. 'Who's Tito?'

'Sorry,' I said. 'You probably know him as Hector.'

He didn't. Apparently, they'd been boyfriends, but the host knew him by a different name altogether. Suddenly it struck me that Tito had never been my Lord Alfred Douglas. *De Profundis* wasn't our story. There was nothing deep or meaningful about the times we'd shared. He was more like Algernon from *The Importance Of Being Earnest* – a frivolous man who lived a double life, pretending to be someone he wasn't. Not Bosie but a mere Bunburyist.

Chapter 5:
Take On Me

Single once more and no longer a virgin, I threw myself back on to the scene with gay abandon. By day I attended lectures on queer dramatists like Edward Albee, Jean Genet, Joe Orton and Tennessee Williams. At night I wandered the bars and clubs of Soho in search of adventure, making the most of happy hour and offers of free entry for those under the age of twenty-five. I got drunk on premium-strength lager and went home with anyone who'd have me.

I was struck by a quote from Williams, which I duly noted in my diary. He observed that the world is often violent and mercurial and that the only defence we have is love – for each other and for the art we choose to share. Truth be told, I wasn't producing much in the way of art. But I did feel compelled to share a lot of love – mainly through the medium of sex.

If Wilde was right and youth was wasted on the young, I figured I didn't have a moment left to lose. I was already nineteen going on twenty. In another five or six years I'd be too old to qualify for free entry, which seemed to indicate some kind of cut-off point. People joked that 'nobody loves a fairy when she's forty' – but on the gay scene, you were considered over the hill at thirty.

I soon found my tribe – at alternative venues like The Bell in King's Cross and Heaven's midweek club night, Pyramid, where the DJs included Mark Moore (who later found fame with S'Express) and the music ranged from The Cult to Pet Shop Boys. I much preferred mixed clubs to men-only spaces. People were friendlier, and there were still plenty of opportunities for casual sex. I took full advantage of them. When our lecturer for American Drama showed us the film version of *A Streetcar Named Desire* and Vivien Leigh uttered Blanche DuBois's immortal line about always depending on the kindness of strangers, I knew exactly what she meant.

It was at Pyramid that I first saw pop icons Boy George, Marilyn, and Marc Almond mingling with mere mortals. I'd been a huge fan of Almond's since the early days of Soft Cell, and had followed his progress from Marc and the Mambas to his latest incarnation as a solo artist. I'd recently been to see him in concert, where I managed to push my way to the front and was thrilled when he took the bangles I offered and added them to the growing collection snaking up his skinny arms. Seeing him at Heaven was too exciting for words, so I simply stared in disbelief.

It was also there that I first met Simon Hobart, who would later kick-start the whole '90s gay indie scene with the club Popstarz. Back then he was an '80s goth with a gravity-defying hairdo, and wore a studded leather jacket with large silver rings hanging from the epaulettes.

I thought they looked fantastic and asked him where I could get some.

He looked at me with an amused grin. 'They're cock rings!'

'Ah,' I said, sagely. 'I see.' In truth, I was still none the wiser.

My own appearance had changed somewhat. I'd grown my hair into a floppy fringe and was dressed in second-hand suit trousers with a billowing white shirt and cream brocade waistcoat purchased from Kensington Market. It was while shopping there that I ran into Morten Harket of A-ha, who'd recently had a big hit with 'Take On Me'. Harket was trying on leather jackets and was even more devastatingly handsome in the flesh. Given the chance, I'd have taken him on in an instant. But I was too star struck and tongue-tied to even say hello. I dreamed about him for weeks afterwards.

From the same market stall, I bought an imitation pearl and diamanté brooch. I completed my outfit with a pair of patent leather shoes, which were the least practical footwear I've ever worn. The night bus home from Trafalgar Square only went as far as Richmond. By the time I walked the remaining two miles to Strawberry Hill, my feet would blister and bleed. But such was the price of fashion. The look I was aiming for was a little bit New Romantic, a little bit *Another Country*, a little bit *Brideshead Revisited*.

I didn't meet my Sebastian, but after several more visits to Heaven I did meet a young man called Mark, who took me home to a tower block in Wapping and was rather alarmed at the tide-mark of make-up I left in the bathroom sink.

Wapping back then wasn't the gentrified area it is today: there was no Canary Wharf, no Docklands Light Railway. 1985 was the year Peter Ackroyd's novel *Hawksmoor* was published, and much of the local landscape hadn't changed since the architect's day. The famous St Anne's church in Limehouse and St George-in-the-East in Shadwell were both a short distance away. Butler's Wharf on the south side of the Thames was still an artists' space, strongly associated with people like Derek Jarman. In 1984 it was featured in the *Doctor Who* serial 'Resurrection of the Daleks'.

Mark was what we'd now call a 'gay geek'. He collected *X-Men* comics and spent a fair portion of his salary at Forbidden Planet. He worked for a set designer and his flat looked like an empty stage set. The walls were bare and there was hardly any furniture. The bed was a thin mattress on the floor.

41

He also had the strangest music collection I'd ever seen. I was still at an age where I judged people according to their taste in music. By rights, Mark shouldn't have passed the test. For starters, he had an unhealthy obsession with Ruby Keeler. Among his favourite albums were the soundtracks to *42nd Street* and *Gold Diggers Of 1933*, which seemed positively perverse in a man barely a year older than me. But there was something of the young fogey about Mark. He was also fond of Barbra Streisand, who I loved, and Barbara Cartland, who I certainly didn't. He'd listen to her warbling 'A Nightingale Sang In Berkeley Square' and try to persuade me that it could be enjoyed ironically. I wasn't convinced.

Mark made it clear that he didn't care much for my taste in music either, considering it 'trendy' and therefore a bit suspect. He had no time for Marc Almond, David Bowie or The Smiths. In fact, one of the few contemporary artists we agreed on was Kate Bush. Mark was also keen on Jimmy Somerville, who was neither sufficiently trendy to arouse his suspicion nor too outlandish for his tastes. Like a lot of gay men, Mark preferred his divas to be female. If we ever encountered an overtly effeminate gay man in a bar or on the Tube, he'd turn to me and stage-whisper, 'Get you, sister!'

Jimmy scored extra points for his politics. The theatre where Mark worked was of the left-leaning, fringe variety. He wore a red-star badge on his black bomber jacket. This didn't necessarily mean anything. In 1985, half the gay men in London wore Russian insignias on their bomber jackets. But in Mark's case, it was more than just a fashion statement. His boss was a lesbian feminist who came from South Wales and wasn't afraid to speak her mind, as Welsh women are wont to do. Consequently, he was well versed in sexual politics and the hierarchies of oppression, and carried a fair amount of gay male guilt. When we first met he was reading the Anne Dickson guide to assertiveness *A Woman In Your Own Right*.

His boss's name was Marion, though she and her girlfriend had pet names for each other that Mark also used, such was the closeness of the bond between them. In fact, Mark had pet names for everyone. One friend was referred to as The Octopus, though never to her face. Another was known as Rabbit, presumably because they talked too much.

Compared to them, I got off lightly. His pet name for me was Pawsie. He said it was because I reminded him of a puppy – easily excitable and just about house-trained. If I had to compare Mark to an animal, it would be a stork. He was tall and angular and would often cross his arms like a large bird folding in its wings. Sometimes my enthusiasm proved too much for him. When I became obsessed with Jean Cocteau, he bought me the latest biography for Christmas. Inside he wrote, 'I'm not sure if this present is a good idea. I dread the consequences!' In another book on Lord Byron he wrote, 'I hope you find this useful, though God knows what it'll do to me!'

Mark had an unfortunate habit of measuring himself against other people. I suppose we all do this to some extent. I know I do. But in him it was so all-consuming, it thwarted his ambitions and seemed to deprive him of any joy. He was a gifted cartoonist, though he never pursued this as a career and his cartoons were often an expression of his frustration with himself. Shortly before we met, he'd dated the horror writer Clive Barker. Together we attended the launch party for his *Books of Blood* series. When Clive's career took off with *The Hellbound Heart*, later the basis for the film *Hellraiser*, Mark was conflicted at best. He seemed to think that success was rather like a pie – if someone else did well, there'd be less left for him. Given that he harboured no writing ambitions of his own, I found this extremely odd.

I don't mean to sound so hard on Mark. I'm sure I wasn't the easiest person in the world, either. Still new to the gay dating game and extremely needy with it, I could also be incredibly insensitive. Weeks after we first slept together, I wrote a poem about waking up at 5 a.m., lying beside his pale naked body and asking myself, 'What is it brought me here to this bare room, bare boy, bare room? My god sleeps a million miles from here, a collage of tan and limbs that is not you.' Hardly the love poem of the century, though for some strange reason I saw fit to share it with him. I'm sure this really helped with any self-esteem issues he might have had.

Despite the fact that we were clearly unsuited, we became boyfriends, after a fashion. As I was rapidly discovering, most of the gay men I met weren't looking for the same thing I was. They didn't want a monogamous relationship. They wanted sexual freedom. Partly, they were making up for all the experiences they hadn't had as closeted gay teenagers. Partly, they were behaving as many straight men would, given half the chance. Mark was no exception, though he at least had the decency to be upfront about it, which was more than could be said for the previous object of my affection. There was no Ron lurking in the background, though there was a Graham and one or two others Mark was more than happy to talk about.

One night I decided to surprise him by travelling halfway across London and turning up unannounced on his doorstep. He wasn't home but his flatmate let me in. I waited until it was too late to travel all the way back to Strawberry Hill, and fell asleep in Mark's bed. He arrived home the following morning, smelling of sex and claiming to have spent the night at a friend's house. I chose to believe him.

Another time, he phoned me a little later than arranged, saying he'd only just got home from work. I could tell from the tone of his voice and the background noise that he was lying.

'Put your flatmate on,' I said, at which point he admitted that he wasn't home at all but visiting a gay couple he sometimes had sex with.

For a while I kidded myself that I could win Mark over. When this failed, I decided to play him at his own game and embarked on a series of affairs of my own. Annoyingly, he seemed to find this rather amusing.

Still, we remained together for several years, so I suppose that makes him my first proper boyfriend. In fact, he was my first in many ways. The first man I took home to meet my parents, though at the time I told them we were just friends. The first to take me home to meet his mum, though the nature of our relationship was never openly acknowledged. The first to bring up the issue of safer sex. 'We should start using condoms,' he told me one day, which sounded bizarre at the time. And it was during our first year together that I contracted my first STI.

I woke one morning literally itching for a pee. When I went to the toilet it felt like I was pissing razor blades. I rang Mark, who casually informed me that he had NSU and that I should go to the clap clinic. He told me NSU stood for 'non-specific urethritis' and that it wasn't necessarily sexually transmitted.

'So, how did you get it?' I asked.

'From having too much sex,' he replied, which seemed to beg more questions than it answered.

Sexual health clinics have changed a lot since the mid-'80s – and thank fuck for that. For starters, people didn't say STI then but STD, which stood for 'sexually transmitted disease' and sounded all the more Victorian and doom-laden for it. When you arrived at the clinic, you took a ticket from the machine on the wall and waited until your number was called. It was like signing on for the dole, with added social stigma and an unexpected amount of cruising.

When I was finally ushered in, the handsome young male nurse at St Thomas' Hospital asked me if I was the active or passive partner during penetrative sex. (People didn't use the terms 'top' and 'bottom' back then; at least, nobody I ever met.)

Nervously, I told him I was neither – or possibly both, though not at the same time.

He told me to drop my trousers and lower my underwear. Then he produced a cotton swab and inserted it quite a long way inside my penis. I flinched, but the worst was yet to come.

He asked me to lie on the bed, roll over on to my side and bring my knees up to my chest. Then he produced a phallic-shaped metal instrument, smeared it with KY jelly and pushed it up my backside.

At this point, I yelped in pain.

He leaned closer and whispered in my ear. 'Not like the real thing, is it?'

Chapter 6:
Pride (In The Name Of Love)

I attended my first Gay Pride march in June 1985. It was the Pride featured in the 2014 film of the same name, with the Welsh miners and the marching band. Having recently fled Wales and everything it represented to me, I confess I didn't appreciate the significance of this at the time. But, as the film demonstrates, the groundbreaking work of Lesbians and Gays Support the Miners was instrumental in garnering the support of the National Union of Mineworkers, who would later pressurise the Labour Party into incorporating lesbian and gay rights as part of the party programme. The miners helped pave the way for the equality measures introduced over a decade later under Tony Blair's government.

Not featured in the film, but certainly present on the day, was Divine – the larger-than-life drag queen who starred in trashy films by John Waters, which were often shown at the Scala cinema in King's Cross, and who was enjoying a second career as a disco diva, bellowing songs like 'Native Love', 'Shoot Your Shot' and his 1984 hit 'You Think You're A Man'. When Divine performed the single on *Top Of The Pops*, there were a record number of complaints. But the gay scene welcomed him with open arms. He'd already appeared at Heaven. Now the club invited him to be their guest performer for Pride. But, due to licensing restrictions, he wouldn't be performing on the back of a float or on a sound stage in the park. No, he'd be standing on the roof of a hired pleasure boat as it sailed slowly along the Thames.

The 1985 Lesbian and Gay Pride march began in Hyde Park and ended in Jubilee Gardens, where there were food and drink stalls, live entertainment and political speeches. It's quite possible that some people missed Divine's performance. But for those who didn't, it was pretty memorable. Dressed in a body-hugging silver-blue gown, gyrating to the beat in his usual outrageous fashion, he screamed along to 'You Think You're A Man' as the backing track boomed from makeshift speakers. If you ask me, he knocked the Welsh miners into a cocked hat. Who needs a marching band when you have an enormous drag queen from Baltimore floating by on a boat?

It's fair to say that not everyone was as big a fan of Divine as I was. Some lesbians objected to drag as a misogynistic parody of women. Some gay men found his act problematic as a stereotypical representation of male homosexuality. All things considered, Divine was pretty divisive. But as I soon discovered, Pride was beset by divisions. In those days, there was even a separate march for women called Lesbian Strength. I couldn't see the sense in lesbian separatism, believing – perhaps naively – that we were stronger together. But I could understand why lesbians were angry. I was angry, too. Luckily for me, some of my fellow marchers had devised a way to express this anger with a chant we could all gaily sing along to. It began with 'Give me a G!' and ended with 'What else is gay? Angry!'

What were we all so angry about? Where shall I begin? In 1985, the age of consent for gay men was twenty-one, compared to sixteen for heterosexuals – a fact brought home to me by Bronski Beat and their 1984 album *The Age of Consent*. We had no employment or partnership rights. You could be fired from your job or evicted from your flat simply for being gay. Police harassment was rife. There were no out-and-proud gay police officers marching beside us at Pride back then. There were plenty of so-called pretty policemen who spent their time and taxpayers' money hanging around public toilets, luring unsuspecting men into committing what were essentially victimless crimes.

Contrary to popular belief, the 1967 Sexual Offences Act didn't make male homosexuality legal. It partially decriminalised homosexual acts between consenting adults in private. The legal definition of 'private' meant that public displays of gay affection could and often did lead to prosecution. If a nosy neighbour saw two men hugging or kissing in their own home, they could be reported to the police. In the years immediately following the '67 Act, the number of men convicted for consenting homosexual offences in England and Wales actually went up, with far more men sent to prison than before. The punishment for a man aged twenty-one or over having sex with a sixteen- to twenty-year-old was increased from two to five years.

In June 1985, I was nineteen years old – two years below the legal age of consent and sexually compelled to break the law on a regular basis. And things were about to get a whole lot worse. A mysterious new 'gay disease' was already making headlines. Soon we'd be engaged in a battle against Clause 28, which forbade the 'promotion of homosexuality' and gave the homophobic tabloid press a field day.

But my abiding memory of that first Pride is one of celebration. I'd never seen so many lesbians and gay men gathered together in one place, and in broad daylight. I'm sure there were plenty of bisexuals and a fair few trans folk, too – though at the time there wasn't the same awareness of these identities as there is now. As the crowds filed from Marble Arch and assembled in Hyde Park, it seemed to me that all of gay life was there – butch dykes, drag queens, muscle boys, leather men, lipstick lesbians and everything in between. Activist types rubbed shoulders with scene queens. Older men and women mingled with bright young things. There were whistles and pink balloons, floats, banners and placards – Coal Not Dole, Comrades of Dorothy, Gay's the Word, Lesbians and Gays Support the Miners.

To fully appreciate the impact of this on my newly out nineteen-year-old self, you need to remember that London then was a very different city to London as it is now. There was no visibly gay café culture in the West End in 1985, no gay couples holding hands on Old Compton Street, no glass-fronted bars packed with shiny people happy to be seen drinking in a gay establishment. In the '80s, gay pubs had blacked-out windows. Many of the venues I frequented were literally underground. Before the growth of the Soho gay village in the early '90s, gay life tended to be tucked away in areas like Earl's Court (aka Girls' Court) and only came out after dark. Prior to my first Pride, almost all of the gay men I'd met were creatures of the night.

There were historical and sociological reasons for this. Despite years of protests and consciousness raising by the Gay Liberation Front, gay liberation was still very much a work in progress. There was still the sense that homosexuality was something to be kept hidden. When tabloid journalists referred to 'the twilight world of the homosexual' or wrote about someone's 'gay shame', they weren't being ironic and they weren't far wrong. Dimly lit basement bars like the Brief Encounter on St Martin's Lane were full of married men in search of a quick queer encounter before hot-footing it to Charing Cross and the last train back to suburbia. As a young man, I was on the receiving end of their furtive looks and wandering hands more times than I care to remember.

So to see hundreds of lesbians and gay men marching proudly through the centre of London was exhilarating. To march beside them felt incredibly empowering. To see the shocked faces of onlookers when someone waved and shouted 'Hello, Mum!' was hilarious. To witness Divine performing on a pleasure boat as masses of people congregated in Jubilee Gardens was something close to a religious experience.

For me personally, Pride wasn't just a celebration. It was an affirmation. It was the first day in my life that I felt truly safe. That feeling wouldn't last long. But for now, I was ready to take on the world.

I returned to my college hall of residence with a new-found confidence – and, yes, a sense of pride. No more would I be intimidated by the meatheads with whom I was forced to share a roof. If they came in late at night and woke me up with their drunken horseplay, I'd repay them the next morning by playing 'You Think You're A Man' at maximum volume. If our paths crossed in the shower room and they made juvenile jokes about dropping the soap, I'd answer back, 'Sorry, mate. You're not my type.' Though if I was being completely honest, there were one or two I'd have happily given a good seeing-to.

Of course I wasn't the only gay student at St Mary's. Some months earlier, I'd made friends with a couple of fellow students on the Drama course – a gay guy called Rob and a lesbian called Jayne. We shared a confidant, my personal tutor Gerard, who also gave lectures about Bertolt Brecht and Peter Brook. For a long time, Gerard remained the only adult I'd come out to. I wanted to tell my parents, but when I tried to broach the subject during half-term, my mother's reaction suggested that this wasn't a conversation she was ready to have yet. I discussed the situation with Gerard, who advised caution. I was away from home, the newspapers were full of stories about a deadly new gay disease, and my mother would only worry. I decided to follow his advice.

Rob lived further along the corridor at the Old House – the only other Drama student in a building full of rugger buggers. Jayne shared my passion for clothes. We used to say that, as stylish young lesbian and gay students with busy social lives, we really ought to qualify for an extra clothing allowance. We were only half joking. Jayne and Rob introduced me to *The Rocky Horror Picture Show*, which I'd never even heard of and they both knew off by heart. I introduced them to the clubs I'd discovered. First I took them to Pyramid at Heaven, and later we went to the gay Monday night at the Hippodrome, where we saw Quentin Crisp perform his one-man show.

But as the summer term drew to a close, my increasingly strident stance put a strain on our friendship. Rob in particular was worried that I was drawing undue attention to us as the college queers. I was summoned to Jayne's room and told in no uncertain terms to tone it down a bit or start looking for new friends to hang out with. It was all very reminiscent of that scene in *The Naked Civil Servant* where Crisp is turned away from an underground gay dance, accused of spoiling it for the others.

I didn't tone it down. If anything, I dialled it up. St Mary's didn't have a lesbian and gay society. I took it upon myself to do something about that. Being granted an audience with the principal, Father Beirne, would be nothing short of a miracle, so instead I booked an appointment with the vice principal, Miss Cosgrove. Needless to say, my demands fell on deaf ears. St Mary's was a Catholic college, and Miss Cosgrove was a good, God-fearing woman. Of course she wouldn't support me in my attempt to turn Strawberry Hill into Surrey's answer to Sodom and Gomorrah. I could have reminded her that the building in which we stood was erected by Horace Walpole, who was hardly an advert for hot-blooded heterosexuality. But I don't think this would have swayed her, and I didn't want to risk being sent down.

Undeterred, I made it my mission to be as flagrantly gay on campus as I possibly could, wearing eye make-up to lectures and distributing leaflets about lesbian and gay rights at the college library. I also dropped out of my Religious Studies course and decided to major in Drama and English instead. Though it pains me to say it, I don't think this was any great loss to the Religious Studies department, who probably thanked the Lord and heaved a collective sigh of relief.

In the final week of my first year at St Mary's, we had a ball – or two, to be precise. For those graduating, there was the formal Going Down Ball. For everyone else, there was the Paupers' Ball, where the dress code was more relaxed but fancy dress was actively encouraged. Given his rather coy stance regarding public displays of homosexuality, you can imagine my surprise when Rob arrived at the Paupers' Ball dressed in a tailcoat and fishnet stockings straight out of *Rocky Horror*. 'Well,' I thought, channelling my inner Frank-N-Furter. 'How about that?'

For my own costume, I borrowed a female friend's leotard, teamed it with a pair of black and silver leg warmers and made a matching cape from a spare piece of fabric. I draped a 'feather boa' of silver tinsel around my neck and had my face painted with the Aladdin Sane lightning bolt. A photograph taken that night shows me posed provocatively against the corridor wall at the Old House – one arm high above my head, one leg raised towards the camera, exposing a bare thigh.

I'm not alone. Pressed up against me in a silk jockey's outfit with riding boots and a face full of make-up is one of the rugger buggers. My left hand is splayed against his hip, revealing black polished nails. I'd love to say I had my wicked way with him later, but that was the full extent of our physical intimacy. Still, it felt like a conquest of sorts.

Chapter 7:
Club Tropicana

Growing up, my mother always told me I had champagne tastes on a beer income. At no point did this become more apparent than during my second year at college. I didn't suddenly develop a taste for champagne. I still preferred a pint of snakebite. But I did develop a taste for some of the finer things in life – particularly expensive clothes and premium-brand cosmetics. Much as I liked to think of myself as a bit of a bohemian, the truth is I wanted nice things, too.

Partly this was due to the magazines I was reading. So-called style mags like *Arena* and *The Face* promoted a glossy lifestyle I desperately wanted but could hardly afford. Each month I'd flick through their pages, feasting my eyes on the hunky male models in their bomber jackets, cycling shorts and chunky boots. I was particularly taken with a Latino model called Zane, who once sported a white polo-neck jumper with a pair of black briefs and what looked like a utility belt complete with knuckledusters. Not that I would ever have gone out looking like that. Even with a full student grant, such sartorial excesses were way beyond my budget – the jumper alone cost a small fortune.

A large part of my grant went on accommodation. I was no longer living in halls of residence but in my first gay flat-share. Plans to share a flat with Jayne and Rob had fallen apart when it transpired that I was expected to take a tiny box room while they each had a large double room. So I did what any self-respecting gay student with a bit of initiative did in those days and called Gay Switchboard.

Staffed entirely by volunteers, Switchboard offered a wide range of services, from counselling and referrals to information on HIV/AIDS. They also provided a list of contacts for people looking for accommodation. I was given the names and telephone numbers of several gay men with rooms to rent. Some were close to college, but the one I chose was situated halfway between Strawberry Hill and Waterloo. Since I was spending so much of my time in the West End, I figured it made sense. My flatmate was a guy called Bryan, who lived in an Edwardian top-floor flat on a wide tree-lined road close to Southfields Tube station and Earlsfield main line. The day I came to view the flat, he was wearing shorts and listening to 'Everything She Wants' by Wham!

It soon became apparent that Bryan's musical tastes were far less left-field than mine, tending towards soulful dance and pure pop. He disliked David Bowie and was devoted to Madonna, while I had yet to be converted. He also loved Sade and was simply wild about Wham!

Truth be told, I was a bit of a closet Wham! fan myself. I loved their first few singles and vividly recall their first appearance on *Top Of The Pops*, if only because it was one of the gayest things I'd ever seen. There was George Michael in his sleeveless leather jacket and bare ankles, luring Andrew Ridgeley away from his girlfriend and a life of heteronormativity. 'Young Guns' couldn't have been more homoerotic if it tried. It even sounded like the title of a gay porn flick.

By the time George was posing in his budgie smugglers for the video to 'Club Tropicana', Wham! were huge and it was time to hide my love away. It was hard enough being a closeted homosexual and teenage freak in South Wales in the early '80s. Within my small peer group, to admit to liking Wham! would have amounted to social suicide. But I still had the early 12-inch singles, hidden behind my Bowie records, along with *Guilty* by Barbra Streisand. If only I'd taken Barbra's advice. The truth is, I had nothing to feel guilty for – and we all know that guilty feet have no rhythm. For a gay man, that was a far greater crime.

Bryan worked for Yorkshire Television, drove a flash car and had a high disposable income. He was the living embodiment of that much maligned '80s breed, the gay yuppie or 'guppie'. He was also mixed race, unapologetically gay and had an ongoing dispute with the family who lived downstairs and were known as the Judges. Mr and Mrs Judge took a dim view of having a dark-skinned gay man living above them, and would complain at the slightest disturbance. When Bryan was involved in a car accident and arrived home from hospital wearing a neck brace, the eldest of their daughters told him, 'I wish you'd died in that car crash.' For a good, Christian family, they obviously didn't have much truck with their saviour's instruction to love thy neighbour.

Bryan became an older gay brother figure to me. Though our tastes and temperaments were rather different, we had enough in common to cement a friendship. Within weeks of me moving in, he'd introduced me to the gay scene in nearby Earl's Court – Bolton's, Brompton's and Copacabana. We even ventured to the infamous gay leather bar The Coleherne, where I was dumbstruck by the sight of a man in full leather with the head of his cock poking through a strategically placed hole in his trousers.

My favourite venue was the basement club Banana Max, where a giant screen played the latest videos by Whitney Houston, Diana

Ross and The Communards on heavy rotation and the ultraviolet lighting gave everyone an unnatural glow. Earl's Court was a popular gay tourist destination and the club attracted men of all nationalities – Americans, mostly, but also Australians, Greeks and Italians. Lots and lots of Italians. These weren't the first Italian men I'd ever encountered. Growing up in South Wales, an Italian barber used to cut my hair. An Italian family lived a few doors down the street. But I'd never been surrounded by such an assortment of gay men before. It was all so cosmopolitan.

Banana Max also boasted a barman called Kenny, who had the most perfect flat-top haircut I'd ever seen and quickly became the object of my unwanted desire. Men with flat-tops were highly prized in 1985. I had a friend called Lawrence whose search for a boyfriend was thwarted by the fact that he would only consider candidates who sported this most fashionable of hairstyles. Once it became clear that Kenny was never going to sleep with me, I decided to model myself on him instead, investing in a pair of denim dungarees identical to the ones he wore and striving for a flat-top – which never really worked and was soon abandoned in favour of a side parting and the vaguest hint of a quiff. Kenny watched this transformation from behind the bar with a bemused grin.

It was at Banana Max that someone offered me my first line of cocaine. Back then, drugs weren't as widely available on the gay scene as they became a few years later. Cocaine was something I associated with pop stars, in particular my idol David Bowie. It seemed impossibly glamorous and highly aspirational. How could I resist? That first line burned my sinuses and gave me the urgent need to empty my bowels – neither of which felt especially glamorous. But for the next half-hour I was on top of the world. My social anxiety dissipated. I could talk to anyone and say anything. If a cute guy caught my eye, I didn't stand around waiting for him to speak to me. I walked right up to him and introduced myself.

Cocaine gave me confidence. It didn't worry me that it was rumoured to be addictive, or that Bowie was once reduced to a walking corpse due to his dependency on the drug. The only thing that concerned me was the cost. Coke was prohibitively expensive for someone on a student grant. If this was the life I wanted to lead, I needed to get a job.

So, in October 1985, I signed up with a hotel and catering agency in the West End and began working a few days a week, whenever my college schedule would allow. I mopped floors, cleaned toilets and worked as a hotel porter, dressed in a nylon uniform that hadn't been cleaned since the last member of agency staff wore it, and usually stank of body odour.

For several weeks I worked in the linen room deep in the bowels of a large, five-star hotel on Piccadilly, sorting the dirty sheets, pillowcases, towels and facecloths that fell through a chute in the ceiling. Often the sheets were soiled and the towels had been used to mop up all manner of bodily fluids. It was dull, repetitive, unrewarding work. There was no job satisfaction because the job was never done. No sooner had you filled one linen basket than there was another waiting to be filled.

But there was one consolation. At the time, I was studying Samuel Beckett, the Theatre of the Absurd, and *The Myth Of Sisyphus* by Albert Camus. For months I'd been unable to get my head around the notion of absurdism. After a few weeks in the linen room, it all became clear. My job was truly absurd in the philosophical sense, devoid of meaning or inherent value. I was just like Sisyphus, forever rolling a boulder up a hill, only to watch it roll back down again.

Living with Bryan was an education in many ways. One night, when he was out with his boyfriend Dave, I turned on the television and the video recorder sprang to life. On the screen were three heavily muscled, orange-skinned men having sex. I'd never seen gay porn before. It wasn't nearly as readily available then as it is now. Before the internet and the relaxation of laws around the distribution of sexually explicit material, most gay porn videos were third-generation copies imported from abroad or sold under the counter in the sex shops of Soho. It wasn't until the early '90s that graphic filmed depictions of gay sex were permitted under the guise of safer sex education – and even then there was a ban on erections. But thanks to Bryan's porn stash I was able to appreciate the pioneering work of directors William Higgins and Matt Sterling and the enthusiastic performances of porn stars such as Steve Henson, Kip Noll, Al Parker and Jeff Stryker.

Stryker was by far the most famous gay porn star of the day, known for his habit of growling, 'You like that, doncha?' as he pleasured some eager young pup with his famously large appendage. So influential was he that it wasn't unusual to come across gay men who modelled themselves on his behaviour in the bedroom, adopting an American accent when really they came from Barrow-in-Furness. Edmund White once observed that when we're young, gay porn is a substitute for gay sex – and when we're older, gay sex becomes a substitute for gay porn. He could have been talking about half the men I met during this period.

In March 1986, George Michael released 'A Different Corner' – his second single as a solo artist, after 'Careless Whisper' the previous year. The tasteful black-and-white video showed him dressed all in white, in a white room. The single rocketed up the charts, and with good reason. It was the epitome of blue-eyed soul – a white man, in a white room, dressed all in white and singing in a style commonly associated with black artists. His hair was longer, and the designer stubble he would sport for the next decade was already in place. He looked gorgeous.

That same month, I was promoted from linen porter at the Piccadilly Hotel to receptionist at Champneys health club, which was housed in the basement. The hourly rate of pay was the same, but I made up for it in tips from wealthy hotel guests who'd give me a pound or two in exchange for fresh towels or a glass of freshly squeezed orange juice. The club also sold Clarins skincare products, a fair number of which found their way into my bag. The lost-property cupboard was always full of the latest designer sportswear. If something wasn't claimed within two or three weeks, it would mysteriously disappear. Many were the occasions when I'd leave work looking like the Michelin Man, with several layers of unclaimed clothes hidden under my jacket.

We had two regular celebrity guests. One was Diana Ross, who we were all under strict instructions to address as 'Miss Ross' and avoid making eye contact with. The other was George Michael, who came to use the sunbed and wasn't the least bit starry. He tended to keep a low profile and time his visits when the club was less busy. The only special treatment he received was in the form of a large and powerful hairdryer, which was ordered from upstairs and ceremoniously brought out whenever he took a shower. The regular dryer in the men's changing room was no match for his hair, which went curly when wet and required a serious blow-dry to straighten it out and maintain his current public image.

Part of my job was to ensure that no wet towels were left in the men's changing room. This provided me with the perfect excuse to wander in when young Mr Michael was taking a shower. We were the only two people there. Not only did I see Gorgeous George stark bollock naked but, judging by the smile he gave me, I was left in no doubt that the rumours were true.

Chapter 8:
Reasons To Be Fearful

1986 was a year of living dangerously. I hadn't experienced homophobic violence since I was bullied at school. My life was better now. I'd moved to London, come out, ruffled a few feathers and found a new social circle where being gay wasn't grounds for a good beating. Even the meatheads at St Mary's had drawn the line at childish pranks. Occasionally I'd be walking the streets of the West End and some white-van man would wind down his window and shout verbal abuse, but it never escalated into anything physical.

In 1986, all that changed. Walk down one street and you'd probably be okay. Turn a corner and you took your life in your hands. In the preface to the recent reprint of his debut novel *Ready To Catch Him Should He Fall*, the author Neil Bartlett describes London in 1986 as an unsafe place for a visibly gay man like his twenty-eight-year-old self, a city impacted by the first wave of the British AIDS epidemic and the extraordinary outpouring of homophobic hostility it unleashed in the media and on the streets.

I'm seven years younger than Bartlett but my experience wasn't very different to his. Like him, I was visibly gay. I wore faded Levi's with a studded belt and Doc Marten boots. A wallet chain hung from my hip and leather bracelets adorned my wrists. The lapels of my suit jacket bore badges proclaiming my political affiliations and sexual leanings. I had both my ears pierced and wore large silver earrings similar to those sported by George Michael. But while George was still passing himself off as straight, I was the kind of gay man who didn't go unnoticed.

1986 was the year I was chased by a gang of youths and physically assaulted close to Wapping Tube station. I escaped with a few bruises but was shaken for weeks. It was the year I was punched in the face by a smartly dressed man on a train heading into Waterloo. He came at me unexpectedly as the doors opened and he alighted at Battersea. It was also the year I went to a house party in Putney, hosted by a young woman called Maria who I knew from school. Her flat was on the second floor and the party was full of boozed-up straight men, including a few faces I recognised from my home town.

No sooner had I arrived than a group of them cornered me in the living room. 'Are you a poof? We always wondered about you.'

'I don't see how it's any of your business,' I replied and turned away. Reflected in the darkened window, I saw someone charge at me. I'm sure he had every intention of pushing me through the glass. I quickly stepped aside, at which point another man grabbed me by the shoulders and shoved me hard against the wall, bashing my head as he did so. His mates laughed and egged him on.

I looked around for help, but people were either too scared to intervene or simply not interested. Eventually Maria appeared. She ushered me to the door and told me to run before my attackers came after me. Nobody thought to call the police. Nobody asked the aggressors to leave. Nobody rang me later to see if I was okay. I never saw Maria again.

So yes, I was familiar with the outpouring of homophobic hostility Bartlett describes. I'd experienced it first-hand.

What I hadn't experienced, at least not then, was the impact of the AIDS epidemic. In March 1986, the BBC broadcast a documentary called *AIDS: A Strange And Deadly Virus* as part of its flagship *Horizon* series. The previous year, fifty-eight AIDS-related deaths had been recorded in the UK, according to the current affairs programme *TV Eye*. A man living with AIDS had even been detained under the Public Health (Infectious Diseases) Regulations 1985.

But for me and my immediate circle of friends, this barely registered, at least not on any conscious level. We never discussed it. Maybe it was the recklessness of youth, coupled with the determination to make the most of the few freedoms we enjoyed. Maybe it was the fear that if we talked about it, that would somehow make it more real.

I was still seeing Mark, despite his apparent lack of emotional commitment and refusal to give up his other affairs. I think he regarded monogamy as a bourgeois construct – or perhaps he just wasn't that into me. Our relationship was often fraught – but for reasons more to do with low self-esteem than high expectations, I refused to walk away, finding comfort in one-night stands and kidding myself that this made me happy.

Not that there weren't moments of pleasure. There were. Dressing up for a night out. Catching another man's eye on the Tube and feeling desired. Meeting some handsome stranger on the dance floor at Heaven and going home with him afterwards. Even the walk of shame the next morning brought me joy. Taking the train or sitting on the bus in last night's clothes, smelling of sex, convinced that everyone could tell and not caring if they did.

But for all the bravado, there was no denying that the age of sexual anxiety had arrived. Though Mark and I continued to have penetrative sex, I avoided it with anyone else, fearing that the condom might break and developing an aversion bordering on paranoia. I'd always been fearful. First there was the fear of my father. Then there was the fear of who I was and how others would react. I was never safe. Now, as people started talking about safer sex, the very basis of my identity seemed to pose an existential threat.

The first time I caught crabs I had a total meltdown. Mark found this hysterically funny, though he wasn't so amused when I contracted gonorrhoea. Neither was I. It didn't seem fair. I'd taken all the precautions – I thought I was being careful. The risk of disease triggered my deepest fears and made me even more anxious. This in turn brought out my compulsive side. I'd drown the anxiety in drink and go through the whole process again.

Despite our differences, Mark and I had a lot in common. We were both creative and loved the theatre, though he preferred realism and I was drawn towards the experimental excesses of Steven Berkoff and Lindsay Kemp. A poster for Kemp's iconic performance piece *Flowers* hung on my wall, together with the film poster for Fassbinder's *Querelle*. Genet cast a long shadow.

Together, Mark and I saw the West End production of *Torch Song Trilogy* starring Antony Sher and Rupert Graves and the Bush Theatre production of *Kiss of the Spider Woman* starring Mark Rylance and Simon Callow. Both plays had a profound impact on me. *Torch Song Trilogy* introduced the idea of gay family and adoption, which were completely alien to me at the time. *Kiss of the Spider Woman* explored the relationship between two very different men – one an effeminate gay window-dresser convicted of gross indecency, the other a hyper-masculine revolutionary and political prisoner. Both plays warned of the inherent dangers of living as an out gay man. In *Kiss of the Spider Woman*, Molina's overtures towards his straight cellmate place him at constant risk of violence. In *Torch Song Trilogy*, Arnold's partner is beaten to death by queer bashers. Danger, it seemed, was everywhere – and there was worse to come.

In the summer of 1986, *The Normal Heart* opened in London. Larry Kramer's landmark play about the early days of the AIDS epidemic had already been a big hit in New York. Largely auto-biographical, it tells the story of Ned Weeks, a gay writer, activist and founder of a prominent HIV advocacy group. The role of Ned was originally played by Brad Davis, star of *Querelle* and *Midnight Express*, who was a bona fide gay icon and would later die of an AIDS-related illness.

The London production of *The Normal Heart* opened at the Royal Court with Martin Sheen in the starring role, before transferring to the West End, where his part was played by Tom Hulce, fresh from his success in *Amadeus*. Tickets for the Albery Theatre weren't cheap. But I was determined to get the best seats available, and Mark and I ended up sitting in the front stalls. The play was a powerful call to arms, the performance only slightly marred by the smartly dressed, middle-aged man sitting a few seats away, who chatted to his female companion throughout the first act. During the interval I went over and asked him to please be quiet as he was spoiling my enjoyment of the play. 'What do I care?' he replied haughtily, looking at me like I was something he'd trodden in.

As I soon discovered, a lot of people didn't care – even nice middle-class people who went to the theatre. Four years after the death of Terrence Higgins, AIDS was still mainly associated with gay men – and in many people's eyes we were expendable. By December 1986, over 600 cases had been reported in the UK – compared to 108 two years previously. Eighty-six per cent of those affected were gay or bisexual men.

I didn't realise it at the time, but one of those men was someone I knew. There was a student at St Mary's who I'll call Peter. We weren't friends but sometimes attended the same lectures. It wasn't until he disappeared one term that I discovered he was gay and had an American boyfriend. I remember thinking this was terribly glamorous. All things American were very popular on the gay scene in the mid-1980s – 501s, Ray-Bans, Madonna.

Shortly afterwards, Peter returned to college looking pale and gaunt. After a few months he disappeared for a second time, never to be seen again. Peter was the first person I knew who died of AIDS. He was a little older than me – a mature student. He'd have been twenty-two or twenty-three when he died.

My second year at college was far more fulfilling than my first. The Drama course in particular I found hugely inspiring. We were each encouraged to keep an 'observation file', which was a writer's notebook by another name. I made notes about books I'd read and plays I'd seen, people I encountered and conversations I had. It was during this period that I first began to fantasise about becoming a writer, though at the time I thought my future might lie in the theatre. With the extra money I earned at the health club, I saw as many live shows as possible, fuelling my imagination with fringe productions of *The Maids* and *The Cabinet of Dr Caligari* and provocative performances by Michael Clark and Lindsay Kemp. Kemp in particular made a huge impression on me, just as he had on my musical idols David Bowie and Kate Bush.

When I wasn't attending lectures or working on my observation file, I tried my hand at making masks. This was one of the practical courses on offer in year two, and one which best reflected the kind of theatre I was most interested in. Soon my observation file was filled with thoughts about masks and their meanings in drama and in life. I read Mishima's *Confessions Of A Mask*, about an adolescent boy tormented by his homosexuality and desire to be normal – a phase I recognised only too well. I quoted John Updike's assertion about fame being a mask that eats into the face. I contemplated the use of masks in Lindsay Kemp's *Flowers* and Oscar Wilde's famous observation: 'Man is least himself when he talks in his own person. Give him a mask, and he will tell you the truth.'

As part of our exam, we were asked to design masks for a play of our choosing. I chose *The Balcony* by Jean Genet – a play about role-playing and the power of appearances. Most of the action takes place in an upmarket brothel, while outside a revolutionary uprising threatens to destroy the city. Like many of Genet's plays, *The Balcony* is self-consciously theatrical and explores the tension between reality and illusion. The characters are archetypes, each playing a part – Chief of Police, Judge, Bishop, General, Thief. I pondered the meaning of masks in Genet's work, and how informed it was by his exaggerated sense of himself as an outsider, a thief, a criminal lover of men.

Having designed and made the masks, I then had the bright idea of seeing how they worked onstage by putting on a production. The head of department wouldn't hear of it, insisting that I was getting ideas above my station and should wait until my final year, when we would be taught all we needed to know about directing. Luckily, my personal tutor Gerard took a different view and actively encouraged me, securing rehearsal space and a date in the diary when the theatre was available. I roped in some fellow students and threw myself into rehearsals.

As a showcase for my skills at mask-making, the production was a success. At one point, a female character cried floods of tears, made from rolls of blue ribbon concealed inside her mask and pulled from her eyes by her male interrogator. It looked and sounded suitably dramatic. The scene was set to Bowie's 'V-2

Schneider'. Earlier, the entire cast danced onstage to 'Venus in Furs' by The Velvet Underground.

As a piece of theatre, the production was a bit of a mess. My heavily edited version of the play didn't make a whole lot of sense. I'd spent so much time worrying about the music and visuals, I hadn't given enough thought to the basics. The young actors gave it their best shot, but without proper direction many scenes fell flat. I learned a lot, though – and the experience would stand me in good stead when it came to directing my exam production the following year.

I turned another corner in 1986. That September, I turned twenty-one. No longer a criminal lover, I had now reached the gay age of consent. Clearly a celebration was in order. I hadn't dyed my hair since first arriving in London two years earlier. For the first time since my mid-teens, my floppy fringe was the colour nature intended. Obviously, this wouldn't do, so to mark the occasion I decided to throw caution to the wind and go platinum blond.

A little more caution probably wouldn't have gone amiss, as my first attempt resulted in a shade of yellow that was less platinum, more citrus. In other words, I looked a right lemon. Mark found it hilarious but I persevered, and after a second application of Recital Super Blonde and a suitable toner I finally achieved the colour I was after.

Bryan kindly offered to throw me a birthday party. A small group of friends came to the flat and we all got drunk on champagne. If I'm completely honest, turning twenty-one was a bit of an anti-climax. I'd been happily consenting to gay sex for the best part of two years. On the inside, I didn't feel any different. On the surface, it was another story. I wasn't just legal. I was legally blond! The change felt as dramatic and transformative as the play I'd recently directed. Mark said it was like sleeping with a different person. I began to wonder who that person might be – and whether there was any truth in the old adage that blonds have more fun.

Chapter 9:
Sign O' The Times

My earliest memory of 1987 is being at a club called Busby's and dancing by myself on an empty dance floor to 'Sign O' The Times' by Prince. It was late February, a month before the album was released, and I was probably wearing bleached denim dungarees and Doc Marten boots, with my hair recently cut into a blond crop. The symbolism of dancing alone didn't strike me at the time, but in retrospect I think it says a lot about my state of mind and the direction my life would soon take.

Sign O' The Times and Marc Almond's *Mother Fist* were the two albums I listened to the most that year. I don't think it's a coincidence that they both referenced AIDS – Almond with his anthem to the joys of masturbation, and the accompanying interviews where he talked about safer sex and his fear of infection; Prince with his cautionary tale of a skinny man who dies of the big disease which had already claimed more American lives than those lost in Vietnam. But for now, such thoughts were far from my mind. I was twenty-one and enjoying sexual freedom for the first time. I felt invincible.

It was at Busby's that I was seduced by a Greek boy called Yannis, who pursued me around the club and later told me it was my dungarees that first caught his attention. He liked the way they clung to my buttocks. I remember thinking this was the nicest thing anyone had ever said to me.

It was also at Busby's that I first met Derek Jarman, who would later become a personal friend and a public figurehead for AIDS in the UK. Pop music was my gateway drug to queer art. Just as the music of David Bowie had introduced me to the work of Jean Genet, so Adam Ant and Toyah Willcox introduced me to the films of Derek Jarman, starting with *Jubilee* and *The Tempest*. I'd recently seen his latest film *Caravaggio*, which marked the film debuts of Sean Bean and Tilda Swinton and featured the impossibly beautiful Dexter Fletcher as the artist as a young street urchin. Like most of gay London, I immediately developed a crush on Dexter.

I was currently reading Jarman's first memoir, *Dancing Ledge*. In the book, he describes the battles to get his arty and unapologetically gay films made. He recalls encounters with David Bowie, Marianne Faithfull and Amanda Lear. He also writes about sex. In one passage, he recalls how he avoided passive anal sex until his early thirties. Inhibition and social conditioning made it too traumatic. It was only by learning to overcome his sexual anxieties and allowing himself to be penetrated that he was able to reach full, emotionally balanced manhood. This leads him to conclude that heterosexual men only experience half of love.

In another chapter, he recalls visiting a restaurant and observing a handsome young Italian man who catches him staring and flashes a cocky grin. Jarman describes the restaurant melting away, until all he can see are the Italian's dark, cruel eyes and dazzling white teeth. After a minute, the writer averts his gaze, feeling as if he's just shared a night of passion.

This was provocative, eye-popping reading material for a naive twenty-one-year-old. Jarman's words struck several chords. Like him, I'd experienced anxieties around sex. Like him, I'd seen strange boys in bars and restaurants and gone weak in the presence of beauty. Derek always had an eye for gorgeous boys, and that night at Busby's was no exception. I desperately wanted to go over and tell him how much his work meant to me, but he was surrounded by a group of intimidatingly attractive friends. They flocked around him like actors at an audition. Perhaps they were.

Finally, I plucked up the courage to introduce myself, apologised for the interruption and congratulated him on his latest film. He couldn't have been more charming, insisting on buying me a drink, introducing me to his friends and asking about my college course and plans for the future. One thing he said has stayed with me ever since: 'If you really want to write or create art, you'll find a way.'

I left the club on a high. I'd met a man I admired greatly and he hadn't disappointed.

There was plenty of disappointment in other areas of my life – a sign of the times, you might say. Most of my gay friends were people I'd met on the scene. Very few shared my interests in the arts and politics. Many saw Pride as a waste of time. It seemed to me that the rising tide of homophobia in the media and on the streets called for a collective, community response – and I wasn't seeing much sense of community within my social circle. Clearly, I was mixing in the wrong circles. But finding like-minded gay men back then was far harder than it is today, when common interests can be shared and connections made on social media. In those days, you went home with someone first and checked their bookshelves later. Not that this didn't have its compensations.

To make matters worse, in April David Bowie released what many fans agreed was the worst album of his career. It was called *Never Let Me Down* – which seemed like a bitter commentary on how many of us felt at the time. When the video for lead single 'Day-In Day-Out' was first shown on television, I felt a deep and burning sense of betrayal. Bowie was the man who'd introduced me to outsider artists like William Burroughs and Jean Genet – and here he was singing a banal slice of soft rock and riding around on roller skates! It was the first Bowie album I didn't rush out and buy. I'm sure my one-man boycott really troubled him.

Disillusioned, I buried myself in books, drawing inspiration from gay classics like *City Of Night*, *Dancer From The Dance* and *Giovanni's Room*. I immersed myself in the lives of historical queer figures like Lord Byron, Jean Cocteau and Oscar Wilde. I went to see Neil Bartlett perform *A Vision Of Love Revealed In Sleep* in a derelict warehouse at Butler's Wharf, where Derek Jarman had previously lived and worked. Like Jarman, Bartlett's work fused a queering of history with a furious response to the homophobia that was still very much alive and kicking. I was blown away. Inspired, I invested in an electric typewriter and began writing plays, short stories and novels I would never finish.

Still the dance floor called – and I came running.

1987 was the year Daisy Chain opened at The Fridge in Brixton. It's hard to express now just how exciting it was. A converted cinema and one-time roller disco, the club was owned by Susan Carrington and Andrew Czezowski, former punks who had previously run the infamous Roxy. They made a striking pair – she with her Peter Pan collars and purple pixie cropped hair, he with his flash suits and gold teeth.

Renowned for its pyrotechnics and strong visuals, with a large stage and room for close to 2,000 clubbers, The Fridge was already well established by the time Daisy Chain first opened its doors. Hosted by drag queen Yvette the Conqueror, with a sweet muscle boy called Polly on the door, on any given night you'd see a number of celebrities – Michael Clark, Michelle Collins, at least two-thirds of Bananarama. The 'Nanas were often there and usually quite drunk. When I met them at a party many years later, Sara told me they loved going to The Fridge because they only lived a few miles away and could make it home in a taxi without being sick. No wonder they were so adored by gay men. Polly's main claim to fame was that he appeared on the cover of their *Wow!* album – shirtless, with his back to the camera and his face out of shot. I suppose it was fame of a sort.

The whole notion of 'scene celebrities' was still new to me – and it wasn't something I took very seriously. There were DJs I admired, and club kids who'd gone on to achieve success in the worlds of pop or fashion. Boy George was once the cloakroom attendant at Blitz. Steve Strange was a door-whore before fronting Visage and having a massive hit with 'Fade to Grey'. Princess Julia appeared in the video and was involved in various music and fashion projects of her own. But the idea that someone could be famous simply for dressing up and parading around a nightclub struck me as faintly ridiculous.

It was at Daisy Chain that I first encountered Leigh Bowery. I was on the dance floor, lost in music, when this apparition appeared before me with a bald head and lightbulbs shining from both his ears. His face and head were painted white, with enormous false eyelashes and a grotesque clown mouth, and his fleshy chest was tightly bound in some kind of corset to give the appearance of breasts. At first I thought I was tripping. It wasn't unusual for me to take a dab of speed or a dot of acid when I went clubbing. But no, he was really there – larger than life and crashing into people as he spun around the dance floor on roller skates.

I think it was the roller skates that irritated me the most. First David Bowie and now this ridiculous exhibitionist. Later, I came to appreciate Bowery and his influence on the London club scene. He was a performance artist, and clubland was his stage. But back then he just annoyed me. One night at Daisy Chain he and Michael Clark climbed up on top of the enormous speakers, high above the dance floor. They were hauled down by the security staff and asked to leave. 'But I'm Michael Clark!' the most celebrated dancer of his generation protested. 'I'm a friend of the club! You can't throw me out!'

But throw him out they did. When I left an hour or so later, he and Bowery were hanging around outside, still complaining and seemingly off their faces. I hadn't yet heard of Ecstasy, but I suspect that may have had a part to play in the night's celebrity drama.

For my end-of-year exam production, I decided not only to direct a play but to adapt one. Once again, the head of Drama at St Mary's took a dim view of this but my personal tutor backed me up. The source material was Cocteau's novel *Les Enfants Terribles* – the story of two siblings, Elisabeth and Paul, who cut themselves off from the world and indulge in a series of psychodramas known as The Game. Paul is in love with a boy called Dargelos, who injures him with a snowball containing a stone. Isolated at home with Elisabeth, brother and sister egg each other on, pushing themselves to ever-greater emotional extremes.

It didn't escape my attention that Paul and I shared a name, or that I too had schoolboy crushes on the wrong kind of boys. Whenever I thought of Dargelos, I pictured the sporty lads I'd obsessed about as a teenager.

The script I wrote was drawn from key scenes in the book, interspersed with moments of pure physical theatre expressing the characters' interior lives. The roles were played by two students called Carol and Liam, who were both excellent. The play opened with the brother and sister dancing to 'After All' by David Bowie. A later scene saw Elisabeth attempting to physically restrain and crush her brother, choreographed to 'Jewel' by Propaganda. A large screen hung above the minimal set, with a series of images created by my cousin Oliver, who was studying art at Saint Martins.

The costumes were designed by the college wardrobe mistress, Gina, who created a white and silver princess dress for Elisabeth and a blouson and knickerbockers for Paul. The make-up was designed by yours truly and heavily influenced by Lindsay Kemp. The external examiner also identified shades of Steven Berkoff. He awarded me the highest grade ever awarded for an exam production at St Mary's.

There was only one senior member of staff who neglected to congratulate me. Years later I bumped into him, a married man, in a gay sauna.

'Ah,' I thought. 'So that's what your problem was!'

My three years at St Mary's passed so quickly, it's only now that I realise how formative those times were. For my Going Down Ball, I borrowed a dinner suit and cummerbund from Bryan, teamed it with a wing-collar shirt and bow tie, and wore as much make-up as my face could possibly accommodate. My hair was spiky blond with dark roots, and diamanté studs glinted in my earlobes. How I survived the train journey from Earlsfield to Strawberry Hill without being beaten up, I don't know. But I arrived in one piece and lined up with my fellow graduates to be welcomed by our vice principal.

When Miss Cosgrove offered me her hand, I pulled out my silk pocket square, stepped back and gave her a courtly bow. I'd been to see Christopher Hampton's production of *Les Liaisons Dangereuses* and was channelling Alan Rickman as the Vicomte de Valmont. Though when my friend Jason Ford recently saw a photo of me taken that night, he said I looked more like the Vampire Lestat. I chose to take this as a compliment.

Chapter 10:
The Only Way Is Up

I graduated from St Mary's with a combined honours degree in Drama and English and no career plans. Encouraged by the glowing response to my exam production, I applied for a job as an assistant director at the Orange Tree Theatre in Richmond, but failed the interview. Maybe I didn't sell myself properly, or maybe I simply had the wrong accent. The job went to a fellow student who hadn't done quite as well at college but who came from a middle-class background and whose parents regularly attended the theatre. Then, as now, it was far harder for working-class kids to get a foot in the door.

To save money, I moved from my swanky gay flat-share in Southfields to a tiny box room way up on the ninth floor of a tower block in Kennington. My stepdad kindly drove down from South Wales and moved me and my belongings in his van. When we arrived at the grim, grey block with its narrow lift smelling of urine, he turned to me and said, 'It's probably best if we don't tell your mother.' I agreed.

My new flatmate was an actor and singer called Vaughan Michael Williams, who performed with a gay cabaret troupe called The Insinuendos. Well known on the London gay scene, they sang topical songs about sexual politics and the absurdities of modern life, often setting new lyrics to familiar show tunes. They were a sort of male version of Fascinating Aïda, though nowhere near as successful.

Shortly after I moved in, Vaughan announced that he fancied me, which made things rather awkward as the feeling wasn't mutual. But by unspoken mutual agreement, he never mentioned it again and we soon became friends as well as flatmates. Vaughan was funny and charismatic, a talented performer and a natural-born storyteller. In short, he was the kind of man I aspired to be. He was also the first person I'd met who made his living as a gay artist, and an overtly political one at that. We were bound to get along.

Of course, we had our disagreements. He disapproved of my taste in music, dismissing Bowie and Prince and denouncing Sinéad O'Connor as a wailing banshee. Vaughan was a keen Barbra Streisand fan and also introduced me to the music of Bette Midler. In doing so, he was in direct breach of the gay code of conduct described in Armistead Maupin's *Tales Of The City* books – which he was quick to loan to me and I was equally quick to devour. According to Maupin's gay everyman character Michael 'Mouse' Tolliver, Streisand and Midler were the S and M of gay culture. You could be into one or the other, but not both at the same time.

Another of Vaughan's musical icons was Nina Simone, who I promptly fell in love with. *Baltimore* remains one of my all-time favourite albums. He also adored Stephen Sondheim and would play the original cast recordings of his musicals so often that I soon knew them off by heart. To this day, I can't hear 'I'm Still Here' from *Follies* or 'No One Is Alone' from *Into The Woods* without thinking of Vaughan and the times we shared.

When he wasn't overseeing my musical education, Vaughan lectured me about my poor diet. He espoused the virtues of vegetarianism, though he often ate fish and sometimes chicken. He impressed upon me the importance of a regular skincare routine, stressing that I should cleanse and moisturise twice a day and never go to bed without first removing the eyeliner he regarded with barely disguised disdain.

He also thought I dressed badly. My clothes were either too big, too small or not really my colour – the predominant colour being black. 1987 was the year I became a Buffalo Boy. The fashion was popularised in the pages of *The Face* by stylists Judy Blame and Ray Petri. It was best exemplified by the famous cover image of thirteen-year-old Felix Howard in a black Crombie, white polo neck, and homburg hat adorned with a feather and the word 'Killer' in newsprint.

But many Buffalo Boys took liberties with the style, adding their own personal touches. Newspaper headlines were cut out, laminated or sealed with Sellotape, and attached to hats and jackets. The toes of Doc Marten shoes were cut open to reveal steel toecaps, and laces replaced with kilt or blanket pins. Hair was shorn close at the back and sides and greased on top. Chunky silver jewellery was worn around the neck and wrists and on the fingers. Rings were often so chunky they looked more like knuckledusters. The overall look was butch, even brutal, but with a queer twist. Some Buffalo Boys wore skirts or kilts. Others, like me, drew the line at skirts, preferring knee-length shorts with black-and-white striped socks. No longer blond, my hair was now dyed jet black – another sartorial decision of which Vaughan heartily disapproved. 'It makes you look too pale!'

Despite our differences, Vaughan and I and often socialised together. He introduced me to the nearby Royal Vauxhall Tavern, one of the oldest gay pubs in London, where Lily Savage performed weekly. Earlier that year, police had raided the venue wearing rubber gloves. Eleven men were arrested and cautioned with the absurd offence of being drunk in a pub.

Lily was furious and urged the crowd to resist arrest. Legend has it that when an officer asked for her name, she replied, 'Lily Savage'. Pressed to give her real name, she replied, 'Lily Veronica Mae Savage'. Such is the stuff of which queer resistance was made. The so-called rubber gloves raid became a pivotal moment in the relationship between the police and the gay community, and Lily was crowned queen of Vauxhall. These days, of course, Lily is better known as television's Paul O'Grady.

It was also thanks to Vaughan that I had one of the most unexpected and exciting sexual encounters of my life. On Saturdays he subsidised his income by working at the Zipper Store in Camden, selling gay leather and fetish wear. One particular Saturday I woke up late with a raging hangover and heard someone moving around the flat. Pulling on some shorts, I wandered into the kitchen and there, sitting at the table, was a young man – a very handsome, very smiley, floppy-haired young man who looked like he'd stepped out of a Merchant Ivory film, dressed in nothing but a towel. His name was Richard and he was The Insinuendos' new pianist. The mutual attraction was obvious from the start, but in my hungover and slightly anxious state I was too fearful of rejection to make the first move. So we chatted for a bit before moving into my tiny bedroom, where we sat on the narrow single bed and proceeded to play a game of chess.

Yes, really. We played chess. It was only when the game was over that Richard said, 'I'm feeling kind of horny, actually,' and things became more intimate. It was probably the most fun I'd ever had on a Saturday morning – and I say that as someone who grew up watching *Saturday Superstore*. Richard Thomas went on to become a highly successful composer, best known for the award-winning *Jerry Springer: The Opera*. All these years later, we're still in touch.

The tower block where Richard and I consummated our friendship was one of those tall buildings that narrowly survived the great hurricane of October 1987. The night of the storm, I was in bed with a boy I'd picked up in Soho, and was either too drunk or too distracted to feel the earth move. I remember looking out from my ninth-floor window the next morning and seeing all the trees down below flattened. Later I heard that another tower block had been hit so hard, the roof had blown off.

It was while I shared a flat with Vaughan that I wrote a radio play about Lord Byron, adapted from an earlier film script I'd written at college. We even booked a studio and recorded a demo, with Vaughan as Byron and various friends voicing other parts. Nothing further ever came of it.

Disheartened but in dire need of money, I found a job at a telephone market-research company, interviewing Peugeot drivers about their latest model of car and cold-calling housewives to discuss their favourite varieties of soup and brands of washing powder. One morning, a gay out-of-work actor called Norman rang a woman in the north-east of England who told him she couldn't possibly talk now as it was snowing. 'Haven't you heard the news? We've had three inches!'

Quick as a flash, Norman replied, 'Three inches? And you call that news?'

Everyone working in the phone room seemed to be involved in the arts, and I soon became friends with an actress called Linda Rogers, a dancer called Simon Griffiths and a musician called Steve Mackey.

Though straight, Steve was something of a gay heartthrob and an outrageous flirt. I made no secret of the fact that I fancied him rotten and he made no attempt to dissuade me from wasting my time. He once came to dinner and spent the evening lounging on my bed and running his fingers through his hair, which cascaded down to his shoulders, lending him a distinctly Pre-Raphaelite look. All he needed was a 'man dress' and a pack of playing cards, and he'd have been a dead ringer for David Bowie on the cover of *The Man Who Sold The World*.

But Steve was more butch and less sexually ambiguous than Bowie. Later, he cut his hair into a sharp wedge, joined a band and told anyone who'd listen that soon he'd be famous. None of us took him seriously until one day the band's singer came to meet Steve from work – a geeky-looking guy in glasses by the name of Jarvis Cocker.

By the time Pulp were storming the charts, Simon was dance captain on a cruise ship in the Caribbean. Like me, he was gay and came from South Wales. I nicknamed him Bonnie after Bonnie Tyler. He retaliated by nicknaming me Shirley after Ms Bassey. It was largely thanks to Simon that I became a Fongette. Together with Adrella and Lily Savage, Regina Fong was one of the holy trinity of drag queens who ruled the London gay scene in the late '80s. She billed herself as a Russian princess – Her Imperial Highness, the Last of the Romanovs – and held court every Tuesday at The Black Cap in Camden. Simon and I went to pay homage most weeks.

I'd seen plenty of drag acts before, but none quite like Regina. She didn't sing, tell jokes or mime along to Shirley Bassey numbers. Instead her act was built around a variety of jingles, sound effects and snippets of popular culture – Cilla Black, Anneka Rice on *Treasure Hunt*, Cybill Shepherd advertising L'Oréal hair dye. There'd also be singalongs to the theme tune to *Skippy The Bush Kangaroo* and 'Tell Me What He Said' by Helen Shapiro. It was ridiculous in the true theatrical sense – absurd, surreal, laugh-out-loud funny, and incredibly hard to explain to anyone who hadn't witnessed it first-hand.

The show involved a large element of audience participation. Regina's power over her audience was something to behold. Regulars would shout requests for favourite clips. If she deigned to perform them, everyone was expected to join in, complete with choreographed routines, one of which involved holding up our hands and miming speed-typing in time to Leroy Anderson's tune 'The Typewriter'. If someone got it wrong or failed to show sufficient enthusiasm, she'd halt the performance and start all over again. We Fongettes loved it, willingly subjecting ourselves to the same silly rituals week after week.

Before becoming a drag queen, Reginald Bundy had been a chorus boy and stage actor. His drag career began with a trio called The Disappointer Sisters. Later, Regina would go on to perform with Neil Bartlett in an expanded theatrical version of *A Vision Of Love Revealed In Sleep* at the Drill Hall and a new play, *Night After Night*, at the Royal Court. Reg died from cancer in 2003, aged fifty-six.

I was still harbouring theatrical ambitions of my own. I enrolled on an MA course at the Polytechnic of North London, studying Modern Drama and Film. My friend Linda and I put on a one-off performance of *Les Enfants Terribles* at the Diorama, with her in the role of Elisabeth and me playing Paul. The play was performed in the round, and I remember feeling sick with nerves. But the production was well received and gave me the boost of confidence I needed to continue working on other projects.

Then everything changed.

One night in early December 1987, I arrived home to find Vaughan crying on the sofa. Since he was seven years older than me – part of the age group most directly affected by the AIDS epidemic – my first thought was that someone he knew had died or, worse, that he'd tested positive. Imagine my shame when he told me that the reason he was so upset was because the government was implementing a bill to ban local authorities from 'promoting homosexuality'. A similar bill had been proposed earlier that year but its progress was impeded by the general election and it subsequently failed. Now it was back with a vengeance, proposed by Conservative MP David Wilshire and supported by leading Tories including Michael Howard and Michael Portillo.

In a party conference speech that's been quoted many times since, Margaret Thatcher stoked the flames of homophobia, claiming that children who should be taught 'traditional family values' were being told 'they have an inalienable right to be gay'. What became known as Clause 28 stated that a local authority 'shall not intentionally promote homosexuality or publish material with the intention of promoting homosexuality'. It also forbade 'the teaching in any maintained school of the acceptability of homosexuality as a pretended family relationship'. It was a pernicious piece of legislation, and led to a climate of fear in which teachers felt unable to support lesbian and gay students or justified in their own homophobic attitudes. Lives were blighted by Clause 28 and the subsequent culture of silence around gay sexuality at school.

The Insinuendos were strong advocates of theatre in education and regularly performed at schools and colleges, raising awareness around gay rights and promoting safer sex. One of their songs, sung to the tune of 'Three Little Maids from School Are We', called for more honest sex education to help tackle homophobia. As Vaughan saw it, the government was openly declaring war on lesbians and gay men.

Many people agreed. The Stop the Clause campaign was the biggest lesbian and gay rights movement this country had ever seen. On 20 February 1988, more than 20,000 people marched through the centre of Manchester. Two months later, an enormous rally was held in London's Jubilee Gardens, with performances from Boy George and Sinéad O'Connor. The protests led to the creation of the Stonewall group, dedicated to lobbying MPs and protecting the community from further political attacks on our human rights.

Far smaller, but no less newsworthy, were the actions of a group of women calling themselves the Lesbian Avengers, who famously disrupted the BBC *Six O'Clock News*. As newsreader Sue Lawley announced the day's headlines, the women stormed the studio shouting 'Stop the Clause!' One handcuffed herself to Lawley's desk, prompting her to remark, 'I'm afraid that we have been rather invaded.'

When the House of Lords voted to pass the bill, two women from the same group abseiled from the public balcony down into the chamber, using a washing line purchased from Clapham market and smuggled in under one woman's donkey jacket. *The Guardian*'s lesbian cartoonist Kate Charlesworth came up with a winning slogan: 'Abseil makes the heart grow fonder.'

One of the women involved in the protests was employed as a supervisor at the market-research company where I worked. Another I knew from The Bell.

Their fearless style of activism would inspire a generation – and determine the course of my life for the next five years.

Chapter 11:
Transition, Transmission

As the community rallied against Clause 28, I attended a party with Vaughan and was introduced to a woman called Kristiene Clarke. She was tall and elegant, with long auburn hair and a brown fedora hat like the one worn by Bowie in *The Man Who Fell To Earth*. Clearly we were destined to meet.

We clicked immediately and decamped to a quiet corner, where Kris proceeded to tell me about a television documentary she was producing. It was all about gender expression and what we'd now refer to as transgender identity. The ironic, tabloid-mocking title of the documentary was *Sex Change: Shock! Horror! Probe!*

Afterwards, I asked Vaughan why Kris was so interested in the subject.

'Maybe you should ask her,' he said.

As it turned out, I didn't need to. The next time I saw Kris, she brought it up. She was the first trans woman I'd ever met – at least knowingly – and we soon became friends. She told me how she'd previously identified as a gay man. She now lived as a woman and was in a relationship with another woman. I found her personal journey fascinating. She'd lived so many lives, seen the world from so many perspectives. The only person I could think of who'd done that was Virginia Woolf's *Orlando*, and *Orlando* was fictional. How could I not be intrigued?

Much to the annoyance of those around me, I became more than a little obsessed with Kris. Even Vaughan, who'd known her for years, found my fanboy crush irritating. At the time I put this down to jealousy, but in hindsight he probably had a point. I'm sure I was annoying. But I'd never met anyone quite like Kris before, and was eager to learn everything I could from her. I'd always had a tendency to throw myself into new friendships feet first and Kris was no exception. For months she was all I ever talked about.

The friendship served us both well. It was largely thanks to Kris that I took my first steps towards becoming a journalist. My first-ever commission was an interview with her about her documentary. While I still harboured dreams of having my play about Byron produced in some form or other, she persuaded me that freelance journalism was a far better way of paying the bills than working for the market-research company. Instead of cold-calling people and asking them about their favourite washing powder, I'd be interviewing people with something interesting to say – starting with her.

Spurred on by her enthusiasm, I rang the editor of London's free gay weekly newspaper *Capital Gay* and floated the idea. Much to my amazement, he said yes. His name was Michael Mason and he was to become a key figure in my life for the next few years. But Kris wasn't done yet. She suggested I try the London listings magazine *City Limits*, too. To be honest, I think she saw me less as an aspiring journalist and more as her personal publicist. So I phoned an editor at the magazine, explained that I was already interviewing Kris for *Capital Gay* and was commissioned to write a shorter piece putting the documentary into a broader context. The editor wanted a few quotes from Kris, together with comments from the director of an earlier documentary series called *A Change Of Sex*, which followed the personal journey of Julia Grant.

Grant was the first trans woman to publicly share her story on British television. She was the subject of five hour-long documentaries, directed by David Pearson. *George And Julia* was screened in 1979 and attracted nearly nine million viewers. The film introduced us to Julia at the start of her transition. Born and raised in Blackpool, she'd moved to London after a failed marriage and was working on the gay scene as a drag queen, lip-syncing to numbers like 'Non, Je Ne Regrette Rien' by Édith Piaf.

In 1978, Julia began living, working and dressing as a woman, which was a precondition for receiving treatment at the Charing Cross Hospital – the main clinic in the UK working with transgender patients. The film showed her in consultation with her NHS-appointed psychiatrist and even followed her into the operating theatre. Subsequent films caught up with her later in life, running the Hollywood Showbar in Manchester and making plans to marry her male partner. She also wrote two books about her life. *George And Julia* was published in 1980. A second memoir, *Just Julia*, followed in 1994. She remained an active member of Manchester's LGBTQ+ community until her death in 2019 of bowel cancer.

In many ways, Julia Grant was a pioneer. By allowing a TV crew to film her personal journey, she helped to change the way trans people were viewed by the general public. But by today's standards, the documentaries seem voyeuristic and prurient. The film Kris produced and directed took a very different approach, featuring a variety of trans men and women and using their experiences to explore the whole notion of gender. It questioned how gender roles were perceived, and focused on the cultural and political challenges faced by transgender people in the UK. Interviewees included Stephanie Anne Lloyd, founder of Transformation – specialist suppliers for trans women – and Stephen Whittle of the campaign group Press for Change.

The piece I wrote for *Capital Gay* appeared the week before the transmission date. It ran to a full page and was headlined 'Coming to a TV near you', which made me squirm but didn't seem to bother Kris in the slightest. Being new to the world of freelance journalism, I hadn't thought to agree a fee. I soon discovered that the paper didn't pay a word rate. Writers' fees were calculated by someone physically measuring each column of printed text with a ruler. For my full-page feature I was paid the princely sum of £40. *City Limits* paid even less, but I didn't mind. I'd been published. I'd seen my name in print. Finally it felt as if my career was on track.

I pitched some more ideas to Michael Mason, who commissioned me, and to the editor at *City Limits*, who didn't. With rent to find and bills to pay, it quickly became clear that I wouldn't be leaving the market-research company any time soon.

The morning after Kris's documentary was screened there was a heated discussion in the phone room at work. One senior member of staff found the whole notion of trans people 'a step too far' but was keen to stress that she wasn't homophobic. I pointed out that since half her employees were either lesbian or gay, this was probably just as well – and for all we knew, there might be someone working here who was trans and hadn't come out yet. Others applauded the film and the way it explored what we'd now call gender identity. Then, as now, the focus of the discussion was mainly on trans women. Very little was said about trans men.

It's important to remember that, in 1988, trans women weren't anything like as visible or as vocal as they are today. There was April Ashley, one of the first British people known to have had gender reassignment surgery, who surgically transitioned in 1960 and was exposed by the *Sunday People* a year later. There was Jayne County, proto-punk icon, who was rumoured to be the inspiration behind Bowie's gender-bending glam rock stomper 'Rebel Rebel'. Bowie fans were also aware of Romy Haag, the Dutch cabaret performer and nightclub manager who dated the Thin White Duke during his Berlin period in the late '70s.

More recently, and far more mainstream, there was the model Caroline Cossey, aka Tula, who appeared in the 1981 Bond film *For Your Eyes Only* and was famously outed by the *News Of The World*. At the height of her career, Tula graced the pages of *Vogue*, *Cosmopolitan* and *Harper's Bazaar*. She was also the first transgender model to pose for *Playboy* magazine. In 1980, she appeared in an ad for Smirnoff, where she was pictured water-skiing behind the Loch Ness monster. The tagline read, 'Well, they said anything could happen.' By 1988, Cossey was regularly monstered by the press, and appeared on TV chat shows where she was subjected to all manner of intrusive questioning and asked to explain herself over and over again.

Through my friendship with Kris, I was introduced to several trans women who shared similar stories of self-discovery and social discrimination. Among them were singer Adèle Anderson of Fascinating Aïda and the magician Fay Presto. In due course, I would interview both Adèle and Fay for *Capital Gay*.

Fay was well known on the gay scene, where she'd perform card tricks and other close-up magic, often at fundraisers of one kind or another. She took me for afternoon tea at The Savoy and told me her story – or at least those parts of it she was willing to disclose. Prior to training as a magician and joining the illustrious Magic Circle, she'd worked briefly as a laboratory assistant and pursued a career in sales. Of the various jobs she'd held before her transition, her favourite was working as a motorcycle courier. It was the perfect cover, she said. Nobody knew what was going on under the helmet.

Shortly after my interview with Fay was published, she wrote a letter to my editor, thanking me for my sensitive handling of her story. I didn't know it at the time, but she'd been badly treated by the press in the past and was extremely wary of journalists, even those working for a gay newspaper. Treating me to tea at The Savoy was a kind gesture. It also meant that the interview was conducted on neutral ground.

Adèle invited me to her flat in East London, where the walls were adorned with theatre posters, and she regaled me with stories of her colourful past. In her student days, she'd been a member of the Gay Liberation Front and identified as a radical drag queen, before reading about April Ashley and beginning her own transition. When she first auditioned for Fascinating Aïda she was asked, 'Are you a man?' and replied that she wasn't – 'because it wasn't the correct question.' When the management discovered that Adèle was trans, they urged founder Dillie Keane to fire her, fearing that she would jeopardise their career. Dillie refused.

The trio went on to enjoy enormous success together and are still going strong, while Adèle simultaneously pursues a solo career as both a singer and actress. Her many film and television credits include *Lady Jane, Hotel Babylon, New Tricks* and *The Romanoffs*. As she says herself, she is often cast as a trans woman – a part for which she is eminently qualified. We remain firm friends to this day.

In many ways, Kris's documentary was ahead of its time. It was no surprise to me when her film-making career took off. Soon she was making films for *Arena*, the BBC arts programme spearheaded by Alan Yentob, who directed the legendary *Cracked Actor* documentary about David Bowie back in 1975. Among Kris's subjects were Sandra Bernhard and Armistead Maupin. In fact, I put in a word for her with Bernhard when I interviewed the comedian for a newspaper.

This wasn't entirely altruistic on my part. No sooner had I embarked on a career as a journalist than I was hoping to make the transition to television. For a while I had ambitions of becoming a TV researcher. I applied for several positions and got nowhere. Kris said she'd help me but nothing ever came of it. It would be years before I got my first break in television – not as a researcher but as a writer and presenter. But in the meantime, my future lay in print media, and 'transmission' had one meaning in my life: the fear of infection.

'You are being safe, aren't you?' Kris asked me one day. A friend of hers had recently tested positive for HIV and she was worried that I'd be next.

'Of course,' I replied. But deep down I didn't know how true this was. The advice seemed to be changing all the time. Was oral sex without a condom safe? How high was the risk of transmission if your gums bled when you brushed your teeth? Was any sex between men safe, really? Or was it all just a question of luck?

Fuelled by gloating tabloid headlines about 'the gay plague' and doom-laden TV adverts featuring black granite tombstones and a grave voiceover by John Hurt, these anxieties were never far from my thoughts. Sometimes I'd have nightmares and wake up in a sweat, convinced that I was showing symptoms. The slightest sniffle would have me anxiously checking every inch of my body for telltale signs – a sore throat, swollen lymph nodes, an unexplained skin rash. Once I had an allergic reaction to a change of washing powder and spent a week convinced that the itchy redness was somehow AIDS-related.

I was twenty-three years old. In under ten years I'd gone from contemplating suicide to facing the very real prospect of an untimely death.

As the months flew by and television programmes warned of the dangers of 'sexual permissiveness' and gay men 'dicing with death', it seemed inevitable. I started tape-recording entire seasons of *Roseanne* and *The Golden Girls*, anticipating a time when I might be housebound or in hospital and in desperate need of some light entertainment.

Too afraid to get tested, I drowned my fears with booze and lived for the moment, partying harder than ever and looking increasingly unwell as a result. I was like a circus performer frantically spinning plates, convinced that if I stopped for just one moment, my world would come crashing down.

And sure enough, it did.

Chapter 12:
A Family Affair

My living arrangements with Vaughan came to an abrupt end when I decided to apply for the government's Enterprise Allowance Scheme. This initiative gave a guaranteed income of £40 per week to unemployed people who set up their own business. Rather than being officially unemployed and run the risk of being caught out or forced to take any job that came along, I'd be self-employed as a writer and still able to claim government support. I'd also qualify for housing benefit, which meant I could spend less time at the market-research company and more time working on what really mattered to me, which was writing.

The only problem was, Vaughan was already claiming housing benefit and wasn't declaring the rent I paid him each month. His self-justification for this was that his earnings were too low for him to get by without subletting, and that we hadn't discussed the possibility of me claiming benefits before I moved in. I tried appealing to his gay socialist principles but to no avail. So there was nothing else for it. I needed to find somewhere else to live.

As luck would have it, my cousin Elaine had recently arrived in London and was also looking for accommodation. She was currently staying with her brother Oliver in Blackheath but was keen to find a place of her own. We signed up with a local letting agency and were soon housed together a short distance from Oliver's place, at the top of Shooters Hill Road. The letting agent was a petite blonde woman with a posh telephone voice who rejoiced in the name of Marjorie Baptiste. We called her Marge.

I hadn't seen much of Elaine since we were both small children, but we immediately hit it off. She was a little shy at first but soon came out of her shell. We shared a similar sense of humour and enjoyed many of the same things – listening to music by Marc Almond, pottering around Greenwich Market in search of vintage clothes, and spending Sunday afternoons watching old Barbra Streisand movies. Many were the times we sat weeping together at *The Way We Were*.

My memories of this period aren't misty and water-coloured, though – mostly, they're sunny and bright, like the yellow walls of Elaine's bedroom. Sometimes we hosted house parties or went to parties thrown by friends in the local area. At some point in the evening, one of us would wrest control of the record player and put on some classic disco, which was Elaine's cue to demonstrate her interpretative dance skills. At one party in nearby Deptford, she acted out the lyrics to 'I Will Survive' with such conviction, she walked out of the door and found herself inside a broom cupboard. Undeterred, she styled it out until the song ended before re-emerging in time for 'Bad Girls' by Donna Summer.

But mostly we went out clubbing. Elaine had never been to a gay venue before but took to the scene like a duck to water. I say 'duck' – at some venues, women were more commonly referred to as 'fish'. On several occasions I got into altercations with misogynistic gay men who made my cousin feel unwelcome and should have known better than to cross a fiercely protective young Welshman after a few pints. You'd think that people who'd been on the receiving end of prejudice would show a little more awareness. But as I was rapidly learning, this wasn't always the case.

Our favourite weekend club was The Bell, partly due to the music policy and partly because it was mixed and women of all sexualities were more than welcome. There weren't many places where a gay boy about town and his female sidekick could dance together to everything from Kate Bush and The B-52s to New Order and Pet Shop Boys without attracting the wrong kind of attention.

The right kind of attention was more than welcome. Elaine was a big hit with the gay boys at The Bell – and one or two of the girls. When a lesbian friend of mine called Paula took rather a shine to her and speculated that she might be gay or possibly bisexual, Elaine refused to rule anything out. I joked that she was 'MissElaineous' – a nickname which soon stuck and she embraced proudly. If anyone asked her outright to nail her colours to the mast, she'd smile and say, 'You do what you can!'

The Bell was also a place where I sometimes pulled, but we didn't have long to make our mark. Clubs in those days closed far earlier than they do today. Even on a Saturday night, 2 a.m. was considered positively decadent – and was dependent on venues selling food, which in this case meant a hatch in the corner where you could purchase burgers and chips to help absorb all the excess alcohol.

Elaine and I would usually have a few drinks at home first, to help get us in the mood and steel ourselves for the long journey ahead. Going to The Bell took commitment. We'd take a bus from Shooters Hill to Blackheath main line station, a train to London Bridge and then a Northern line Tube to King's Cross. This could take anything between an hour and ninety minutes. Once we'd queued to get in, queued for the cloakroom and stood waiting at the bar for that all-important first round, we'd dance for two or three hours until the club closed, then begin the longer journey home. Neither of us could afford a cab fare so we relied on the night bus. First we'd take a bus from King's Cross to Trafalgar Square. Then we'd wait for another bus all the way back to Blackheath. If we missed one bus, the next wouldn't be along for up to an hour.

Sometimes we'd fall asleep on the second leg of the journey, or take the wrong bus by mistake and wind up somewhere like Barnehurst or even Dartford. But however late we arrived home, we'd always treat ourselves to a late-night/early-morning snack – usually a lentil bake, cooked from scratch, which took over an hour to prepare and ensured that we slept really badly and were sufficiently tired and emotionally fragile to wallow in our regular Sunday afternoon Streisand sobfest.

Elaine was a strict vegetarian who seemed to live almost entirely on pulses. As a teenager, she'd struggled with her weight and was now committed to healthy eating and exercise. We invested in a small trampoline known as a rebounder, and would start the day with a fresh fruit salad followed by half an hour bouncing along to whichever dance tracks had recently taken our fancy. 'Love Eviction' by Quartz Lock featuring Lonnie Gordon was a particular favourite. 'Tell It To My Heart' by Taylor Dayne was another. Elaine was also a keen runner, while I joined a gym in nearby Woolwich and threw myself back into weight training.

Gradually our idea of healthy living became more extreme. We read books like *Ultrahealth* and *Raw Energy* by diet gurus Leslie and Susannah Kenton and convinced ourselves that apple fasting was the way forward. For two whole days we ate nothing but apples. On the second night, we went to the cinema with Oliver. The film he'd chosen was *Babette's Feast*. My stomach rumbled so loudly I'm surprised we weren't thrown out for causing a disturbance.

For the best part of a year we stuck to a diet plan called Fit For Life. Devised by husband-and-wife team Harvey and Marilyn Diamond, *Fit For Life* promised many things. Clearer skin! Better digestion! More energy! A healthier body! A permanent solution to weight loss! Of these, the first four appealed to me more than the last. My skin was often blotchy and I regularly suffered from heartburn and indigestion – partly due to a hiatal hernia and partly thanks to a diet high in spicy, processed foods and alcohol. Freedom from indigestion sounded wonderful, and a better complexion was a bonus. More energy would also be nice. I often found it hard to motivate myself in the mornings, usually due to the hangover. I wasn't so bothered about losing weight but who didn't want a healthier body? Especially when we were living through a gay male health crisis?

Being the all-or-nothing kind of person I am, I threw myself into Fit For Life – not with gusto, as this implies a certain amount of enjoyment in the food I was eating, but with the dedication and zeal of a religious convert. No bleached white bread for me, thank you very much! None of your nasty processed foods! Keep those sugary drinks well away from me! And don't even think about offering me a piece of that chocolate! Not when I can have carob instead – the chocolate substitute with none of the nasties!

I vividly recall going through our kitchen cupboards and throwing away perfectly good food which didn't pass the Harvey-and-Marilyn test. Their mantra was: 'Is this food going to clog me or cleanse me?' If the answer was 'clog' then out it went. Together with Elaine, I binned cans of soup and baked beans, frozen pizzas, crackers made with bleached white flour, salted peanuts and other savoury snacks. So what did we eat? To begin with, lots of fruit. Like Leslie Kenton, the Diamonds were very big on fresh fruit. Apples, pears, cherries, grapes, melon – you name it, they loved it. Every day began with fruit – on its own, in a fruit salad or juiced. But it had to be fresh and not canned. Canned fruit was a definite no-no. And nothing but fruit was allowed before lunch.

There were also restrictions on which foods could be eaten together. Lunch might be a chicken salad or a sandwich made with wholemeal bread – but never a chicken salad sandwich. Complex carbohydrates and proteins weren't allowed in the same meal. If you wanted a sandwich, it came with salad and not a lot else. If you wanted chicken, it came with salad – but that didn't include potato salad or pasta salad, only raw vegetables. Cooked vegetables were also allowed, but in smaller quantities. Food combining was challenging, but the benefits far outweighed the inconvenience. It was claimed that the diet could help with allergies, headaches and eczema and even cure symptoms of disease.

The authors didn't describe Fit For Life as a diet but a new way of eating that could be incorporated into your daily lifestyle. Elaine and I were all for trying out new things. But these weren't small lifestyle changes. They were drastic. Basically we survived on large amounts of raw fruit and vegetables, brown rice and pasta, handfuls of nuts and seeds, a small amount of dairy, the odd glass of wine and the occasional indulgence like a baked potato – but never with grated cheese as this was strictly forbidden.

We'd spend a small fortune on dairy-free mayonnaise, banana chips and carob beanies at the local health-food shop, where every item seemed to cost £5 and was sold to us by a woman who seldom smiled and looked anything but healthy. We'd go out clubbing with little or no alcohol in our system and pieces of fruit or raw nuts in our bags for the journey home. I once brought back a young man I met at The Bell. As we climbed into bed he asked if I was wearing some kind of body lotion from the Body Shop.

'No,' I replied. 'Why do you ask?'

He grinned. 'Because your skin smells like strawberries!'

They say you are what you eat. That night I was at least 70 per cent fructose.

Another time, after months of adhering to this regime, Elaine and I were enjoying the sunshine in Greenwich Park and decided to reward ourselves with an ice cream. Minutes later we were rolling around on the grass in agony. Our now-delicate digestive systems just couldn't handle it.

For Elaine, extreme dieting was simply about staying trim and healthy. For me, there was an unspoken, ulterior motive. The books I read promised a level of health and protection against diseases I hadn't thought possible through dietary changes. Now I was willing to believe that restricting what I ate really could help 'cleanse' and 'detoxify' my body. I was desperate to rid my body of toxins because, in my mind, those toxins might include a deadly virus.

The irony was, by sticking so rigidly and for so long to this radical new eating plan, I became so painfully thin, rumours spread that I was already ill.

Just as Gerard had become a father figure to me, so Elaine became more like a sister than simply a cousin. The elder of my two sisters and I rarely spoke, and my youngest sister Jac had just started at Brynteg Comprehensive, where she was taught by some of the same teachers who'd encouraged me years earlier. Though our surnames are different and physically she takes after her father far more than our mother, her teachers had little trouble identifying Jac as Paul Burston's kid sister. We're alike in many ways – both keen observers, both opinionated and outspoken when we feel the need arises. Despite the twelve-year age gap, we've been close since she was small.

But for a few years we didn't communicate as often. By the time I was living with Elaine, Jac was adapting to life at her new school and going through puberty, with all the challenges both entail. I remembered myself at that age and knew from personal experience how all-consuming those changes can be. There were things I didn't share with my sister because I thought she was too young to understand, and there were things I didn't share with her because I was too afraid to admit them even to myself.

But Jac was no fool. Even as a small child, nothing escaped her attention. By the age of eleven, she knew her older brother was gay and she knew what AIDS was. Unbeknown to me at the time, she was worried that I'd get ill and die.

When I came home to visit that summer, she noticed how gaunt I looked and worried even more.

Encouraged by the recent success of *Les Enfants Terribles* at the Diorama, I decided to stage the production for a week-long run at the Etcetera Theatre in Camden. My parents kindly loaned me the hire fee and came to London to see the play. I'm not sure what they really made of it, but they said all the right things and my mum kept the programme and some press photos in a scrapbook, so I know they were proud of my achievement.

The critics were less than impressed. Writing in *City Limits*, the theatre critic Lyn Gardner praised Linda's performance but described me as 'too self-conscious' and the production as pretentious. I consoled myself with the knowledge that some of my greatest heroes had often been dismissed as pretentious, including Bowie and Cocteau himself.

One night Vaughan came to see the play with his new boyfriend. His only comment to me afterwards was, 'Where are your politics?'

I remember feeling deeply wounded by this. So what if my play wasn't overtly political? It was certainly overtly gay. Surely that was enough? Just because I didn't eat, sleep and breathe gay politics the way he did, that didn't make my creative endeavours any less worthwhile.

Vaughan and I hadn't seen much of each other since I'd moved out. I'd assumed it was because he felt guilty or awkward about the reasons for my departure. But now I thought perhaps he was simply busy with his new boyfriend. I'd only ever known Vaughan as a single man. Maybe he was one of those people who dropped his friends when a new love interest arrived on the scene. I'd certainly been guilty of this myself in the past, so who was I to judge?

A few weeks later Vaughan invited me over to his place for dinner. The room where I'd once slept was now occupied by another young gay man, who was out for the evening. Apart from that, the flat looked exactly as I remembered it. The upright piano still stood in the living room, with books and pages of sheet music stacked on top. House plants still covered the windowsills and trailed from every available surface. The window blinds still looked a little dusty. The furniture hadn't changed.

But something had. No sooner had I arrived than I knew instinctively that something wasn't right. Vaughan looked different somehow and was acting strangely – far less gregarious than usual and clearly distracted. The conversation was stilted. Finally I asked him how things were going with the new boyfriend.

'We broke up,' he said.

'I'm sorry to hear that. What happened?'

'He couldn't handle the fact that I've gone off sex since I discovered I'm HIV-positive.'

That was how he told me – and then he immediately changed the subject. Nothing further was said, though I remember the gnawing feeling deep in the pit of my stomach and the struggle to stop myself from crying. Somehow we made it through dinner and I took the Tube to London Bridge and the train back to Blackheath, where I told Elaine the news and cried uncontrollably for hours.

With the awful, inescapable knowledge of Vaughan's diagnosis, my whole world seemed to tilt on its axis. I kept thinking back to the night of the great hurricane and the flattened trees below my window. I thought about the time I came home and found him crying on the sofa. It all felt so prescient somehow. Suddenly HIV wasn't something I simply read about in the papers. It was up close and personal. I started grieving for Vaughan long before he became seriously ill. I remember feeling ashamed of this – and even more ashamed of the other feelings he stirred in me. In the time I'd known him, he'd had far fewer sexual contacts than I had. Compared to me, Vaughan was practically celibate. If this could happen to him it could happen to anyone. It could easily happen to me – and probably already had. My healthy-living plan went out of the window. What was the point in watching what I ate and depriving myself of cigarettes and alcohol? What was the point of anything?

I started drinking regularly again – not too heavily at first, but quickly escalating to the point where one bottle of wine with dinner wasn't enough. I could feel myself spiralling out of control, slipping back into self-destructive patterns of behaviour I recognised all too well. I needed an outlet, some other way of channelling my emotions, something more constructive.

Then, one day, I opened a copy of *Capital Gay* and saw an advert for a public meeting at the London Lesbian and Gay Centre. People were planning to form an AIDS activist group based on ACT UP in New York. And I thought, 'I could do that!'

Chapter 13:
We Can Be Heroes

1 December 1989. World AIDS Day. An unmarked white van is slowly snaking its way through Parliament Square towards Westminster Bridge. The driver is an ex-military man named Alan. Packed in the back are a dozen men and women, none of us from a military background, all of us personally embattled in one way or another.

Halfway across the bridge, the van suddenly stops. The rear doors fly open and we jump out, carrying a thick iron chain. Dodging the traffic, we padlock the chain to either side of the bridge, before handcuffing ourselves to it and tossing the keys into the Thames below. Some of us are holding bunches of flowers, the kind you might place on a loved one's grave. We link arms as a show of solidarity and begin our protest. 'Act up! Fight back! Fight AIDS!'

I joined ACT UP shortly after Vaughan told me he was HIV+. By the time I was chaining myself to Westminster Bridge some ten months later, it had completely taken over my life. Some people found this hard to deal with. It was all I ever talked about. But Elaine understood. She was there for me when many others weren't.

ACT UP stood for AIDS Coalition to Unleash Power. There was no formal structure or hierarchy, but rather a variety of sub-groups dedicated to direct action, fundraising, media liaison, outreach and so on. I volunteered to be part of the action group. Not everyone could afford to get arrested. Some had family to think about or jobs to protect. But everyone was equally welcome. Some people made placards or banners for our actions. Others acted as legal observers – like Elaine, who observed me being arrested more times than either of us can remember.

Archive photographs from the time tend to show angry gay men in black leather biker jackets. There were certainly a fair few of those, myself included. But there were also a lot of women involved in ACT UP London – Stacey Baker, Ché Feenie, Emma Hindley, Jo Mackie and Maureen Oliver, to name just a few. Most were lesbians. Statistically, lesbians remain one of the lowest-risk groups in terms of the transmission of HIV. But many were personally affected by the crisis, or felt a strong sense of political solidarity with gay men. As was often asked at the time, had the situation been reversed, would gay men have stepped up in quite the same way? I'm not sure they would have.

At that very first meeting I met a beautiful young biker boy called Spud Jones, who quickly became one of my closest friends. As I soon discovered, activism can be a powerful bonding agent. Spud was the singer in a band called Tongue Man, who released punky, noisy, unapologetically gay records with titles like *Joys Of A Meatmaster*. He was never destined to appear on *Top Of The Pops*.

But another member of ACT UP often did. Jimmy Somerville had been part of the soundtrack to my life from 'Smalltown Boy' through to his recent hit 'Don't Leave Me This Way' – the Communards cover of a disco classic, interpreted by many as a tribute to those recently lost to AIDS. His new solo single 'Read My Lips (Enough Is Enough)' was a protest song calling for increased funding to tackle the pandemic. The title came from a phrase used by President George Bush and adapted by the New York queer art collective Gran Fury, who provided much of the artwork for ACT UP, including images of same-sex couples defiantly locking lips. Together with Erasure's Andy Bell – at that time, one of the few celebrities who was open about his HIV status – Jimmy toured the UK, raising much needed funds to help cover our legal costs.

ACT UP was committed to 'non-violent direct action', sometimes referred to as 'civil disobedience' – otherwise known as breaking the law. The aim wasn't simply to vent our anger – though for me this was certainly part of the attraction – but to raise awareness of the issues affecting people living with HIV and AIDS, be they welfare cuts, discrimination in the workplace, homophobic reporting in the press, or the failure of prisons and other services to provide free condoms and needle exchanges to help stop the spread of the virus.

Demonstrations were referred to as 'zaps' and tended to be rather theatrical in nature. Again, this suited me down to a T. For example, ACT UP New York famously staged an enormous 'die-in' at St Patrick's Cathedral and stormed the offices of politicians and drug companies, covering desks and computers with fake blood. ACT UP Paris lowered a giant pink condom over the Egyptian obelisk at Place de la Concorde.

It's fair to say that ACT UP London never reached such dizzy heights. Our first zap involved catapulting condoms over the walls of Pentonville Prison. When it became clear that rubbers wrapped in foil didn't have the density required to scale the prison walls, we inflated the condoms and tried to float them over instead. We also chained ourselves to the gates of Downing Street on the day the Chancellor of the Exchequer, John Major, was due to deliver the budget. As his car approached, a group of us leaped out and handcuffed ourselves to the gates, successfully blocking his path. My photo appeared in one of the gay free sheets under the headline 'Not budging on budget day'. Five people were arrested and referred to as 'the ACT UP five'.

Another time, we invaded the offices of the *Daily Mail*, cunningly disguised as motorcycle couriers. The target of our protest was columnist George Gale, who peddled the kind of victim-blaming AIDS commentary typical of the period. I was sporting rather a luxurious quiff at the time and questioned whether a motorcycle helmet was really necessary as it might flatten my hair. My friend Emma rolled her eyes and reminded me that this was no time for vanity. Photographs taken inside the *Daily Mail* offices show Emma, Jimmy, me and others handcuffed to some railings while a security guard looks on perplexed. My hair looks suitably disarrayed but disappointingly lacking in volume.

But mainly we blocked traffic. As my fellow activist and soon-to-be boyfriend William often said, our battle cry could have been 'ACT UP London, lie down!' Joking aside, this was one way to guarantee media coverage. If all else failed, at least we'd make the traffic news. So when the government announced benefit cuts to people living with HIV, AIDS and other life-threatening illnesses and chronic conditions, we staged a die-in next to the Cenotaph on Whitehall. A dozen of us lay across the road, clinging on to a large banner and chanting, 'Living with AIDS, dying for money!' I was one of the first to be dragged away by the police, who didn't arrest me but simply dumped me on the pavement. I picked myself up and tried to re-join the protest, only people were packed so tightly together there was no room for me to squeeze in. I had to outrun the police and approach the demo from a different angle, lying back down in the road but facing the opposite way to everyone else. The moment was captured by photographer Gordon Rainsford and remains one of my favourite ACT UP photos. I might look a right poser, but it's a pose with purpose. My 'Action = Life' T-shirt is clearly visible. The look on my face is one of grim determination.

There weren't a lot of laughs at ACT UP. Some people were literally fighting for their lives. But there was certainly a lot of camaraderie and the zaps gave me a real buzz. The planning meetings were more life-zapping. During one interminably long meeting, myself and another young gay male activist became so frustrated we went off and had sex together in the toilets. When we returned, the same few people were still debating the same issue, round and round in ever-decreasing circles. My friend and I pushed back our chairs, sat down on the floor and started painting placards for an upcoming demo.

I've heard it said that living through the AIDS crisis was like living through a war – and in some ways, it was. But it was a war in which the usual rules of engagement didn't apply. Only small, isolated pockets of the population were affected. The vast majority were either blissfully unaware or couldn't have cared less. Our war dead were rarely shown the respect they deserved. Our war heroes largely went unrecognised. It's only now, more than thirty years after the UK's first AIDS unit was opened by Princess Diana at the Middlesex Hospital on Tottenham Court Road, that a permanent memorial is finally being built.

While hundreds of young men lay dying, politicians talked about containment measures, mandatory testing and the issuing of 'AIDS-free' identity cards. A senior police officer named James Anderton insisted that gay people and those with AIDS were 'swirl-ing around in a human cesspit of their own making'. According to the tabloids, we were perverts and plague-carriers who should be rounded up and quarantined on an island somewhere. It was even suggested that people with HIV should be branded with tattoos spelling out their diagnosis. Graffiti began to appear around London. 'G-A-Y – Got AIDS Yet?' And 'AIDS – Arse Injected Death Sentence'.

Before he was diagnosed, Vaughan had been an active member of the residents' association. When word spread that he was ill, someone wrote in red paint on his front door: 'House of AIDS'. Even after the paint had been scrubbed off, the stain remained. I wanted to track the culprit down, name, shame and report them. But even if I could, what good would it have done? Things would only have escalated. I no longer lived at this address. Vaughan did, and he hardly ever left the flat.

Thirty years before Covid-19 forced the entire world into lockdown, a vilified, vulnerable community was facing a different pandemic – one that carried added social stigma and brought very little public sympathy. There was no national minute of silence for those lost to AIDS, no candles on doorsteps or calls for the country to pull together and beat the virus. We were on our own.

I'd grown up with the stigma of being gay. Now there was a whole new layer of guilt and shame to contend with. Even among gay men, it wasn't uncommon to hear derogatory comments about those living with HIV. The gay scene has always prized youth and beauty above all else – and suddenly there was this wasting disease that turned beautiful young men from objects of desire into objects of pity, fear and even contempt.

Internalised homophobia had a lot to do with it. It was around this time that I interviewed the American gay activist Phill Wilson, who was visiting London to host a workshop promoting safer sex. He said something that has stayed with me to this day. There's no point in giving people the information they need to save their lives if you can't convince them that their lives are worth saving. So many gay men grow up internalising years of homophobia. We're literally taught to hate ourselves. Is it any wonder that some of us struggle with self-esteem issues or develop patterns of behaviour that put our health and even our lives in danger? Is it any wonder that we might even project those feelings on to one another?

Yes, there was a lot of community fundraising and grass-roots support for those affected. Without it, charities like the Terrence Higgins Trust wouldn't exist. But there was also a lot of shaming – a sense that people with AIDS were somehow letting the side down. There were good gays and there were bad gays – and there were people like me, who desperately wanted to make a difference and did it the only way we knew how, by literally putting our bodies on the line.

Whenever I post photos from my ACT UP days on social media, people invariably remark on what heroes we were. I didn't feel like a hero. All my life I'd been called a coward, a sissy, the kind of boy anyone could beat up and frequently did. I knew what it felt like to be bullied and not fight back. When AIDS arrived I felt I had no choice. I was like a cornered animal. My only option was to come out fighting. I don't think anyone in ACT UP thought of themselves as being particularly brave at the time. We were just a group of desperate men and women doing what we had to do. But, looking back, I'm surprised at how courageous we were. In our own way, we were heroes – and not just for one day.

Which brings us back to that cold December day on Westminster Bridge. As zaps go, this is one of our most successful. We raise the chain to allow emergency vehicles to pass under, but otherwise we succeed in blocking the traffic for quite some time.

Then the police arrive. They're wearing rubber gloves and wielding bolt cutters. They sever the chain at both ends and reel us in like fish on a line, cutting through our handcuffs as they haul us into the paddy wagon. Our fellow activists gather round and chant, 'The world is watching you! The world is watching you!'

The world isn't watching. The world is – for the most part – turning a blind eye. But the gay-press photographers are here and we do make the local radio news, so at least some people are made aware of our protest.

We're carted off to the police cells and held for four hours. I share a cell with a man with AIDS who is denied his medication. Later, we make our way back to the London Lesbian and Gay Centre for a debriefing. Hanging from our wrists are the remains of the handcuffs we wore earlier. The butch lesbian on the door tries to refuse us entry, insisting that the cuffs are a celebration of sadomasochism and offensive to women. I barge in anyway. The irony of being arrested at a human rights demonstration and then policed by a member of my own community isn't lost on me. Nor do I find it remotely funny.

I risked arrest and a criminal record many times with ACT UP. In most cases, I was taken into police custody, cautioned and released without charge. The one time I was arrested and prosecuted for my actions, I wasn't breaking the law. The target of the zap was Australia House on the Strand, in protest at the Australian government's decision to ban people with HIV from entering the country. The action began with a group of us storming the building and staging a sit-in. When the police forcibly removed us, a number of people lay down in the road outside. I was standing on the pavement, chatting with a handsome young television reporter from the BBC, when a police officer arrested me and charged me with obstructing the highway. The arresting officer clearly wasn't very bright. At the time of my arrest, there was a large film camera pointed in my direction and a sound engineer with a boom microphone hovering nearby.

For reasons best known to themselves, the CPS chose to prosecute. And so I had my day in court. I won't pretend I wasn't nervous. To be honest, I was terrified. But as I stood in the dock at Bow Street Magistrates' Court, I comforted myself with the thought that two of my heroes, Oscar Wilde and Quentin Crisp, had once stood here. I had the best barrister legal aid could buy, in the form of a fierce Irishwoman called Grainne McMorrow. Plus, I had a star witness – the TV reporter who was present at the time of my arrest and was willing to testify on my behalf. Originally from Canada, he was now based in Manchester but happy to travel down to London. With his testimony, the case was thrown out of court and the arresting officer was given a stern ticking-off by the magistrate. I turned to look at the policeman and grinned triumphantly.

Incidentally, the name of that young TV reporter was Tyler Brûlé – the same Tyler Brûlé who went on to launch the hugely successful style magazines *Wallpaper** and *Monocle*.

Reader, I dated him.

Chapter 14:
Love Is The Drug

Dating Tyler was never going to be straightforward. I was on benefits. He earned a decent wage as a TV reporter. His star was already on the ascent. I was a total nobody. He was a Canadian based in Manchester. I was a Welshman living in deepest South London. We were worlds apart.

This may help explain why we only ever had two dates. The first was in London, when he came to give evidence at my trial. I was already bedazzled by the fact that Tyler appeared on television. I was even more impressed when he sent a car to collect me from Blackheath and drive me all the way to his hotel in Soho. This certainly beat public transport.

But no sooner had I arrived than my imposter syndrome began to kick in. I'd never been invited to such a swanky hotel before. I'd only ever worked in one. (To this day, each time I check in at a smart hotel, part of me expects the head of housekeeping to summon me to the linen room.) I'd heard of gay couples being turned away from hotels and guest houses and had visions of us being forcibly ejected the moment someone clocked the fact that Tyler and I were quite possibly on a date.

I needn't have worried. This was Hazlitt's in Soho. They did things differently there.

I've never been great at keeping a diary but I did keep one that year. Reading it back now, what strikes me is how little I write about ACT UP. I write about plays I'd seen – Peter Hall's revival of *Orpheus Descending* by Tennessee Williams, a musical called *Poppy* by Peter Nichols – and a play I was working on, about the so-called Acid Bath Murderer, John Haigh. I write about the men I fancied at the gym and my frustration at not being able to find a decent boyfriend or a proper job. At one point, I liken myself to one of Elaine's jacket potatoes, 'about to explode'. That one throwaway remark is probably the most revealing of all.

One diary entry describes the ACT UP demo at Australia House and mentions the fact that ten of us were arrested – including Jimmy Somerville, which generated a fair amount of press coverage. Even *The Sun* ran an even-handed full-page piece, which was rare for the time.

The same entry recounts a trip with Vaughan to Amsterdam. It was somewhere he'd always longed to visit. His friends clubbed together to pay for the trip and it was agreed that I'd be the one to accompany him. He was already pretty ill by then. Photographs from that weekend show him looking worryingly pale and gaunt. I was terrified that he might die on me. What would I do? I'd just turned twenty-four. I was in a foreign city where I didn't speak the language. How on earth would I shoulder such a responsibility?

Thankfully, my fears were unfounded. Together we visited the Homomonument, the first monument in the world commemorating lesbians and gay men killed by the Nazis. We took a boat trip on the canal and Vaughan took a photo of me dressed in double denim with an ACT UP badge proudly pinned to my jacket and a smile on my face which I wasn't really feeling. It's one of the few photos of me smiling at that age – and it's totally forced. After the boat trip we got stoned on hash cookies in a coffee shop. Later, Vaughan visited a gay bathhouse, while I ventured to a club called The Cockring, where I met 'a very cute boy called Marc' and 'chose to go home with him and do it properly'. When it came to sex, I was still quite prudish, preferring to take out rather than eat in.

But most of my diary entries for that period are devoted to Tyler. I write about first laying eyes on him at an ACT UP meeting, how quickly things became flirtatious, how happy I was feeling despite having hardly any money and little hope of my ambition to become a published writer ever being fulfilled. One diary entry ends: 'If I wasn't so tired – a night full of dreams about Tyler – I'd be dancing!'

The dream soon turned sour.

A few weeks after my court case, Tyler invited me to spend the weekend with him in Manchester. He covered my train fare and took me to an expensive restaurant, where he insisted on paying and I became painfully conscious of the gulf between us. It wasn't just that we dressed differently – him all clean-cut in his chinos and preppy, button-down shirt; me in my leather biker jacket, ribbed vest and torn jeans. He was only a few years younger than me but had already achieved so much, and seemed far more ambitious and goal-oriented than I had ever been.

By the time I arrived back in London, I knew that I wouldn't be visiting Tyler in Manchester again any time soon. But it was all very amicable and I was happy for him when he went on to enjoy such enormous success.

ACT UP continued to dominate my life and most of my conversations. I must have driven my non-activist friends mad. In fact, I know I did, because a number of people told me so. I'd try to rein myself in, but then another friend would get ill and I'd throw myself back into the maelstrom of meetings, demos and arrests.

For all the courage I displayed during my clashes with the police, I was still largely driven by fear. Shortly after that trip to Amsterdam, I went to visit Vaughan in hospital. His urine bottle was full, and when I went to empty it, the contents spilled over my hand. I knew the risk of infection was virtually zero. But that didn't stop me from obsessively checking my hands for tiny cuts or grazes and scrubbing them until the skin was red-raw.

Like many others I knew, I hadn't taken an HIV test. I was too afraid of what the result might be. The only available treatment then was AZT, which many claimed was toxic and was actually killing people. So what was the point in knowing? I'd always been good at repressing things. I'd had a lot of practice. I adjusted my sexual behaviour but still the nagging doubts remained. What if I've already got it? Will I get ill? How quickly will I die?

ACT UP offered a way of channelling my fears into something more constructive. Our slogan, after all, was 'Action = Life' – a positive spin on the ACT UP New York slogan, 'Silence = Death', which we felt was too nihilistic. But like the New York chapter, we were 'united in anger'. To me, this sounded far more empowering than 'riddled with sexual anxiety, compounded by grief'. Though this would have been closer to the truth.

The same year I dated – briefly – a young Canadian, I fell for a young American. (And don't think I didn't play that Bowie song over and over. Of course I did.)

I met him at the London Lesbian and Gay Centre following a tortuously long ACT UP meeting in which everything was debated and nothing was decided. There were internal rows over politics, and accusations of entryism and takeovers by Trotskyists. In other words, the same arguments that have always divided those broadly on the left and continue to do so to this day. It was the Judean

People's Front versus the People's Front of Judea – in ripped jeans and leather jackets.

I stormed out of the meeting and up to the bar, where someone caught my eye, smiled and made the last few hours melt away. His name was Chris, he came from California and he was quite possibly the most beautiful man I'd ever seen. Within minutes of meeting him, I knew I was falling hopelessly in love. Hopelessly, because he already had a boyfriend.

To give Chris his due, he told me this as soon as we started chatting. Not that it stopped him from offering to buy me a drink and flirting shamelessly.

After a couple of pints, they called last orders.

'So what happens now?' I asked.

He grinned. 'That depends.'

'On what?'

'On whether you invite me home.'

I could hardly believe my luck. I'd seen Chris around but always assumed he was out of my league. He had model-boy looks – bright eyes, thick dark eyebrows, kissable lips and a perfect quiff. He reminded me of a young Matt Dillon. Now here we were, jumping on the Tube together to London Bridge, then taking a train to Blackheath station and a bus on from there. He must really, really like me!

It turned out he did. But he also really, really liked his boyfriend. So for a while I was his bit on the side. At first, I didn't mind. Sex with Chris was the best I'd ever had. When we weren't busy pleasuring each other, we smoked – first thing in the morning, last thing at night. Smoking in bed felt sexy because everything about Chris felt sexy. My habit spiralled out of control – twenty a day, then thirty. Even now, the sound and smell of a Zippo lighter takes me right back to that place and time.

Smoking wasn't my only vice. I was also addicted to Chris. And like any addiction, it became increasingly hard to handle. I'd wait expectantly for him to call, thrilled at the thought of seeing him again, then sink into a dark depression when he didn't ring. When we were together, it was wonderful. When we were apart, it was agony. I was falling for him big time and wanted him all to myself.

One achingly long bank holiday weekend I sat waiting by the phone for three whole days. When he didn't call, I rang his flatmate and pushed him for information. Was Chris out with his boyfriend? How were they getting on? Was he serious about me? Did his flatmate think we might have a future together? Christ, it was pathetic.

Whether it was my clinginess that tipped Chris over the edge or he was simply waiting for an excuse to break up with me, I'll never know. But the next time I saw him, he told me it wouldn't be good for either of us if we 'started a relationship'.

Personally, I thought we were already in a relationship, but apparently I was alone in this. We agreed to part as friends and that was it. Goodbye, young American.

A few weeks after being dumped by Chris, I met a guy called Steve at the gym in Woolwich. I can barely remember him now, but according to my diary he made quite an impression. He was a few years older than me, handsome and had 'a gorgeous body'. Not that I ever saw it in any other context than the communal showers at the gym.

One day he waited until I'd finished my workout, followed me into the changing room and watched me undress before casually asking if I had a boyfriend. When I told him I didn't, he smiled and informed me that he was going to the West End gay club known as Bang that night. 'Maybe I'll see you there?'

He didn't see me there. Or rather, I didn't see him. Maybe he was at the club or maybe he changed his mind. I never found out. There's no mention of Steve after that one diary entry. We never banged or even went on a date. He joined the ranks of all the other men I met, immediately pictured myself settling down with, was briefly disappointed by and soon forgot about.

Rereading these diary entries, it strikes me that my increasingly desperate search for a boyfriend was every bit as tumultuous as my life as an AIDS activist – and it doesn't take a genius to work out that these two things may have been related. Love and loss are hard to handle at any age. I'm in my fifties now and I'm still learning. But when you're twenty-four they can feel overwhelming.

Like many gay men of my generation, I didn't have a gay adolescence. I didn't come out or lose my virginity with another man until I was nineteen. Those teenage years I spent repressing my desires and denying the fact that I was gay led to a kind of arrested development. In many ways, my twenties were my delayed adolescence.

And here I was – little more than a teenager at heart, living through the horrors of the epidemic, desperate for something solid to cling on to and looking for love in all the wrong places. It's no wonder my emotions ran high. The stakes were even higher, and I was so painfully young.

I think it was the need for something to hold on to, the craving for something permanent, that led me to get my first tattoo. That, and the fact that my friend Spud had biker tattoos adorning both his arms and I thought they looked really sexy. People warned me that tattoos were painful. What nobody told me is that they're also addictive. No sooner had my first tattoo healed than I went back for seconds. On my upper-right arm I had an elaborate skulls-and-dagger design, and on my left, a phoenix.

The symbolism of this may seem a little obvious. In fact, it was inspired by my admiration for Pat Phoenix of *Coronation Street* fame, who came to my home town when I was young to open an amusement arcade called Stardust. For reasons I didn't fully comprehend at the time, I'd always had a soft spot for Elsie Tanner, the scarlet woman played by Phoenix on the nation's favourite soap. And so it was that one small boy with stardust in his eyes and a large number of older women with shopping trolleys waited in the rain for over an hour to see their idol.

When she finally arrived, stepping out of a big black car in a fur coat and sunglasses, we all surged forward, eager to get a good eyeful of the woman who made Weatherfield seem as glamorous as Hollywood. And it was then that Pat Phoenix touched me. On the upper-left arm, just below the shoulder – where I now have a tattoo of a phoenix.

Of course, if anyone ever asked me, I didn't tell them this. Tattoos were supposed to be butch and sexy and there's nothing remotely butch or sexy about this story. So I'd simply say that the phoenix was a symbol of rebirth, a creature that dies in flames and rises again from the ashes. The tattoo was a personal tribute to the fiery spirit of AIDS activism, to our defiance and fight for life in the face of a deadly disease.

This much, at least, was partly true. Tattooed beneath my flaming phoenix I have a row of skulls and a ribbon banner inscribed with the words 'Love and Rage'. These were the two emotions that consumed me at the time. Looking back, it's hard to say which had the greater hold.

Chapter 15:
Rage Hard

Growing up in South Wales, I was familiar with the work of Dylan Thomas. In the sixth form I joined a reading group and read his poetry. I was particularly taken with 'Do not go gentle into that good night' and its incitement to rage against death, rather than accept it passively. By my mid-twenties, my understanding of this poem had deepened considerably.

As a young gay man about town, I was equally familiar with Frankie Goes To Hollywood's fifth and final Top Ten hit 'Rage Hard', the chorus of which draws heavily on Thomas's poem. The video features Holly Johnson, Paul Rutherford and the lads as rock revolutionaries, inciting an audience of enslaved people to rise up and cast off their chains.

As the '80s drew to a close, I was raging harder than ever. I was an active member of ACT UP, busy chaining myself to railings, getting arrested and bending the ear of everyone I met with the importance of our actions.

I was also starting to make a name for myself as a journalist, first as a regular freelancer for *Capital Gay*, then as a contributor to publications like *City Limits*, *The Face* and *Gay Times*. The work was enjoyable but poorly paid. So in the autumn of 1989, I secured a part-time job at GALOP – then known as the Gay London Police Monitoring Group, now rebranded as 'the LGBT+ anti-violence charity'.

I worked for GALOP two days a week, taking calls from men who'd been queer-bashed or arrested for consenting sexual offences. Police entrapment was rife in the late '80s and early '90s. Officers would stake out public lavatories, luring men into committing acts of indecency with so-called pretty policemen. Names would be released to the local press and lives ruined. It's no wonder so many gay and bisexual men viewed the police with suspicion.

In the spring of 1990, I attended the inaugural meeting of OutRage! The self-styled 'queer direct-action group' was founded in response to a wave of homophobic murders – in particular the killing of actor Michael Boothe, who was kicked to death in West London – as well as a huge rise in the number of gay and bisexual men arrested for consensual sexual offences. The group's demands to the police were 'protection, not persecution' and 'policing without prejudice'.

OutRage! borrowed heavily from ACT UP. Many of the same people were involved, including co-founder Simon Watney. Their methods were very similar. Like ACT UP, the group was committed to non-violent direct action and civil disobedience. Juggling my involvement in ACT UP and OutRage! with my job at GALOP wasn't always easy – and there were other challenges, too.

Vaughan died on 19 February 1990. The date is etched into my memory and stitched on to the panel a group of us made in his name for the AIDS Memorial Quilt. Laying the panel at a public ceremony in Trafalgar Square, my legs gave way beneath me and I stumbled to the ground, shaking with grief. It was one of the hardest things I've ever had to do – harder even than the night he died.

Difficult to the end, Vaughan's dying wish was that his friends be summoned to his bedside and instructed to have a party. He'd been hospitalised for weeks by then and had lost the power of speech, so communicated his instructions with the aid of a note-pad. He wanted music, balloons and party streamers. No sad faces or signs of mourning were allowed – only smiley, happy, party people.

I didn't know if I could do it. My former tutor and friend Gerard told me I'd regret it if I didn't. He kindly drove me to the Middlesex Hospital on Tottenham Court Road and waited for me in the car park. Meanwhile, in a private room with several equally distressed friends, I put on a brave face, danced around and waved my pink balloons as a dying man took his last breath. He was thirty-one years old.

Shortly after Vaughan died, Brian Kennedy passed away. I'd met Brian through my job at GALOP. He was a member of the Gay Business Association, who were keen to work with us and develop a better working relationship with the police. He was also a journalist – and an outspoken one at that. Brian edited the 'Out in the City' section at *City Limits* and published his own quarterly magazine, *Kennedy's Gay Guide*. He told me I reminded him of himself when he was my age and asked me to cover for him at *City Limits* while he went on holiday.

I didn't know it then, but Brian wasn't really going on holiday. He was going into hospital. His first bout of serious illness was soon followed by a second. When he was discharged from hospital the second time, he invited me to his flat, told me he had AIDS and asked if I would take over his role at *City Limits* and also edit *Kennedy's Gay Guide* on his behalf. How could I refuse? I was grateful for the work, but the fact that these career opportunities came my way as a direct result of the AIDS crisis left me feeling conflicted, to say the least.

The day Brian died I was just about to leave my flat to visit him in hospital when his flatmate phoned and told me I was too late. His heart had stopped half an hour earlier. He was thirty-seven years old. I went into the *City Limits* office a few days later, sat at a dead man's desk and broke down crying.

It wasn't all doom and gloom at *City Limits*. I had some wonderful times working for the magazine and made some friends for life. It was there that I first met Suzanne Moore, Deborah Orr and Sam Taylor – fellow working-class kids who'd made it into the overwhelmingly middle-class world of journalism. I also met a fair number of celebrities. A few months into the job, I went to cover Elizabeth Taylor's visit to the London Lighthouse hospice for people with HIV and AIDS. Taylor had long been considered a gay ally thanks to her friendships with Montgomery Clift, James Dean and Rock Hudson. But it was with the arrival of AIDS that her status as a gay icon was secured. Taylor spoke out at a time few public figures did, raising awareness and funds through her own personal AIDS foundation. After her death, it was even claimed that she ran the LA equivalent of the Dallas Buyers Club, procuring experimental AIDS-treatment drugs and distributing them from her Bel Air home.

Of course, none of us knew this at the time. But nobody at the London Lighthouse that day was left in any doubt that they were in the presence of a bona fide Hollywood legend. Flashbulbs exploded the moment she arrived. Unfortunately, a photographer from *The Sun* was among those invited, so many people were reluctant to come forward, fearing that their picture would appear in a newspaper hardly known for its sympathetic coverage.

I had no such qualms, and cornered Taylor in the cafeteria for an autograph. She was tiny, with jet-black, heavily backcombed hair – and yes, her eyes really were a startling shade of blue. The wattage of her star power was truly dazzling. So much so that I mumbled my name and she signed the press photo 'To Michael' before hastily correcting her mistake.

Under Sam Taylor's editorship, I was sent to interview Rupert Everett, who had just published his first novel and gave a charming, if slightly defensive, account of himself, complaining that magazines like *City Limits* often had it in for people like him, who happened to come from more privileged backgrounds than the average left-wing hack. I wondered if this explained his decision to dress for the interview in a flannel shirt and backwards baseball cap.

I also interviewed Jason Donovan, who was starring in *Joseph And The Amazing Technicolor Dreamcoat* and had recently become the target of an outing campaign similar to those being waged in the US. Days before our interview, posters of Donovan appeared around Covent Garden with the words 'Queer as Fuck' emblazoned across his chest. We sent a photographer along but our lawyer advised against publishing the images. A friend at *The Face* ended up using them instead, and Donovan famously sued the magazine for libel. His complaint was that suggesting he was gay implied that he was a hypocrite. Gay activists were angered when his lawyer described the suggestion that his client was gay as 'a poisonous slur'.

My interview made the cover of *City Limits*. It was headlined 'Jason Talks Straight' and implied that perhaps he wasn't all he seemed. Donovan was enraged and went on Michael Parkinson's radio show to denounce me as 'a frustrated homosexual'.

Me, frustrated? I should have sued.

The controversial outing campaigns of the late '80s and early '90s were a direct response to the AIDS epidemic. Many of those targeted were politicians who were gay in private but straight in public and working against the interests of the community during a time of crisis. AIDS gave gay politics a whole new level of urgency. But it wasn't the only immediate threat to life.

In March 1993, GALOP started receiving calls from men who'd encountered someone they thought might be a serial killer. By June that year, Colin Ireland had murdered five gay men, earning him the nickname the Gay Slayer. Though he insisted he was straight and had previously been married twice, Ireland frequented London's famous gay leather bar The Coleherne, targeting men who were into S&M and inviting himself back to their homes. There, he would restrain them under the guise of some sexual bondage game before killing them. His first victim was Peter Walker, who Ireland bound and then suffocated by pulling a plastic bag over his head. The next day, he called a journalist at *The Sun*, informing them of what he'd done and indicating that he wanted to make a name for himself as a serial killer.

Despite this, Ireland managed to avoid detection for months. He was highly organised, carried a murder kit of rope and handcuffs, plus a full change of clothes. After strangling or suffocating his victim, he would clean the crime scene of any forensic evidence and remain there until the following morning, to avoid arousing suspicion.

It was all eerily reminiscent of the 1980 gay serial-killer thriller *Cruising*, starring Al Pacino. The murders were heavily publicised by the mass media, and London's gay scene was on high alert. The phones at GALOP never stopped ringing. Some were crank calls. Others came from men who either knew one of the victims or had seen someone fitting Ireland's description but weren't willing to speak to the police directly. It took months for the police to connect the killings, despite the fact that the victims were all gay and the murders all followed the same pattern. Had the connection been made sooner, it's possible that lives might have been saved.

It would be nice to think that lessons were learned from the Colin Ireland enquiry. The Metropolitan Police are certainly better at dealing with gay victims of crime today. I know because I've been one. But just a few years ago, history repeated itself when the so-called Grindr Killer Stephen Port drugged and murdered at least four men over a twelve-month period from the summer of 2014. The bodies were all found in the vicinity of his flat – the first outside his front door and the other three in a nearby graveyard. Despite the force's own LGBT advisory group warning that there was a gay serial killer at large, investigating officers at Barking & Dagenham Police insisted that the crimes weren't linked. Key witnesses weren't questioned, a suicide note faked by the killer was taken at face value, and the victims were characterised as drug addicts. A sister of one of the victims described the attitude of the police as 'shocking'. Again, it's hard to avoid the suspicion that the lives of young gay men simply weren't seen as important enough.

By the time Colin Ireland was arrested in July 1993, I'd left *City Limits* and was gainfully employed as the Gay Editor at *Time Out*, documenting London's rapidly expanding lesbian and gay scene. My position at *Time Out* had previously been held by Michael Griffiths, who was much loved and had become too ill with HIV to continue working. This was the second time my career as a journalist was advanced as a direct consequence of the AIDS crisis, and the sense of guilt was palpable.

I wasn't long into the job when a friend called to inform me that another gay journalist I knew had been rushed into hospital. Just as I had done at *City Limits* a few years earlier, I broke down crying at a dead man's desk and had to be escorted from the building.

With the benefit of hindsight, I can see that this was the point at which I should have sought professional help. I was struggling to cope. I felt burned out and racked with survivor's guilt. The personal losses from AIDS and the Ireland murders all seemed to blur into one. So many men, so many deaths. Why them and not me?

For several years now, I'd been living with the fear of death hanging over me. Vaughan was the first of a growing number of friends who died young while the world carried on as normal. I was still only twenty-seven years old and my life was anything but normal. It isn't normal to be burying your friends in your twenties, or to live in a state of constant anxiety that you might be next. It isn't normal for the deaths of so many young men to be treated with such contempt. A counsellor could have helped me to process my grief, alleviate my guilt and lay some of my fears to rest. Instead, I did what I had always done in times of stress. I turned to drink.

My relationship with alcohol had been problematic for some time. And now, as a journalist, I was constantly being invited to bar openings, film screenings, press nights and book launches where the booze flowed freely. If I went to a club, I was given free drinks tickets. The gay scene was booming – and alcohol was the most popular social lubricant. Even at *Time Out*, it wasn't uncommon for journalists to go for long boozy lunches, returning to the office half-cut and putting their lunch bill through as expenses. And where there was alcohol, cocaine often followed. It was the '90s, after all.

Several people told me my drinking was getting out of hand. Among them was my long-suffering partner William, who'd stood beside me in ACT UP and picked me up so many times when I was down. William was a social worker. It was in his nature to want to help. But I didn't listen. I was in denial. I was hurting. And I was angry – so very angry.

In 1993, Patrick Wilde's stage play *What's Wrong With Angry?* opened at the LOST Theatre in Fulham. I wrote about it in *Time Out*. The play told the story of a love affair between two British school boys and was later made into a film called *Get Real*. It tackled the unequal gay age of consent and the impact of Section 28 on young people – issues close to my heart and legitimate justifications for anger. But *What's Wrong With Angry?* also summed up my emotional state that year. I wasn't just angry, I was vociferously so.

For me, gay journalism was a natural extension of gay activism. It was a means of getting a message across. The kind of activism I was involved in wasn't always polite – and neither were some of my columns. The editor of *Time Out*, Dominic Wells, had hired me on the basis of my spiky public persona and forthright opinions. He was looking for a troublemaker and he came to the right place. Soon the letters page was full of people taking issue with the opinionated new Gay Editor.

One morning, I bumped into publisher Tony Elliott in reception. 'I see you've been busy lighting fires everywhere,' he said.

I didn't know how to respond. Was he annoyed with me?

Then he grinned. 'Keep it up!'

'I will,' I said – and I was true to my word. The truth is, I liked being a troublemaker. What I didn't realise then was just how much trouble I was getting myself into – or where it would lead me.

Chapter 16:
Deeper And Deeper

Confession time. I wasn't always a diehard Madonna fan. Her first album passed me by. 'Like A Virgin' didn't turn me on. Neither did 'True Blue', though I liked 'Live To Tell' and loved the video for 'Open Your Heart', which featured Felix Howard of *The Face* and Buffalo Boy fame.

But the moment I heard 'Like A Prayer', I was converted. Elaine and I went to see the Blond Ambition tour at Wembley and had what can only be described as a religious experience. Like me, Elaine enjoyed the theatricality of the show and the homoerotic performances of the male dancers. After two years in London, my shy cousin from South Wales had blossomed into a self-determined young woman who knew the gay scene like the back of her hand. Of course she believed in the power of Madonna. The woman was practically her role model.

By 1993, Madonna was well into her imperial phase. Her last album, *Erotica*, hadn't sold as well as previous albums – largely because it was overshadowed by the backlash to her coffee-table book, *Sex*. But her legions of gay fans couldn't have loved her more – and she still commanded widespread media attention. There were books written about her – and not just the usual celebrity biographies. Academic books. Essay collections. Works brimming with feminist discourse and queer theory. Some colleges even offered courses in Madonna Studies. Not since David Bowie had a pop star's cultural impact been taken so seriously.

Like Bowie, Madonna is a magpie. Like him, she constantly reinvents herself, experimenting with different looks and musical influences and enjoying varying degrees of commercial success. And like him, she's sexually subversive. She once told a journalist she was on a mission to bring 'subversive sexuality into the mainstream', and at no point in her career was this more explicit than in the early '90s. She'd always presented herself as unapologetically sexual. In the video for 'Justify My Love' she took it further, flirting with androgyny, lesbianism and sadomasochism. Now she launched an all-out assault on the new puritanism espoused by politicians on both sides of the Atlantic.

Several commentators complained that there wasn't much love in *Sex*, as if this was the point. Madonna had written plenty of songs about love. This was a book about her sexual fantasies – love had little to do with it. As she states in her introduction, sex and love are not the same thing. Some critics found this hard to grasp. The book's metal packaging was described as cold and clinical, with the title stamped into the front cover, industrial style. But there was plenty of humour between those metal covers – Madonna grabbing a slice of pizza in the nude, Madonna as a daffy LA housewife tottering across her lawn, Madonna as a bunny girl astride a dog, Madonna hitchhiking naked.

I was one of the first British journalists to get a sneak peek at *Sex*, weeks before the book was published and the *Erotica* album and single were released. I knew the publicist and was invited to the offices of Simon & Schuster for a preview. First, I had to sign a non-disclosure agreement, confirming that I wouldn't breathe a word about what I'd seen until publication day. Then the book was ceremoniously placed before me, still sealed in its silver foil packaging. The publicist opened the package, telling me there was supposed to be a CD of the new single inside, though she couldn't find it. She left the room and I began turning the pages. Suddenly the CD fell out. I hurriedly popped it into my bag, just before the publicist reappeared, saying the CD was definitely there. I must have blushed because she promptly made her excuses and left, allowing me time to retrieve the CD from my bag, return it to its rightful place and absolve myself of any wrongdoing.

I had a few reservations about the *Sex* book. As other critics would point out, Madonna was heavily influenced by Cindy Sherman and the work of several underground queer photographers. There's certainly an element of what we'd now call cultural appropriation. In some sequences, Madonna comes across as a bit of a tourist.

But looking back at *Sex* some thirty years later, it strikes me as an extraordinarily brave thing for a woman in Madonna's position to have done. In the early '90s, with AIDS raging through the gay community, homosexuality was associated in many people's minds with death and disease. Very few pop stars of Madonna's magnitude were vocally supportive of gay people. Even fewer were out. George Michael was still firmly in the closet – and would remain so for some time yet. Neil Tennant didn't come out until 1994 – to me, as it happens. Even Bowie was shying away from his bisexual past, marrying supermodel Iman and telling *Rolling Stone* that he was always a 'closet heterosexual'. Same-sex desire wasn't something mainstream pop stars talked about.

And yet here was one of the most famous women in the world, openly celebrating homosexuality, lesbianism and bisexuality, in a book featuring guest appearances by Naomi Campbell, Isabella Rossellini and gay porn star Joey Stefano – not forgetting male model Tony Ward, who Madonna had recently dated and famously described as having 'an ass you could serve drinks off'. The book contains an image of Madonna about to bury her face in Ward's backside and also makes the assertion that anal sex is the most plea-surable way to get fucked. As an art project, *Sex* may have been, as one wag put it, 'virgin on the ridiculous'. It did, after all, feature Vanilla Ice. But it was culturally and politically important precisely because it was sex positive at a time when so little else was.

Journalists who previewed the book were promised that press copies would be delivered to their desks on the day of publication. When that day finally dawned, no book was forthcoming. Instead I received an apologetic phone call from the publicist. Apparently, Madonna had decided that everyone should pay for their own copy. Well, she did say she was a material girl.

In 1993, Our Lady of Reinvention returned to London for the launch of The Girlie Show, which drew heavily on the *Erotica* album and opened with the star dressed as her alter ego, Mistress Dita Parlo, complete with a mask and riding crop. My sister Jac, who was fifteen at the time, travelled down from South Wales with a friend to see the show – another family member I was happy to welcome into the Madonna fan club. She and her friend got separated in the crowd, and Jac watched the show in the company of some drag queens, who lifted her up when she couldn't see. She loved every second. I was particularly proud to hear her analyse the concert in terms of gender expression and diverse sexuality.

If Blond Ambition was gay, The Girlie Show was positively queer. 'Like A Virgin' was reimagined as a vaudeville song, with Madonna performing in a top hat and tails, singing with a German accent in the style of her heroine Marlene Dietrich. 'Bye Bye Baby' was milked for all its bisexual connotations, with the star making out with male and female dancers. 'Deeper And Deeper' celebrated gay disco, with Madonna descending on a giant mirror ball in a blonde bubble perm wig, before she got serious with her call for tolerance, 'Why's It So Hard', and her tribute to those who'd died of AIDS, 'In This Life'.

It was a fitting showcase for *Erotica* – which remains, in my opinion, one of the most important and underappreciated albums of her entire career.

In 1993, I too was falling deeper and deeper – not deeper in love, but deeper into self-destructive behaviour. I'd go out binge-drinking, end up at some club or other, and either have sex on the premises or go home with someone whose name I'd usually forgotten before I put my clothes back on. The London Apprentice in Old Street was a favourite haunt. Downstairs the DJ played hard house tunes, while upstairs horny punters made their own entertainment in dimly lit corners behind camouflage netting. The air stank of poppers and other, more naturally occurring, fluids. Rumour had it that one morning the house lights came on and a dead body was found among the debris.

I'd also go cruising late at night on Clapham Common, knowing full well how dangerous it could be. The Common was a popular gay cruising site and often attracted the attention of homophobic thugs whose idea of a fun night out involved a few pints and a spot of queer-bashing. When I worked at GALOP, a young man was attacked and left for dead on the Common. Years later, a similar fate would befall Jody Dobrowski, a twenty-four-year-old barman who was beaten to death after visiting friends in Clapham. One night I was chased across the Common by a gang of youths, while my fellow cruisers ran for cover. I don't blame them. In their shoes, I'd have probably done the same.

I managed to escape by zigzagging through a copse of trees and across the top of the Common to the main road. I'd had plenty of practice at outrunning men who meant me harm – and from the sound of them, these men were more drunk than I was. I dreaded to think what might have happened were they not. So I chose not to think about it. I pushed it aside, the way I often did when circumstances called for me to question the wisdom of my actions. I was running scared – from myself as much as anyone.

I used to tell myself that I was addicted to love. It would be closer to the truth to say that I was addicted to sex. For me, the two were inextricably linked. On a political level, I understood Madonna's assertion that sex and love were not necessarily the same thing. It was, after all, one of the central tenets of the gay liberation movement. But one's man liberation is another man's sexual compulsiveness. On a personal level, I found it hard to distinguish between the pursuit of sexual pleasure purely for its own sake and the urge to fill what felt like a void inside. Casual encounters invariably left me feeling even more hollowed out, but I just couldn't help myself. It would be years before I was able to address my behaviour and get to the root cause of it. First I had to admit that there was a problem, and I was still very much in denial.

None of this was particularly easy on William. In 1993, he and I were living together in a top-floor rented flat overlooking the roundabout at Stockwell. However, the spark had gone out of the relationship and we mainly slept in separate rooms. So we did what unhappy couples often do in these circumstances and decided to throw a party.

WigStockwell was named after the drag festival Wigstock in New York, and everyone invited was expected to wear a wig. Some guests were more committed to the idea than others. Suzanne Moore arrived looking like Louis XIV, complete with extravagant facial hair. Oliver and Elaine both made a special effort – he in a punky silver wig and matching biker jacket, she in an '80s bubble perm that she whipped off to reveal a bright red crop. My friend Carl Miller sported a platinum-blond curly wig eerily reminiscent of the one worn by

Madonna in The Girlie Show. A number of my *Time Out* colleagues showed up in wigs and fancy dress, including editor Dominic Wells. Several men came in full drag. Among them was the editor of *Gay Times*, who was a dead ringer for TV presenter Magenta Devine.

William wore three different outfits, disappearing at various intervals throughout the evening for a quick costume change. I wore a blond bob and a pink dress, with a yellow feather boa and red thigh-high boots I'd bought at a charity auction and which once belonged to Lily Savage. They hurt like hell.

As the party started to die down, I changed into a bra top and denim shorts and went out clubbing – first to The Fridge, where I made new friends in the dark room, and later to the original after-hours club Trade, where I passed out in the toilets and was poured into a taxi by a concerned bouncer.

Arriving home the following day, the stairs leading up to our flat were littered with party streamers, bits of tinsel, stray feathers and abandoned wigs. Proof, I think, that a good time was had by all.

It was shortly after seeing Madonna's Girlie Show that I had my first professional encounter with Boy George – a man who knew a thing or two about addiction and had just released a greatest hits album called *At Worst . . . The Best Of Boy George And Culture Club*. The interview was for *Gay Times* and I should start by saying I was a big fan of Boy George. I still recalled that famous first appearance on *Top Of The Pops*, when people asked, 'Is that a boy or a girl?' I bought the first Culture Club album *Kissing To Be Clever* the day it was released and had followed his career with interest ever since. That said, the interview didn't go very well.

He kept me waiting for over two hours. He began by telling me that giving interviews bored him. He bitched about Madonna, Matt Dillon and Andy Bell. Things went rapidly downhill from there. At one point, he asserted that gay men should all be in therapy and were all sexually compulsive and terrified of intimacy. Sensing a certain amount of projection in what he was saying, I asked if the same was ever true of him. 'Yes, definitely,' he replied. 'I'm one of those people who has learned to judge myself by how people respond to me sexually.'

George and I have since kissed and made up, but casting my mind back to that first interview, I can't help thinking he could just as easily have been talking about me.

Shortly after my prickly encounter with George, *Gay Times* commissioned me to interview another of my musical idols, Marc Almond. It was the second time I'd interviewed Marc. The first was for *City Limits* in 1991, a few days after Freddie Mercury died. 'It's been a sad week,' Marc told me then. 'Everyone loved Freddie, whether they liked Queen's music or not.' It was hard for me to fathom at the time. Growing up, many of the boys who called me queer had 'Queen' emblazoned on the back of their denim jackets. Yet Freddie was not only queer but arguably the most popular public figure in the UK to die of AIDS, raising awareness in much the same way that Rock Hudson had six years earlier.

That second interview with Marc took place at his flat in Earl's Court and led to a friendship that lasted for many years. It also led to me being doorstepped by a tabloid journalist working for Piers Morgan, who was then Showbiz Editor at *The Sun*. How did Marc appear, the reporter wanted to know. Did he look at all 'under the weather'? When I phoned Marc to warn him, he informed me that Morgan had already approached his record company, asking whether he'd recently tested positive for HIV. Back at my desk, I rang Morgan to complain. He asked me who I worked for. I told him I was the Gay Editor at *Time Out*. 'You wouldn't know a good news story if it bit you on the arse,' he said. He didn't deny making enquiries about Marc, insisting that knowledge of a celebrity's HIV status was in the public interest. I recently reminded Morgan of this episode on Twitter, when he was claiming to be an ally of the gay community. He responded by blocking me.

Chapter 17:
Queer With Attitude

The idea for *Attitude* magazine sprang from a conversation I had over dinner with my good friends Tim Nicholson and Jane Phillips. They'd recently launched *For Women* magazine and I'd written a few pieces for them, mainly on subjects like gay porn and lipstick lesbians. I also wrote regularly for the *Modern Review* and had gay-themed pieces published in the *Guardian* and the *Independent*. At the time, this was known as 'queering the mainstream'.

Attitude was always intended to be an outward-looking magazine, unlike the bulk of the gay press at the time, which struck me as very inward-looking. I wanted *Attitude* to be read by gay men, bisexual men and people who didn't identify as either. I wanted it to be part of the mainstream. The aim was to produce a magazine that offered a platform for writers who thought outside the box – including those who weren't gay themselves but were what we'd now refer to as 'allies'.

Tim and Jane fell very much into this category. A heterosexual couple, they had the publishing experience and contacts I lacked. Tim was a writer and Jane a designer. Most of their friends and many of their work associates were gay, including the photographer Brad Branson, who'd worked for *Interview*, *Rolling Stone* and

Vanity Fair and who they persuaded to come on board as *Attitude*'s in-house photographer.

Much of the editorial direction came from me. I was still free-lancing for *Gay Times* and growing increasingly frustrated with what I saw as its 'gay is good' world view. In the early '90s, it seemed to me that writers working for the gay press were expected to act less like journalists and more like cheerleaders. One reason my columns in *Time Out* provoked such controversy was that I refused to gush enthusiastically about every gay bar, club, book or film I was asked to review. No other section editor at *Time Out* was expected to do this, so why should I?

My columns were also attracting the attention of the main-stream media, not all of it welcome. When I wrote about the homo-eroticism of the new *Superman* TV series, starring the young, buff and ridiculously handsome Dean Cain, the column was picked up by *The Sun*, which ran with the headline 'Pooferman!' Such 'hilarious' uses of the word 'poof' were pretty commonplace in the tabloid press at the time.

Tackling homophobia was certainly part of *Attitude*'s agenda. But we were equally keen to call out some of the shortcomings of so-called gay culture. We wanted to create a magazine that was edgy and didn't pander to the happy-clappy gay mentality of the time. We wanted to test boundaries, ask difficult questions and challenge the status quo. We also wanted to attract mainstream advertising and sell lots of nice things to gay readers with a high disposable income. I'm aware, of course, that these two goals are somewhat at odds with one another. But the money had to come from somewhere, and I wasn't interested in producing a magazine that would be seen by fewer people than currently read my column in *Time Out*.

Attitude was partly modelled on *Out* magazine, which launched in the US in 1992. It was partly a counterpoint to *Loaded*, the magazine 'for men who should know better', which launched in the same month as us and was unashamedly regressive in its outlook. *Loaded* embodied the 'ironic' New Lad culture that dominated the early '90s. I loathed New Laddism and everything it represented – middle-class, well-educated men aping the kind of behaviour commonly associated with uneducated, unreconstructed, toxic masculinity, and doing it all in the name of irony. It was hideous.

Launching *Attitude* was an exciting prospect, but it was a bold move and by no means certain to succeed. I wasn't willing to give up the security of my part-time job at *Time Out*. Besides, I liked working for *Time Out*. So it was agreed that I'd work for *Attitude* a few days a week. I'd be listed on the masthead as Consultant Editor but was very much the public face of the magazine.

Deciding on the name of the magazine wasn't difficult. For the past few years, I'd been strongly aligned with the brand of 'in your face' queer politics imported from the US, which helped fuel ACT UP and led to the creation of Queer Nation in the States and OutRage! in the UK. It felt more urgent and appropriate to the times than the softly-softly diplomatic approach embodied by the Stonewall group – a lobbying organisation named after a riot, as leading members of OutRage! were fond of reminding us.

In retrospect, I appreciate that both approaches are necessary. At the time, I was firmly in the direct-action camp and saw anything else as a compromise. Queer activists weren't nice gays going for tea at Number 10 and asking politely for a place at the table. We were angry queers kicking down doors and demanding an end to unjust laws. We had that much overused word, 'attitude'.

AIDS had a lot to do with it. A few months before we launched *Attitude*, Derek Jarman died. Since first meeting him in the mid-1980s, I'd interviewed Derek for *City Limits* and *Time Out* and contributed an essay to his 1992 book *At Your Own Risk*. I still have the handwritten letter he sent me, thanking me for our first interview. Like his film-making, his handwriting was exquisite. I was present at the 'kiss-in' organised by OutRage! in Piccadilly Circus, where Derek was photographed and his image appeared in the *Guardian* with the picture caption 'Kiss of Death?' As he wrote in *At Your Own Risk*, if that was how the *Guardian* saw him, what hope did he have with the tabloids?

Others saw him differently. In September 1991, Derek was famously 'canonised' by the international order of gay male nuns known as the Sisters of Perpetual Indulgence. Originally founded in 1979 in Iowa City before moving to the gay Mecca of San Francisco, the Sisters are best described as street activists who use drag and religious imagery to highlight sexual intolerance and satirise questions of morality. By the late '80s, they were also active in the UK.

Never one to shy away from controversy or shirk his responsibilities, Saint Derek of the Order of Celluloid Knights of Dungeness took his saintly duties seriously. Long before same-sex marriages were legally recognised in the UK, he performed a wedding ceremony for a couple of lesbian friends at his beloved Prospect Cottage on the Kent coast. He officiated at the unofficial renaming of Old Compton Street as Queer Street, organised by OutRage! I remember the beatific smile on his face as he paraded through Soho in his golden robes, blessing people as he passed by.

But the knives were out for Derek even as his health deteriorated. It was me who warned him that the *Guardian* was planning a hatchet job, though as he wrote in his final journal *Smiling In Slow Motion*, the warning came a little too late – the interview had already taken place earlier that day. He recounted me calling him at 5 p.m. and wondered if I was right in thinking that the journalist concerned had an agenda.

Sadly, I was. The piece appeared the following week and was mean-spirited, ill-informed and judgemental, with little understanding of safer sex and no compassion for a man who had the courage to live his life so openly at a time when people with HIV were widely demonised.

I feel immensely proud and privileged to have known Derek. I used to visit him at his office on Wardour Street and his flat in Phoenix House on Charing Cross Road. We'd discuss the political issues of the day, swap gossip and go for dinner together at Presto, the small, family-run Italian restaurant he loved so much. After he died, the matriarch, Maria, turned his table into a shrine.

One of the last times I saw him was at a press screening of *Blue*, his final feature film – about his failing eyesight and the complications of living with AIDS. As the film ended and the lights came on, I turned to find him sitting behind me, crying silently. A month or so later, we met again at a production of *The Wasp Factory* in King's Cross. He was practically blind by then and painfully frail. After we parted, I was physically attacked in the street. A man stopped me to ask where Bagley's nightclub was. I pointed him in the general direction and turned away. Then the homophobic abuse started. I was in no mood for this and began to put up a fight, before realising that he was far stronger than me and clearly in an altered state. When he tore off his football shirt to show that he meant business, I ran for cover at The Bell.

Derek was defiantly queer to the end. His public row with Sir Ian McKellen over his acceptance of a knighthood from John Major's government made him a controversial figure. But his death on 19 February 1994 affected a lot of people. Derek was such a force of nature, some of us fooled ourselves into thinking that he'd live forever. Had he clung on for another two years, he might have benefited from groundbreaking new drug treatments. He might even be with us now. But it wasn't to be.

His funeral was held in Dungeness, where he'd grown his famous garden out of shingle and sheer grit – a symbol, some said, of his personal battle to live against all the odds. The service was rather traditional, the mourners anything but. The Sisters of Perpetual Indulgence were there – and so was Maria in her black funeral garb and heavily lacquered helmet of hair. I remember her standing outside the church, consoling a steady stream of grieving gay men. I wept as she held me in her arms, telling me he was at peace now.

Two days after Derek died, I joined a candlelit vigil outside the House of Commons, where MPs were voting on an amendment tabled by Edwina Currie MP to equalise the gay male age of consent. There were an estimated 5,000 lesbians, gay men and their supporters present. The mood was sombre but peaceful.

When word got out that the vote had failed, and that the age of consent for gay men would be reduced to eighteen and not equalised at sixteen, the mood changed. People became angry, and rightly so. Eighteen wasn't a compromise but an insult. You're either equal or you're not. Sir Ian appeared and appealed to everyone to calm down. But it was too late. 'Shame on you!' someone shouted back. Then all hell broke loose. People stormed the building. I was one of them.

The following morning's newspapers talked about 'gays on the rampage' and 'an angry mob' storming Parliament, hurling missiles, marching through central London and blocking traffic. It was all a far cry from the style of activism embodied by Sir Ian, who'd famously gone for tea with the Prime Minister at Number 10. But if the press were surprised at the levels of anger unleashed that night, they obviously hadn't been paying attention. There's only so far you can push people before they fight back. When diplomacy fails, direct action is the only dignified response.

Some sections of the gay press described what happened that night as a riot. It wasn't. Not quite. No bricks were thrown. No arrests were made. But for a moment there, I felt the true spirit of Stonewall – the civil uprising, not the Downing Street tea party.

Attitude launched three months later, in May 1994. My former character witness and one-time fling Tyler Brûlé wrote a very supportive piece for the *Guardian* media pages. I appeared on Sky News, where the presenters expressed surprise that there was any demand for a magazine aimed at 'homosexuals'. I also took part in a late-night discussion programme on Radio 4 about the changing face of modern masculinity. My fellow guests included the editor of *Men's Health* magazine and a woman who'd written a book that divided men into seven character types, each of which conveniently began with the letter 'W'. There were 'warriors', 'wizards', 'wankers' and various others I can't recall. I do remember thinking that they were all conspicuously heterosexual.

I became increasingly annoyed at the direction the discussion took, which seemed to ignore the pink elephant in the room. It probably didn't help that I'd snorted a large line of cocaine shortly before going on air and was determined to get my point across as forcibly and as frequently as possible. Coke can do that to you.

At one point, the editor of *Men's Health* suggested that modern men were far more in touch with their feminine side and the old homophobic taboos no longer existed. I argued that if this were true, *Men's Health* wouldn't constantly address its readers as if they were all 100 per cent heterosexual – and nor would it hide behind the euphemism of 'health' when really it was the male equivalent of a woman's beauty magazine. That went down well.

But not as well as my next comment, which was directed at the author of the book. 'There aren't seven types of men,' I informed her. 'There are only two. Those who are comfortable with the idea of being penetrated and those who aren't.'

At which point, the producer cut off my microphone.

The launch party for *Attitude* was held at Browns in Covent Garden. Andy Bell was there, as was Julian Clary. At one point, Boy George arrived and word spread that he was threatening to slap my face. I managed to avoid him and survived the night with my dignity more or less intact.

The following week, I received something of a slap when my face appeared on the cover of the gay free weekly bar mag *MX* (later known as *QX*) with the cover line 'Paul Burston – Gay or Git?' Such was the enthusiasm with which the gay press embraced the competition.

In any case, *Attitude* launched to great acclaim and quickly became the most talked-about gay magazine in the UK. When Pet Shop Boy Neil Tennant decided it was time to throw caution to the wind and finally confirm that he was gay, it was *Attitude* he turned to. Before long we became the go-to magazine for high-profile celebrities wishing to set the record straight and come out.

My interview with Tennant appeared in our fourth issue, published in August 1994. In his book *Good As You: From Prejudice To Pride – 30 Years Of Gay Britain*, the journalist Paul Flynn describes it as the first major milestone in the magazine's history, and such a far cry from the modern, media-managed celebrity coming-out story that parts of it read rather uncomfortably.

In fact, this particular celebrity coming-out story had been slightly media-managed. At the end of our interview, Tennant asked if he could see the piece before it went to print. Foolishly, I agreed. I then received an angry phone call from his publicist, informing me that Neil was very upset at the way he'd been represented. I agreed to speak with Neil on the phone. He rang me shortly afterwards.

'Hello, Paul. It's Neil Tennant here. How are you?'

'I'm fine,' I replied. 'But I understand that you're not.'

He insisted there were just a few points where he felt I'd been unfair. One of these was when he'd uttered the words 'I'm gay' and I included all the 'ums' and 'ahs' as he built up to it. In fairness, it's common practice for journalists to 'tidy up' quotes so they read better. I agreed to make a few small edits. Otherwise, the piece ran as written.

Shortly after Neil Tennant helped put *Attitude* on the map, I interviewed Donna Summer. Arguably the greatest gay disco diva of all time, she was in the process of suing *New York Magazine* over allegations that she'd described AIDS as God's punishment for homosexuals. Her lawyer was on the line throughout our phone interview, which didn't go too well. Summer was wary and evasive, refusing to answer some questions and responding to others in monosyllables. Years later, I interviewed Summer again in person, when she was due to perform at G-A-Y at the Astoria. This time, she was far more forthcoming and keen to set the record straight. Despite being a born-again Christian, she insisted that she'd never said those things. I believed her.

Her performance at G-A-Y was memorable for several reasons. One, she was Donna Summer. Two, she was in fine voice. And three, when she sang the medley known as 'MacArthur Park Suite', I was so high on Ecstasy I nearly toppled off the balcony. Thankfully, someone grabbed me just in time and I lived to tell the tale.

For my next cover feature for *Attitude*, I secured an interview with Vivienne Westwood, who I knew socially through a former colleague at GALOP. She'd been to dinner at my flat in Stockwell and I'd attended a bonfire party at her place in Clapham Common, where we danced to Elvis Presley.

In the summer of 1994, I escorted her to the after-party for the Stonewall Equality Show – much to the annoyance of the organisers, who were still angry at my coverage of the age of consent vote in *Time Out*. I was what you might call the bad fairy at the party.

Vivienne was wearing a skirt with a long, lace train. As we approached the venue, I noticed that the train was no longer in pristine condition but littered with cigarette butts and other detritus from the filthy London streets. I pointed this out to Vivienne, who replied tartly, 'Fashion isn't supposed to be hygienic!'

On our arrival, Ian McKellen greeted Vivienne while pointedly ignoring me. Someone brought over Edwina Currie, who was guest of honour but still considered a controversial figure by many in the community. Some of us remembered her earlier comments as junior health minister, when she said that 'good Christian people' didn't get AIDS. But unlike Donna Summer, Edwina was being given a free pass.

Vivienne gave Currie short shrift. 'I'm sorry,' she said. 'But I don't know who you are and I'm too drunk to care.'

I have to say, I liked her attitude.

Plenty of people didn't like mine, however. While the magazine enjoyed growing popularity, my reputation as a troublemaker brought its fair share of personal criticism. The editor of one gay magazine publicly accused me of 'making a career out of saying the unsayable' – which struck me as deeply revealing in a way he probably hadn't intended. So there really were things we weren't supposed to say? There was a gay hymn sheet we were all supposed to sing from? I hadn't just imagined that?

'Gay press slams Burston after "cheerleading" slur' ran a headline in the *UK Press Gazette*, referring to comments I'd recently made during an interview. The gay press was always slamming me. Barely a month went by without someone at *Gay Times* or the *Pink Paper* making a statement about me or running a news item decrying something I'd written. I often responded in kind, which was foolish and played into the hands of those who preferred the pettiness of playground politics to mature debate. I guess you could say I had an attitude problem.

Regrets? I have a few. I wish I'd been kinder and less hot-headed. It's all very well telling yourself 'the personal is political', but far too many political disagreements degenerated into personal insults, which is nothing to feel proud about. I was too quick to assume we were out of the woods where the mainstream press was concerned, and too slow to admit when I was wrong. But it's worth noting that many of the opinions I expressed then are pretty common-place today. Blaze a trail and you tend to burn a few bridges in the process.

It's around this time that I was credited – or charged, depending on your point of view – with coining the term 'post-gay'. This was largely thanks to James Collard, who worked at *Attitude* and later moved to New York, where he edited *Out* magazine and in 1998 wrote a piece for *Newsweek* attributing the term to me. I've since heard it discussed by academics and, most recently, by the writer Dustin Lance Black on Radio 4. What I meant by 'post-gay' wasn't that we were living in a world where gay identity no longer mattered. It was that we were living in a world where it shouldn't be the *only* thing that mattered. I was talking less about gay politics and more about gay culture – or the homogeneous gay culture of the time. As Collard wrote in *Newsweek*, 'post-gay' was simply a critique of gay politics and gay culture – by gay people, for gay people.

Shortly before the launch of *Attitude*, I had published a column in *Time Out* that summed up my position and really set the cat among the pigeons. Despite generations of gay activists' insistence that 'gay is good', I argued that not everything marketed to us as gay was necessarily good. In fact, a lot of it was bad – poor service, second-rate goods, naff pop acts, lousy restaurants, and package holiday companies that ripped off gay consumers. This doesn't sound particularly controversial now. Back then I might as well have come out as the gay Antichrist. When I met Neil Tennant for our interview, he told me the column had really struck a chord with him, adding in that withering tone of his that gay culture used to be cutting-edge, whereas now it was just 'nightclubs, music, drugs, shopping, PAs by Bad Boys Inc'.

Others took a very different view. The *Fag & Hag* comic strip in *MX* depicted me holding a free drink and saying, 'I despise gay culture and all it stands for,' with someone replying, 'Why do you dress like such an old poof, then?' Such rapier-sharp wit! The most common accusation was that I was writing from a place of internalised homophobia. I'm not saying I'm a stranger to such feelings. Show me a gay man who isn't. Unless we're extremely fortunate, most of us experience homophobia from an early age. That's bound to leave its mark.

But arguing that we deserve better than much of the rubbish marketed at us is hardly a sign of self-loathing. Quite the opposite, in fact. It's saying we're worth more, not less. Whenever someone accused me of internalised homophobia I was reminded of one of my favourite quotes from Oscar Wilde, the one where he compares the nineteenth century's dislike of realism to the rage of Caliban at seeing his own face reflected in the looking glass.

A rare photo of me smiling as a child – before the bullying began.

My first protest – at not winning the fancy dress competition at Butlin's.

This little Ziggy – Bowie fan, school prefect and unlikely student governor.

Bleach boy at Southerndown Beach in 1984 – the summer I nearly drowned.

Photo taken by Vaughan on a canal boat in Amsterdam, shortly before he died.

'ACT UP London, lie down!' Protesting benefit cuts for people with HIV/AIDS.

Chain of love. Blocking traffic and raising awareness on World AIDS Day.

Derek Jarman – activist, artist, film-maker and friend.

Fashion! The night Vivienne Westwood came to dinner.

On stage at Polari In Heaven with my 'representative on earth', Alexis Gregory.

Portrait of me as a Bowie fan by artist Mark Wardel, aka TradeMark.

Chapter 18:
Union City Blue

Saturday night and Deborah is speeding. From the speakers high above us, the artist currently known as Deborah Harry sings an old song about power, passion and the desire to rearrange her mind. Down here on the dance floor, another Deborah – my Deborah – is well ahead of her. An hour ago, Deborah and I each took half an E and a few dabs of speed. Now, as the music soars and Deborah Harry sings about 'union', we know just what she means. It's this. Us. Here. Now. On this crowded dance floor. Gay men and straight women, dancing together as we've always done. Power. Passion. Union.

I'm writing in the present tense because drugs like Ecstasy do that to you – they put you right there in the moment. You're lost in music and the beat is inside you, together with the chemicals coursing through your veins and rushing to your brain. You're at one with the world, or at least the room, and heaven knows we all need to feel that connection sometimes.

I stepped away from queer activism when my friend and fellow AIDS activist Spud died. There'd been too many losses, too many funerals, and his was the most devastating of all. We'd been so close and shared so much. When he died, it felt as if a part of me died, too.

After his first bout of serious illness, when he was out of hospital but hadn't left his flat in weeks, I persuaded Spud to join me for a drink at Comptons in Soho, which had always been his favourite gay watering hole. It hadn't crossed my mind that there might be danger lurking there. He'd lost a lot of weight and his clothes hung loosely on him. His face was drawn and his usually thick dark hair had thinned considerably.

As we stood at the bar, waiting to be served, a man approached him and said, 'What the hell happened to you? You used to be so handsome!'

I wanted to punch his lights out, but Spud held me back. We left quickly, before things escalated and I did something I'd regret. Spud never went to a gay bar again. In the run-up to the launch of *Attitude*, his health declined sharply. He died on 6 April 1994. He was thirty-three years old.

Something inside me snapped. The anger I'd been carrying around for so long became all-consuming. I found myself picking arguments for no good reason, other than the opportunity to vent. And it was about to get worse. A few months later, I arrived home from work to find a voicemail from a friend in New York, alerting me to the fact that our mutual friend Georg was in hospital.

Georg Osterman was a kind soul and a great talent, who wrote and performed with the Ridiculous Theatre Company. I'd been to stay with Georg and his partner Adam the previous year. It was November 1993, and Kate Bush had just released her album *The Red Shoes*. Georg and I went to Tower Records to buy the CD and played it over and over again. On the song 'Moments Of Pleasure', Bush describes being in New York and an encounter with a man who meets her at the lift waving his walking stick, and doesn't look well at all. As the song played, I had to stop myself from crying. She could have been describing the man sitting in front of me. In the months since I'd last seen him, the once heavily muscled Georg had lost a lot of weight. When he'd met me at the lift the day before, I was shocked at how frail he looked.

And now here was our friend Tim calling to say he'd taken a turn for the worse. I channelled my feelings into the following week's column in *Time Out*:

Now, more than anything, AIDS makes me angry. I'm angry in a way I never thought possible. I'm angry at Tim for being the person who relayed the message, and at Georg for being so sick and drawing me back to that strange place where people just keep dying and there's nothing I can do to stop it. I'm angry at Clive, who slipped away so quietly last month, and at Derek, who made such a noise about living we all thought he would be with us forever.

I'm angry at the distance between London and New York, and the distance between myself and too many of the people I think of as friends – those helpless, hopeless friends who need to have it explained to them time and again that something truly terrifying is happening and it's getting harder and harder for me to meet them half way. I'm angry at anyone who doesn't know what this feels like. But most of all I'm angry at myself. Angry that I've started grieving for someone who isn't even dead. Angry that I can't seem to remember a time when I wasn't grieving for someone. Angry that I shall never grieve for Georg enough, just as I have never grieved for anyone enough. There are too many people to grieve for, and not enough time between funerals to do any of them justice.

So I do what I always do in these circumstances. I prepare to cross out another name in my address book, and implant it in my memory, in the file marked 'People Who Must Never Be Forgotten'.

Reading these words back now, almost thirty years after they were written, I'm struck by two things. One, I don't mention Spud at all – a sign perhaps of just how raw his loss still felt. And two, how desperately sad I sound, and how dangerously close to the edge.

It took me another year to finally pluck up the courage to take my first HIV test. I was terrified that the result would be positive and relieved when it came back negative – relieved and more than a little guilty. I knew I was one of the lucky ones. For the past six years I'd been extremely careful. But there were times before that when I'd had unprotected sex with men I hardly knew. All it took was one unsafe encounter with someone who'd been exposed to the virus that had killed so many of my friends. Yet here I was – negative, spared and riddled with guilt. Why them and not me?

I didn't write about this at the time. It still feels difficult writing about it now. What right had I to be feeling sorry for myself when so many had lost their lives? These days, survivor's guilt is recognised as a symptom of post-traumatic stress disorder, similar to that experienced by those who've survived combat situations, natural disasters or acts of terrorism. Maybe a good therapist could have helped me to understand that what I was feeling wasn't uncommon.

But still I didn't seek help. Instead I sought escapism. I chose self-medication. And the gay club scene offered just the thing.

I took my first Ecstasy pill in 1992 – four years after the Second Summer of Love, the same year the legendary gay club Love Muscle first opened its doors at The Fridge in Brixton. By 1995, Deborah and I were regulars at Love Muscle. She lived just round the corner off Brixton Hill, and I lived up the road in Stockwell. Some nights I was so off my face I walked home alone up Stockwell Road, otherwise known as Murder Mile, dressed in little more than a pair of denim shorts and a string of love beads. Drugs had that effect on me. I was fearless – and reckless.

I first met Deborah Orr when we both wrote for *City Limits*. Like me, she was a major Blondie fan. I think it was one of the first things we bonded over – that, and smoking. Deborah was a serious smoker. I rarely saw her without a cigarette in her hand – full-strength, of course. 'None of that Silk Cut rubbish!' When she talked, it was usually through a plume of cigarette smoke. I think it added to her reputation as the 'fierce Scots hackette' of *Private Eye* infamy.

By the time someone had the brilliant idea of remixing old Blondie tracks for the dance floor, Deborah was editing the *Guardian Weekend* magazine and I was two years into my job at *Time Out*. I was twenty-nine years old. I'd worked for two magazines, edited a third, helped launch a fourth and written for numerous others. I'd had my first book published – a collection of academic essays about lesbians, gay men and popular culture called *A Queer Romance*, co-edited with Colin Richardson with contributions from Bruce LaBruce, Cherry Smyth, Monika Treut, Gregory Woods and others. A second book called *What Are You Looking At?* was on the way. Professionally speaking, things were looking good.

Personally, they were anything but. My relationship with William had run its course. I was still drinking too much, taking far too many drugs and having more casual sex than was strictly good for me, physically or psychologically. Hindsight is a wonderful thing, and it doesn't take a genius to work out that these were the actions of someone who'd experienced some kind of trauma – and not just one, but a whole multitude, one after the other.

I still remember being at a friend's funeral, weeping for someone we'd buried months earlier and feeling really guilty about it. That's what cumulative grief does to you. You're unable to process it properly. Before you've gone through the five stages of grief for one person, another has died, and then another. Denial and isolation give way to anger and depression, then you're right back where you started. It all becomes too much to bear. So you seek help. Or you do what I did and swallow it down, blot it out, do whatever it takes to make the pain go away.

I don't think it's a coincidence that Ecstasy took off in the gay scene the way it did in the '90s. Here you had a community ravaged by illness and grief, living in a climate of fear and shame, and here you had a pill that would take all those feelings away, if only for a few hours. Nor do I think it's a coincidence that many of the songs that filled those '90s gay dance floors were remixes or re-recordings of tracks that came from an era pre-AIDS. Disco was often about survival but now the meanings of the songs had subtly changed – 'Love Hangover', 'Found A Cure', 'I Will Survive'. These were anthems for a generation who'd lived through the worst of times. They were songs for survivors.

Deborah and I danced to them all. Being friends with her wasn't always easy, especially as she was someone I also relied on for work, which meant a certain power dynamic was ever-present. She always said exactly what she thought, no matter how harsh it sounded. She could be caustic and incredibly combative. If you want to understand why, read her brilliant memoir *Motherwell*, which explains a lot.

But she was a good friend in many ways. When my essay collection *What Are You Looking At?* was ready for publication, it was pointed out to me that one essay contained several quotes from 'Lady Lazarus' by Sylvia Plath. The Plath estate were famously protective of her legacy and rarely granted permission for her work to be quoted out of context. I was advised to pull the essay. Deborah made a few phone calls and permission was granted.

She was also incredibly generous. More than once, she helped me out financially when times were tight. And when we went clubbing together, nothing else mattered. Dance-floor Deborah was my favourite. Only she could pick up the one hot straight guy in a club full of gay men. Only she could sing along with me to Blondie and mean every word.

Now she's gone, too – lost not to AIDS but to cancer. But each new death brings back reminders of those terrible times.

One of my greatest regrets is that, a few years before she became ill, Deborah and I fell out so spectacularly it was impossible to put the pieces back together again. Without dwelling on the details, she sided with someone who was causing me a considerable amount of personal distress. I felt angry and betrayed. A friendship of twenty-five years ended in recriminations and acrimony. I wish we'd patched things up before she died. But it's too late for that now. So instead I try to focus on the good times we had together and am grateful for the pieces she commissioned me to write. Of these, the biggest and best was interviewing Blondie in 1999.

Deborah phoned me as soon as the reunion was announced. 'You know Blondie are getting back together?'

I did.

'I want you to interview them for the magazine. But you have to get me her autograph.'

As luck would have it, I knew a journalist in New York called Cathay Che who was a personal friend of Ms Harry and who'd written a book about her, in which I was quoted. I emailed Cathay and asked her to put in a good word for me. She did.

After several years as a solo artist, Deborah Harry reverted back to Debbie for the new Blondie album, *No Exit*. In person, she was everything I wanted her to be and more – witty, beautiful, effortlessly cool. That cover feature remains one of the highlights of my career as a journalist. I met with her and the band three times and was able to build a rapport – a long lunch one day, a photoshoot a few weeks later, an after-show party shortly after that. You rarely get that kind of access any more. These days it's often fifteen minutes in a hotel room with a publicist holding a stopwatch. When I interviewed Beyoncé for *Time Out* in 2002, I was given twelve minutes precisely.

It's hard to imagine now, but the Blondie reunion wasn't a guaranteed success. Their last single had been seventeen years earlier in 1982, and barely scraped into the Top 40. The tabloids were gleefully claiming that Debbie was too old – just as they do whenever Madonna or any other female artist has the audacity to live beyond the age of thirty. But when I first heard 'Maria' I knew the band had a major comeback hit on their hands.

'Do you think?' Debbie asked, seemingly uncertain.

'Absolutely. It's a classic Blondie song. People will love it.'

The interview was published the week the single was released. The cover line on the magazine read: 'Power. Passion. Rapture. Blondie's back!'

And they were. 'Maria' stormed the charts, becoming their sixth UK Number One – and Debbie Harry sent me flowers. The other Deborah couldn't have been happier about that.

Chapter 19:
Outside

'He's out. As in outcast.'

This was the headline in the *Independent* in October 1995, the first time I was profiled. The accompanying interview portrayed me as a controversialist, a troublemaker, the gay journalist other gay men loved to hate. There was some truth in this. I certainly had my critics. But for every letter of complaint to *Time Out* calling for my head, there was often another thanking me for sticking my neck out and challenging the political complacency of the time.

Gay culture was steeped in false optimism, I told the journalist from the *Independent*. 'There's this denial that a lot of us are traumatised. Many gay men simply haven't learned how to talk about it. Small pockets of friends communicate, but the subculture as a whole doesn't. I want gay men to make a fuss not only about what the straight world does to us but about what we do to each other.' Years later, this theme would be explored in a book called *The Velvet Rage* by Alan Downs. At the time, I got little thanks for what my detractors described as 'washing gay men's dirty linen in public'.

In the days before the internet, it wasn't uncommon for journalists to keep their hate mail pinned above their desks as a badge of pride. I had more than my fair share. Some letters were written in green crayon – no, really, they were – and came from homophobes who invariably referred to themselves as Christians. Others came from outraged members of the gay community whose anger seemed to stem from the fact that I wasn't expressing their opinion but my own. Imagine! A gay columnist doing what any other journalist would do and voicing an opinion without first consulting an entire community! What an unspeakable outrage!

Back then, the Gay section at *Time Out* was one of the few gay platforms in the mainstream media. Whenever a gay news story broke, I would invariably get calls from well-meaning heterosexual journalists asking, 'What does the gay community think about this?'

'Hang on,' I'd reply. 'I'll just open the window and ask them for you.'

I was picturing that scene from *Life Of Brian*, where Brian urges the hundreds of followers gathered outside his window to stop and think for themselves. There was no gay community that spoke with one voice, just as there is no single opinion that everyone shares, whether they happen to be gay or not. To suggest otherwise is lazy and reductive. As a gay journalist, I never claimed to speak on behalf of anyone but myself. But I did claim the right to speak.

An epithet often applied to me at the time was 'the *enfant terrible* of gay journalism'. Given my personal history with Cocteau's novel, this might have been fitting, were it not for the fact that I was fast approaching thirty and hardly an *enfant*. In gay years, I was practically middle-aged.

I'd always felt like an outsider. At various times in my life I'd been a stranger to my own family and even to myself. So coming to terms with being an outsider within my own community wasn't a huge adjustment to make. Besides, most of the people I admired were outsiders in some way or other. I figured I was in good company. With hindsight, I think it's possible that my escalating cocaine habit may have contributed in some small way to my heightened sense of self-importance.

1995 was the year I turned thirty and I celebrated with a big party in a club in Piccadilly. I wore a Vivienne Westwood shirt and splashed out on a skinny black designer suit by Helmut Lang. It was the most I'd ever spent on an outfit and the beginning of a new addiction – but that's another story.

My parents drove down from South Wales and my mother insisted on having her photo taken with Marc Almond. 'I've always loved Marc,' she cooed, conveniently forgetting her less-than-enthusiastic comments when his picture first appeared on my bedroom wall fourteen years previously. 'I suppose he's gay as well, is he?' she'd sniffed, leaving me in no doubt that she disapproved.

Deborah Orr and Suzanne Moore were there, as well as my acting pal Linda, who took care of my mum when she got rather drunk on all the free wine and had to be escorted to the Ladies.

'How much has Mum had to drink?' I asked my stepdad.

'Jesus Christ, Paul!' he replied. 'It's got nothing to do with the drink!'

It took me a while to understand, but in a way he was right. It wasn't the drink – or rather, it wasn't just the drink. There were lesbians, gay men and queer people of all descriptions at that party, including some whose physical appearance was confusing for a middle-aged couple from a small town in South Wales who'd only just got their heads around the fact that their son was gay. It was the first time my parents had been surrounded by so many people so unlike themselves. This was way outside their comfort zone.

Remembering how anxious and overwhelmed I felt the first time I went to Heaven, I could hardly blame them.

My birthday celebration doubled as the launch party for my essay collection *What Are You Looking At?* which was reviewed favourably in the mainstream media and largely ignored by the gay press. *Premiere* magazine described it as the work of 'a funny, often waspish writer' and compared me to Oscar Wilde, no less. One of the gay-bar rags dismissed it as 'boring'.

The book included an essay in which I expressed my disillusionment with David Bowie and his recent reincarnation as A Lad in a Suit. I spoke too soon. Shortly after my book launch, Bowie went all experimental again with the release of an album called *Outside*. Arguably his most dystopian – and unashamedly pretentious – concept album since *Diamond Dogs*, it told the story of Nathan Adler, a government official assigned to investigate a series of 'art crimes', one of which involves the murder of a girl called Baby Grace Blue.

The first in what was intended to be a series of albums – or 'a non-linear Gothic drama hyper-cycle', according to the hyperbolic sleeve notes – *Outside* marked Bowie's reunion with Brian Eno, collaborator on his famous Berlin Trilogy in the late 1970s. Just as importantly – to me, at least – it signalled Bowie's return to exploring 'outsider' sexuality and gender performance. This was most notable on the single 'Hallo Spaceboy', which posed questions about sexual orientation. The Bowie of 'Queen Bitch', 'Rebel Rebel' and 'Boys Keep Swinging' was back – and about time, too.

I saw the Outside tour at Wembley. It was a far cry from the crowd-pleasing Serious Moonlight tour of 1983. Bowie sang few of the hits, preferring to showcase the new album and perform fan favourites like 'Breaking Glass', 'The Man Who Sold The World' and 'Teenage Wildlife'. The stage design resembled a building site, with crumpled sheets and splashes of paint, banners and mannequins. It was edgy, self-indulgent and everything I wanted Bowie to be. I seriously doubt there were any Phil Collins fans in the audience.

The support act was Morrissey, who was promoting *Vauxhall And I* – for my money, his best solo album to date and by far the queerest thing he'd done since The Smiths, with songs like 'Billy Budd' and 'I Am Hated For Loving'. He was booked for the European leg of the tour but left after nine dates and wasted no opportunity to slag off 'David Showie' in subsequent interviews. Clearly there was only room for one Queen Bitch on the Outside tour, and that role was already taken.

Remixed by Pet Shop Boys in early 1996, with an extra verse and added vocals by Neil Tennant, the single 'Hallo Spaceboy' put Bowie back on *Top Of The Pops*, wearing eyeshadow, a dog collar and kitten heels. During another television appearance, the look was only slightly marred by the addition of a dangly skeleton earring, but we'll draw a discreet veil over that. For a man fast approaching fifty, Bowie still had it.

Shortly after that performance on *Top Of The Pops*, I ran into Pet Shop Boys at the Groucho Club and we had a few drinks together. Knowing what a huge Bowie fan Neil had been as a teenager, I remarked on how exciting it must have been to finally work with him.

'I think he was more excited to work with us,' came the reply.

The first single from the *Outside* album was the uncompromising 'The Hearts Filthy Lesson', which was used in the serial-killer thriller *Se7en* starring Brad Pitt and Morgan Freeman and will forever be associated in my mind with New York. I had my own filthy lesson in the city that never sleeps – and it could have killed me.

In September 1995, *Time Out* launched a New York edition and the entire London team were flown over for a launch party. Those were the days when advertising revenue was high and magazines had money to burn on transatlantic flights and rooms at the W Hotel. We arrived on Thursday afternoon, excited but jet-lagged, and were due to fly back to London a few days later.

I had a number of contacts in New York and was nominated to source drugs for a group of workmates for the party. I made a few phone calls and headed off to an address in Chelsea for a rendez-vous with a dealer recommended by a friend. After purchasing the required amount of cocaine, the dealer offered me a line. Thinking it was more of the same, I snorted it. Big mistake. It wasn't cocaine. It was crystal meth. This wasn't a drug I'd ever taken before – or one I particularly wanted to try. I'd heard so many horror stories about Tina, as it was commonly referred to in gay circles. Even a single line could cause a stroke or a heart attack.

Luckily for me, I didn't go into cardiac arrest. But it wasn't the pleasurable high I got from Ecstasy or even the ego-boosting rush I got from cocaine. This was something else entirely. I was speeding like crazy, horny as hell and didn't sleep a wink for three whole days.

My memories of the launch party are vague, to say the least. I know there was live entertainment, DJs and drinks because the invitation says so. I know Yoko Ono was among the guests because several colleagues saw her. I also know there was an after-party at the Tunnel club featuring DJ Junior Vasquez, who famously produced remixes for Madonna. At some point after that, drunk on booze and wired on the combination of drugs I'd shoved up my nose, I ended up at a gay sex club in the Meatpacking District. Back then, this wasn't quite the gentrified neighbourhood it is today. They really were packing meat there – and not just in the gay sense of the word.

My friend, the author Tiffany Murray, lived there at the time and remembers it as pretty edgy. 'You could choose your danger, or your spectacle. My male pals would go to The Lure, The Eagle and J's Hangout – they explained the sex party bit later – while I sat under-ground in Jackie 60, the waft of actual meat carcasses drifting down to its basement. I loved it there. I would go alone, sit in the main room and watch the trans hostess of the night perched on a high stool, dressed as Jackie in sunglasses, mumbling, "Jackie 6-0, let yourself go" into the mic, as men in bloody aprons above us banged on the meat truck doors, "Open up, Louie!" As they say now, good times!'

As well as meat packing, the district was known for prostitution and drug dealing. It was a place where you had to keep your wits about you.

My wits had left me several hours, a dozen drinks and countless lines of white powder ago. Not that this put me off in the slightest. I arrived at the underground sex club, paid the entrance fee, which included a free drink, and left shortly afterwards with a hot Latino guy who took me back to his place. We had sex and cuddled for a bit. Then I climbed out of bed and started to get dressed – and that's when things took a turn for the worse.

He didn't want me to go. He insisted that I stay the night – or what was left of it.

I thanked him for the offer but said I'd rather go, and continued putting on my clothes.

Suddenly his whole demeanour changed. He leaped out of bed and started pacing the room. His face looked different. Maybe it was the combination of drugs in my system but I became convinced that this guy meant to harm me in some way. It wasn't helped by the fact that his studio apartment looked like a scene from *Se7en*, or that he'd insisted on locking the door from the inside and pocketing the key.

He didn't seem like a serial killer, but then apparently neither did Dennis Nilsen. Fight-or-flight response kicked in, and I'd never been much of a fighter. Flight seemed the safer option, only the door was locked and my naked jailer was blocking the way. I asked him to please unlock the door. He said it wasn't safe, that we didn't know who was out there. I told him I'd take my chances and really wanted to leave. He refused. I asked him again, louder this time. At which point, he pulled out a kitchen knife and told me to calm down. Because nothing is more calming than someone pulling a knife on you.

I often felt disconnected when I was on drugs. There was a sense that actions didn't have consequences, that I was outside myself or that things weren't really happening. It's partly what drew me to them in the first place. In my sleep-deprived, chemically altered state, I became hysterical. The irony of being held hostage by a hook-up in the Meatpacking District wasn't lost on me. I even laughed.

But this was really happening. The room was real. The man standing in front of me was real. The knife he held in his hand was all too real. Suddenly I was terrified. We'd already had sex. What more did he want from me? Would I be tortured like one of the poor victims in *Se7en*?

I took a few deep breaths, talked myself down and tried reasoning with him, saying my hotel roommate would be wondering where I was. He asked me where I was staying and I told him. I even gave him the correct room number. I was too distraught to think clearly. I agreed to come back later if he'd just let me leave. Much to my amazement, he put the knife away, produced the keys from the pocket of his jacket hanging from the back of a chair, and opened the door.

Outside, the sun was already rising. I hailed a cab back to the hotel and arrived to find my roommate lying in bed, wide awake, staring at the ceiling. Like me, he'd been up all night. I told him about my misadventure and we both had a good laugh. When the phone rang, he answered it, turned to me and giggled, 'It's for you!'

It was my friend from the Meatpacking District, ringing to check that I'd got back safely – and hadn't given him a wrong number.

Needless to say, I didn't make good on my promise to meet him again later.

You'd think, wouldn't you, that an experience like this would be enough to send me running to the nearest NA meeting – or at least take a long, hard look at myself and my increasingly dangerous, self-destructive life choices?

I wish that were the case. But the truth is, I was just getting started.

Chapter 20:
Lust For Life

In 1996 I was approached by an independent TV production company with a view to making a documentary inspired by some of the ideas in my book *What Are You Looking At?* Following a meeting with commissioning editor Jacquie Lawrence at Channel 4, this quickly evolved into what was described as 'an authored polemic' about the state of gay television, which I was to write and present.

It wasn't my first time on TV. Years earlier, I'd appeared on a late-night TV debate show about gay rights and was introduced as 'a practising homosexual'.

'Oh, I'm not practising,' I replied. 'I've perfected it to a fine art.'

I also took part in a programme about safer sex presented by the actress Margi Clarke, where I discussed alternatives to anal intercourse – like mutual masturbation and nipple play. The following night my mum arrived at work and was met by a group of fellow nurses asking, 'Wasn't that your Paul on the telly last night, talking about people playing with his nipples?'

A similar thing happened the next time I went to get my hair cut – and the time after that, and the next. One of the few compensations of losing my hair was not having to endure the regular ribbing from my barber.

More recently, I'd taken part in a Channel 4 documentary called *Sex Wars*, about the supposed conflict of interests between lesbians and gay men. Nailing my colours to the mast, I wore a T-shirt emblazoned with the words 'Nobody Knows I'm a Lesbian'. I also appeared in a documentary about gay men and black divas, singing the praises of Grace Jones while dressed head to foot in black sequins. Since I was talking about divas, I figured I should look the part.

But the programme that became *Queerspotting* was my first time fronting a documentary. It opened with me in silhouette and the pointed caption 'A Homosexual' – highlighting the way gay men had been portrayed on television for years. It included interviews with Julian Clary, the screenwriter Howard Shulman and agony aunt Anna Raeburn. I enjoyed the interviews enormously. I was experienced at this, having interviewed countless people as a journalist. I was less comfortable recording pieces directly to camera and often had to do several takes before the producer was satisfied that I'd given it my best shot.

The documentary received good reviews. At one point during our interview, Julian Clary commented on the ephemeral nature of television, adding somewhat archly, 'Everyone will have forgotten this programme in about five minutes.' Reviewing *Queerspotting* in the *Independent*, the critic Tom Sutcliffe wrote, 'Burston had the courage to leave that comment in.'

My first proper TV break gave me an audience far larger than my usual readership. It also impressed my coke dealer, who happened to be watching the night it was broadcast and made a special trip to deliver bags of fun to the viewing party hosted by a friend of mine. Naturally, this gave me the impetus to get another documentary under my belt as soon as possible.

But first there was the London Lesbian and Gay Film Festival and my hot date with Tony Ward. I say 'hot date'. Madonna's ex was starring in a gay indie film called *Hustler White* by Rick Castro and Bruce LaBruce, and I was interviewing him on behalf of *Time Out*. I did however have a gay porn mag in my bag – the issue of *In Touch* that Ward had posed for many years earlier and which was hastily reissued after his appearance with Madonna in the video for 'Justify My Love'.

Halfway through the interview, I finally plucked up the courage to take out the magazine and ask Ward to autograph it for me. He turned straight to the centrefold, which showed his famous backside in all its naked glory. Across it, he wrote, 'To Paul, god I was hot, love Tony'.

'You don't look so bad now, Tony,' I heard myself simper, and prayed for the ground to swallow me up.

The launch party for the festival was that Friday evening at the National Film Theatre – and there he was again, standing all alone. Naturally I felt it was my duty to rescue him. As the party died down he asked me what I was doing later. I told him I was meeting my boyfriend and a friend of ours at a club called Popstarz at the Hanover Grand.

'Do you mind if I tag along?' Ward asked.

Did I mind? Not at all. So off we went.

Ward caused quite a stir at the club, not least with our friend Aruan, whose birthday it was that night. I told Tony and asked if he'd mind giving the birthday boy a kiss. He didn't mind at all and gave Aruan a full mouth-on-mouth snog.

Afterwards, I asked Aruan how it felt.

Pretty amazing, he said. 'Those lips kissed Madonna!'

I told him Tony was wasted on him. In fact, I've reason to believe that Tony was pretty wasted for most of that night – largely because he kept telling me so.

'Man, I am so fucked up!' he said at one point, his arm draped around my neck.

Had this been a gay porn movie, this is the point at which I'd have said, 'We should go back to my place so you can sleep it off,' and one thing would have led to another.

Sadly, real life seldom lives up to the promises of gay porn, and that's as intimate as things got between Tony Ward and me. I still have that signed photo of his naked backside, though.

My next foray into television was screened in October 1997 as part of a season called *Seven Sins* on Channel 4. Perhaps inevitably, the sin assigned to me was lust. The documentary was made by a husband-and-wife team called Barbara and Rafi Rafaeli and was shot on location in South Beach, Miami.

South Beach is the ultimate gay party town. Like London or Los Angeles, it has a highly developed commercial gay scene, built around gay men's apparently insatiable appetite for sexual adventure. Like New York or Palm Springs, it plays regular host to what are known as circuit parties – an ever-expanding network of large-scale themed events such as the White Party or the Winter Party, held to raise money for AIDS charities and characterised by thousands of shirtless men with gym-fit bodies and chemically enhanced smiles.

For generations, America's elderly and infirm had been retiring to Miami to live out the remainder of their days in the sun. Only now many of the retirees were far younger – and gay. In the bustling gay bars and busy restaurants lining Collins Avenue and Ocean Drive, 'retiree' had become a popular euphemism for a gay man living with HIV or AIDS who'd packed in his job, cashed in his life insurance policy, and adopted a lifestyle that revolved around the beach, the gym and generally striving to look and feel as good as possible for however many years he had left.

Then in the mid-90s along came protease inhibitors. The arrival of this new class of antiretroviral drugs meant that people with HIV were no longer developing AIDS at the rate they had been previously. In many cases, the new drugs stopped the virus in its tracks, reducing a person's viral load and preventing the various illnesses that had taken so many lives just a few years earlier. Clearly this was cause for celebration. But there were unforeseen consequences.

In South Beach, gay men who'd expected to be dead in a few years were suddenly given a new lease on life. For many, this was obviously a blessing. For others, it led to financial insecurity, anxiety, depression, and patterns of self-destructive behaviour I recognised all too clearly.

The producer and director had already selected the interviewees for the film. My job was to front the story and deliver the polemic. It wasn't an easy shoot. Unlike my previous documentary, which had been developed from the start with me as writer and presenter, this film had been in development long before I was added to the mix. The director, Rafi, was laid-back and easy-going. The producer, Barbara, was a more forceful character, with firm ideas about what the film and its presenter should say – some of which I took issue with.

My guide to South Beach was a local gay journalist called George, who wrote a social diary column and sold advertising for a gay free-sheet called *Scoop*. I liked George a lot. He was charming and great company. But like many people employed by the gay press and reliant on gay ad revenue, he was reluctant to say anything on camera that might be construed as remotely critical.

The angle of the film was that South Beach was a gay pleasure-seekers' paradise with a darker underbelly. We featured a local gay artist, whose lover had died of AIDS and whose work paid tribute to lives lost to the epidemic. I talked to handsome young gay men who were clearly struggling with self-esteem, body dysmorphia and dependency issues. Many were having unsafe sex. Few were willing to talk on camera but were happy to be quoted in a newspaper article I was writing.

One guy called John told me the last time he had unsafe sex with a stranger was two weeks ago. 'I met this really hot guy from out of town. We were both pretty messed up, pretty drunk, and he came back to my place. It wasn't like I planned to be unsafe or anything. It just happened. When you're really into someone, it isn't always easy to talk about that stuff. Things happen in the heat of the moment.'

I asked John if he ever worried about contracting HIV. 'Of course. But the way I figure it is, if it's going to happen, then it's going to happen.' His view was echoed by another guy called Greg, whom I met at the Winter Party. 'I'm looking round at all these gorgeous men,' he told me, 'and I just keep thinking that over half of them are probably HIV-positive. And you know, there's a lot of unsafe sex going on now. I mean, I'm usually pretty careful. But sometimes, well, y'know . . . AIDS isn't really something you want to think about on a day like this, is it? Still, that's why God gave us drugs. One more hit and I'll be fine!'

This sense of fatalism was far more prevalent on the gay scene in the mid-1990s than many people cared to admit, but I'd never heard it expressed so explicitly before. The truth is, I could understand where John and Greg were coming from – but I was also required to maintain a professional distance. I was here as a journalist, not to make friends. Nor was it my job to promote South Beach as a gay travel destination, though I'm sure the film's focus on muscular young men sunbathing and dancing shirtless in nightclubs didn't hurt the local tourism economy. My first responsibility was to tell the truth as I saw it, and some of the behaviour I witnessed or had described to me in South Beach was excessive at best, self-destructive at worst.

Thankfully, by 1997 HIV was no longer seen as the death sentence it once was. But it was still a chronic condition – and one with life-altering, even life-threatening implications. The new drugs had made a huge impact, but they didn't work for everyone and nobody really knew yet what the long-term effects would be. Gay health workers warned of the danger of treating protease inhibitors as some sort of morning-after pill, and expressed concerns that the beneficial effects would be offset by a sudden surge in new infections. There was even talk about the possibility of a new, drug-resistant strain of 'super HIV' developing as a result of unsafe sexual encounters between men infected with different strains of the virus.

I'd spent several years as an AIDS activist, so I was well versed in the arguments about bodily autonomy, sexual shaming and personal responsibility. It was an incredibly sensitive subject and getting the balance right wasn't always easy. I'm not entirely sure we did. There was some tension in the film between the visual celebration of gay hedonism and the cautionary tone of my voiceover, which was added in the editing suite back in London.

I didn't want to sound as if I was endorsing everything I witnessed, but nor did I want to come across as prudish or preachy. I may have been personally practising safer sex, but I was still prone to putting myself in dangerous situations. Who was I to judge what risks others chose to take? After some discussion, I insisted that my final words in the film should be less condemnatory and more celebratory. 'If this is lust, it's the lust for life. Rave on, South Beach!'

I got my way. In doing so, I managed to shoehorn in the title of an Iggy Pop song, recorded with David Bowie two decades earlier. Another of Bowie's musical associates, Lou Reed, was also connected to the film. A personal friend of Rafi's, Reed kindly allowed us to use two songs from his classic album *Transformer* – 'Make Up' and 'Goodnight Ladies'. The closing credits for the documentary included the words 'Thanks, Lou!'

To say I was thrilled would be putting it mildly. *Transformer* was produced by none other than Bowie himself. For an obsessive, somewhat fanciful fan like me, it felt as if the film brought us closer together – just two degrees of separation.

When we weren't busy filming, I took the time to explore South Beach. I'd pass by the Versace mansion on Ocean Drive, and once saw the great man himself heading out to buy his morning newspaper. I was never really a fan of his menswear but I loved the way he dressed iconic women like Princess Diana, Kate Moss and Madonna. A year later he'd be dead, gunned down outside his mansion by gay serial killer Andrew Cunanan.

Madonna was strongly linked to Miami at the time. She owned a mansion of her own near Vizcaya, and some of the images from her *Sex* book incorporated local landmarks. The famous photo of her rising from the ocean like a modern-day Venus was taken there, as well as the playful pictures of her hitchhiking naked and posing nude in a pizzeria.

In 1996, Madonna had reinvented herself as a musical actress, starring in Alan Parker's film version of *Evita*. The dance version of 'Don't Cry For Me Argentina' was still big in the gay clubs. One scene in our documentary showed me dancing to the song on a crowded dance floor. What it didn't show was the copious amount of drug taking that took place before the scene was shot. The quality of cocaine in Miami was far superior to any I'd tried before, and I was determined to make the most of it while I had the chance.

One evening I met up with my old friend Simon, aka Bonnie from the market-research company. He was working as a dance captain on a cruise ship docked in Miami and wanted to know all about the documentary I was making. I told him it was part of a season called *Seven Sins*, that it focused on lust and was mainly about a group of gay guys in South Beach.

Simon wasn't a big fan of South Beach. He found it too exclusive and full of 'body fascist types'. Like me, he was still drinking and smoking. But over cocktails at Palace Bar on Ocean, he expressed concern at how heavy my smoking had become – I was up to forty a day by then – and how frequently I visited the restroom to 'powder my nose'.

Did I listen? Did I admit to my friend that my addictive behaviour was escalating in more ways than one? Did I hell. Lust wasn't my only sin. I was also guilty of pride. And we all know that pride comes before a fall.

Chapter 21:
Queen Bitch

My first-ever book tour wasn't a book tour in the usual sense. I didn't travel the country in order to promote a book I'd already published. I travelled in order to research and write one.

Queens' Country was my fourth book – after a slim biography of Marc Almond, published in 1997. It was my first for Little, Brown and the last non-fiction title I would write for many years. The idea came largely from my editor at the time, Andrew Wille. Like me, Andrew was a fan of Edmund White and was looking for someone to write a British counterpart to *States Of Desire*, in which White explores gay lives across the United States. I was also a fan of Bill Bryson, whose recent *Notes On A Small Island* had demonstrated that travel writing could also be funny.

Not that White's book is lacking in humour. He's a witty and often waspish writer. But *States Of Desire* was first published in 1980, at a time when 'the gay community' was still a relatively new concept. Almost twenty years on, this idea was fracturing – and I was one of the gay writers who'd helped take a wrecking ball to it. There wasn't one big, happy-clappy gay community but rather lots of smaller communities – sometimes not very happy at all, and often at loggerheads with one another. Or, to put it another way,

White came to consolidate the idea of a gay community. I came to question it – and to do so with a smile on my face.

I had a lot to smile about. By the time *Queens' Country* was published in 1998, I'd been at *Time Out* for five years. I'd finally been able to buy my own flat and had a handsome Spanish boyfriend who has asked not to be named here and who I'll refer to as Javier. I'd presented two television documentaries and published four books. I was out partying most weekends and networking at the Groucho most weeknights. But until recently, there'd been something missing – and that was a major book deal. My previous books had been what might politely be described as 'cult reads'. I had desperately wanted a mainstream publisher – and thanks to my agent at the time, I now had one in Little, Brown.

For the book, I'd travelled to various destinations across the UK, from Belfast to Edinburgh, Derbyshire to Manchester, Essex to Somerset. I interviewed people I met along the way and explored themes pertinent to the time and place. For example, the chapter on Manchester was called 'Village People' and examined the emerging commercial gay scene that would later be immortalised in the groundbreaking TV drama *Queer As Folk*. The chapter on Essex was called 'The Great Dark Lad' and explored internalised homophobia and the gay obsession with straight or 'straight-acting' men. The chapter on Somerset was called 'A Cottage in the Country' – and I wasn't referring to the kind of cottage that comes with a thatched roof and roses around the front door.

As someone who'd swapped a small-town, closeted life for that of an out-and-proud metropolitan gay man, I confess I had some preconceptions. I expected to find more people who dreamed of escaping as I once had, or whose lives were hemmed in by homophobia. Nothing could have been further from the truth. For the most part, the men I met were openly gay and far more integrated into their local communities than those living a ghettoised existence in gay London.

Nowhere were my preconceptions shattered more than in rural Derbyshire. For a chapter entitled 'A Weekend with the Blues Brothers', I hung out with a group of young gay Conservatives – and thoroughly enjoyed the experience. Had you told me this a decade earlier, I would never have believed you. My host in Derbyshire was parliamentary sketch writer for *The Times* and former Tory MP Matthew Parris. I liked Matthew a lot, though our politics couldn't have been more different. Like me, he was something of a maverick, albeit one who'd been a great personal supporter of Margaret Thatcher. Still, his own voting record on gay rights had been pretty exemplary, even in the days when he preferred to keep his sexuality private. As MP for West Derbyshire, 1979–1986, Parris was one of the first politicians to call for a change in the law surrounding the specifically 'gay crime' of gross indecency and to condemn the use of 'pretty policemen' in police entrapment operations. When we first met, he was on the managing committee of GALOP. By the time I went to stay with him in Derbyshire, he was regularly using his column in *The Times* to raise awareness of gay issues.

In many ways, Britain in 1998 was a very different country to the one it had been over a decade earlier, when my personal gay journey began. After eighteen years of Tory rule, the 1997 general election had seen Tony Blair sweep to power in a Labour landslide. For many people, the mood was summed up by the campaign song by D:Ream, 'Things Can Only Get Better'. And then Princess Diana died. The country went into shock. Endless newspaper articles were written about how the nation's spontaneous outpouring of grief heralded a new, kinder, more empathetic society.

I was deeply affected by Diana's death, as I think many gay men were. The famous photograph of her hugging a skeletal man with AIDS had sent a powerful message at a time when there was very little hope and less public sympathy. I was at London Lighthouse the day she made her last public visit. I remember thinking then how charismatic she was – and how very fragile. The night she died, I was woken by my friend Tim phoning from New York. The following day felt strangely personal, as grieving gay friends gravitated to my flat and we watched the news unfold over bottles upon bottles of wine. And there was Tony Blair, capturing the mood of the country and calling her 'the people's princess' while the Queen totally misjudged the situation and declined to make a public address. It felt as if serious social change was afoot.

But after a year in government, there was still no sign that Blair would make good on his manifesto promises to LGBTQ+ voters. The age of consent for gay men remained at eighteen. Section 28 was still enshrined in law. The armed forces ban was still in place. There were still no employment rights for LGBTQ+ people or partnership rights for same-sex couples. One could be forgiven for thinking that all that talk of gay equality had been a load of hot air.

What had changed – at least in London – was the gay scene. Though still dominated by clubs playing commercial house music for high and horny, usually shirtless men, there were pockets of resistance – alternative scenes within the scene. It started with the mighty indie night Popstarz in 1995 and grew with smaller, quirky clubs like Duckie, Marvellous and Nag Nag Nag. Here the DJs played everything from Britpop to Bowie, glam rock, '70s disco, '80s synth-pop and beyond. Many were the times I danced the night away at Duckie or Marvellous, singing along to 'Starman' or 'Queen Bitch'.

But it wasn't just the music policy that marked a shift away from the gay norm. There was a change in attitude, too. 'The attitude in a lot of gay clubs is really offensive,' Popstarz promoter Simon Hobart told me in an interview for *Time Out*. He was referring specifically to the body fascism and identikit gay Ken dolls found at most of London's leading gay venues. When he first launched Popstarz,

Hobart had set out to offend as many gay sensibilities as possible. Dispensing with the usual style of gay club flyer featuring half-naked hunks, he vented his spleen at the London scene with disparaging remarks about 'E-heads' and 'mindless techno'. Popstarz, the flyer said, was a club for 'people with hangovers, not hang-ups', a place where people 'don't have to take their shirts off to stay cool'.

This was gay clubbing for people who hated gay clubs. Some promoters described themselves and their club nights as 'post-gay' (there's that controversial term again), while others went further and railed against everything they hated about the gay mainstream.

'Gay identity has become meaningless,' Duckie DJ Mark Wood asserted in the same article for *Time Out*. 'What we do is anti-gay in the sense that if gay is everything the gay scene offers you, and everything the gay press tells you you're supposed to like, then everything we do is the complete opposite.'

Radical queer performers like Manchester's David Hoyle, then better known as the Divine David, openly challenged the gay status quo and were regularly heckled or had bottles thrown at them for daring to speak the truth as they saw it. There are no prizes for guessing where my sympathies lay.

This was all documented in *Queens' Country*, together with the heart-warming tale of a gay couple running their own massage parlour in Bristol, stories told at gay youth groups in Belfast, and the dangers faced by men cruising Edinburgh's Calton Hill. Subtitled *A Tour Around the Gay Ghettos, Queer Spots and Camp Sights of Britain*, the book offered a portrait of the UK as seen through the eyes of people who'd been historically despised and disenfranchised but were now out of the closet, out on the streets and demanding a better life for themselves. It was also a book about the pitfalls of identity politics and the shameful ways we as gay men sometimes treat one another.

As I wrote in the introduction, 'These days, adopting a gay identity and lifestyle demands just as much in the way of role-playing as being in the closet, and leaves only a little more space for manoeuvre. Instead of being required to pass successfully as straight by disapproving heterosexuals, one is required to pass successfully as gay by equally disapproving homosexuals . . . In a sense, this book is an attempt to expose some of the lies told by and about gay men in Britain today. It is a book about the kinds of lives gay men lead and the kinds of places in which they lead them; about the injustices of living in a homophobic society and the absurdities of taking your sexuality too seriously.'

Clearly, I was setting out to ruffle a few feathers. Still, the reviews were mostly favourable. *The Face* called it 'a cracklingly irreverent snapshot of gay life'. The *Big Issue* described it as 'funny, provocative, thoughtful and spiky', adding 'Burston is incapable of writing a boring sentence' – which led to endless ribbing from Deborah Orr and probably came as a surprise to some of the sub-editors I worked with at *Time Out*. Even the gay press were supportive. The *Pink Paper* ran a sympathetic profile piece describing me as an 'accidental gay maverick' and the book as 'pistol sharp' and 'seriously funny'. Another gay publication repeated the *enfant terrible* tag in a piece headlined 'Wild Child'. I was now thirty-three years old.

It was left to *Gay Times* to publish the only real hatchet job, suggesting that I'd travelled the country in order to remind myself why I hated gay men so much, then wrote a book about it. Not for the first time, I was denounced as 'bitchy' – a term only ever applied to women and gay men.

Queens' Country was serialised in the *Daily Express* and an extract appeared in the *Independent On Sunday*. Sales weren't as strong as expected but the book did well enough for Little, Brown to offer me another deal – one that set my career off in a whole new direction.

'I think you should write a novel next,' my editor Andrew told me at our next meeting. At this point I was still known mainly as a columnist, and a controversial one at that. I'd written interviews and longer feature articles but had never once had a work of fiction published. What Andrew saw in *Queens' Country* wasn't the work of a polemicist but someone with an ear for dialogue and the strong sense of character and place required by a novelist. *Bridget Jones's Diary* had been a big hit and he was looking for a 'gay male Bridget'. What did I think?

Truth be told, I was never a great fan of Bridget Jones. Among other things, I hated the way she and her sob sisters always had a gay man's shoulder to cry on, a gay man to dispense fashion advice, a gay man with no sex life or romantic interests of his own. There's even a line in the film adaptation where she describes going to a party full of fellow singletons – 'mainly poofs'. Who were these gay men and why didn't they have an ounce of self-respect?

But Andrew had given me an idea. What if I took this genre and subverted it? I'd give him his 'gay male Bridget' – I already had just the man in mind. His name was Martin and he lived across the hall from me in Oval. One day he arrived home from work to find that his live-in lover had moved out without saying a word. I thought this would make a great premise for the tale of a hapless gay singleton, thrown back on to the gay dating scene and having to adapt to a whole new set of expectations and mating rituals. Martin was happy for me to use elements of his story – and even insisted that I name my protagonist after him.

The novel that eventually became *Shameless* began life in diary form, with a very different title. Inspired by a cult film by Russ Meyer, which I'd seen at the Scala Cinema in King's Cross, the contract I signed in 1998 was for a book with the unwieldy working title of *Faster, Disco Bunny, Kill, Kill!*

No, I don't know what I was thinking, either. But I certainly wasn't thinking straight.

Chapter 22:
From New York To LA

It took me two years to complete *Shameless*. I was busy working on other projects. I had a part-time job at *Time Out*, plus regular freelance work for a number of newspapers and magazines. I was also doing a fair amount of research for the book, though this mainly consisted of going clubbing and experimenting with the various drugs my protagonist would be exposed to and the effects they would have on him. If researching a novel can be likened to an actor preparing for a role, I was of the method-acting school of thinking and was doing a De Niro.

At one point, a friend took me aside and said, 'Paul, I think you've done quite enough research now. I think it's time you sat down and wrote the book!'

He was right, and I did. But first I had some business to attend to in New York.

Beneath The Sheets was the title of my third documentary for Channel 4, which purported to go under the covers of the gay press on both sides of the Atlantic. It was a sexy title for a documentary that wasn't particularly sexy, unless you counted the still shots of magazine covers with half-naked hotties. The 'sheets' referred to the gay free-sheets, though other publications were also discussed.

Interviewees included the editor of *Out* magazine, James Collard, who I knew from our days at *Attitude*. I was cast as a kind of detective dressed in what one friend called my Sam Spade outfit, walking the streets of London and New York in a raincoat and trilby hat, with my voiceover added at a later stage.

These days, whenever I see a documentary with a journalist walking self-consciously past the camera, a little part of me dies inside. It's one of the oldest clichés in the book. The less said about this particular journalist in this particular documentary, the better. Let's just say it wasn't my finest hour. But it did involve a free trip to New York. When filming ended, the producers even flew my boyfriend Javier over and we stayed on to catch up with friends and explore the city.

Our host was the artist Tim Hailand, who I'd first met through our mutual friend Georg Osterman – the same Tim who'd called to inform me of Georg's illness a few years earlier and the death of Princess Diana the previous August. I don't mean to make Tim sound like a harbinger of doom. He really isn't. But he is the kind of person who says exactly what he thinks and will often be the one who breaks the news to you, good or bad. You know where you are with Tim – and right now we were in his one-bedroom apartment on West 17th Street while he slept on a friend's couch.

This was my second visit to New York in three years, and a far less messy one than the first. Tim doesn't drink or use drugs, so most of our time was spent shopping, seeing the sights and watching live entertainment – and by 'live entertainment' I don't just mean the muscle boys who danced in their underwear on the bar at Splash, stimulating as they were. Tim was friends with Joey Arias, who'd once appeared with David Bowie on *Saturday Night Live* and was now hosting and performing at a venue called Bar d'O in the West Village, together with fellow drag queens Raven O and Sherry Vine.

The venue has since closed, but back then Bar d'O was the place to go. It had a Weimar-esque, *Cabaret* feel, with Arias performing in various stages of undress and singing so uncannily like Billie Holiday I assumed he must be miming. When it was pointed out to me that, no, that was his voice, you could have knocked me down with a white gardenia.

Tim knew everyone in the '90s New York queer demimonde – Antony and the Johnsons, Kiki and Herb, Lady Bunny, Rufus Wainwright. And those he didn't know, he wasn't shy about introducing himself to. When Tim came to stay with me in London he wasted no time in befriending Pete Burns of Dead or Alive. When Pet Shop Boys visited New York, Tim found out which hotel they were staying at, phoned Neil Tennant and suggested they meet. Apparently, Neil was most amenable. 'Well,' he's reported to have said. 'This is New York!'

Tim's taste in music, theatre and pop culture was remarkably similar to my own. So when he told me I had to see a new rock musical called *Hedwig And The Angry Inch* at the Jane Street Theatre, I booked tickets immediately. Co-written by and starring John Cameron Mitchell, the musical tells the story of Hedwig Robinson, a genderqueer East German singer. The character was apparently inspired by a German divorced US Army wife who was Mitchell's family babysitter when he was a boy and who moonlighted as a sex worker. Others saw elements of pioneering trans rocker Jayne County in Hedwig, as well as lipstick traces of glam-era David Bowie and proto-punk performers Lou Reed and Iggy Pop.

Bowie and Reed had both given the show their blessing, and I was half expecting to see them at the performance I attended. In that respect, I was disappointed. But I loved the show so much I bought the original cast recording and wasn't the least bit surprised when it went on to become an international hit, spawning a film version and turning Mitchell into a bona fide star.

The next time I saw Tim was that October in LA. I was there to interview gay comedian Steve Moore for the *Sunday Times Magazine*. Otherwise known as 'the Happy AIDS Guy' – a term he coined himself – Steve performed at mainstream comedy clubs, and would lull audiences into a false sense of security before suddenly announcing that he was HIV+ and asking for a sip of someone's beer. When the laughter stopped, he upped the ante. 'Don't mess with me, folks!' he'd say, prowling across the stage and grinning mischievously. 'I could open up a vein and take out the whole front row!'

It was a dangerous line to tread and Steve did it with great skill. He'd honed his craft doing stand-up spots and warm-ups for TV sitcoms like *Roseanne*. I still have the signed TV script he kindly gifted me. Thanks to the new HIV medications, Steve was far healthier when I met him than he had been a few years earlier. This formed the basis of one of his jokes: 'AIDS! I hope I never get that again! It was awful!'

Never having been to LA before, I'd asked the magazine to book me into a hotel on Sunset Boulevard, not realising how long the road actually was and thinking I'd be near the centre of things. In fact, I was miles away. But I was staying at the Hotel Bel-Air, so I wasn't complaining – even if the old imposter syndrome kicked in every time I spotted a member of housekeeping.

I was introduced to Steve by Fenton Bailey and Randy Barbato, founders of World of Wonder Productions and the people behind the phenomenally successful *RuPaul's Drag Race*. Back then, they were better known for cult TV shows like *Manhattan Cable* and documentaries exploring the quirkier, often darker side of celebrity culture. Shortly before I arrived in LA, they'd completed work on *Party Monster: The Shockumentary*, about the notorious New York Club Kid Michael Alig, who was imprisoned for the manslaughter of Andre 'Angel' Melendez.

They'd also made a comedy special about Steve for HBO. *Drop Dead Gorgeous* charted a year in the comedian's life and took its title from another of Moore's jokes: 'People keep telling me how good I look. They say things like, "I can't believe you've been exposed to the AIDS virus. You've never looked better!" I figure, hell, pretty soon I'll be drop dead gorgeous!'

When I first met Steve, he was still riding high from all the publicity surrounding the film. *Drop Dead Gorgeous* received gushing critical notices across the board and was nominated for a clutch of industry awards. He'd appeared on *Entertainment Tonight* and the Leeza Gibbons TV chat show. Asked, 'How does a man from Danville, Virginia get his own HBO comedy special?' Steve responded with typical aplomb. 'Well, Leeza,' he said, scarcely missing a beat. 'It took me twenty-one years and a deadly virus. But I'm very grateful!'

I spent several days in Steve's company. I watched him perform at an AIDS charity dinner in downtown Los Angeles and at the world-famous Comedy Store on Sunset Strip. I attended a Halloween party at his house in Studio City. I met him for lunch at a restaurant overlooking Venice Beach, where he told me he wasn't feeling too well. His biggest worry was earning enough money to cover his medical care. Much to his dismay, the success of the HBO comedy special hadn't led to increased ticket sales for his live tour. In Chicago, he'd had to cancel two shows. In Palm Springs, he'd cancelled two whole weeks. One night in the gay heart of San Francisco, he'd opened to an audience of just seven people.

'I couldn't believe it,' he said, clearly still wounded. 'I tell the world I'm gay. I tell the world I'm HIV+. What sort of career could

I possibly expect after that? I thought, surely the gay community would appreciate the risk I'd taken and show up to support me.' But they didn't. Why did he think that was? 'I don't know. I'm not a drag queen. I don't perform my show dressed in a Speedo with a buff body. I'm a forty-three-year-old, not terribly pretty gay man with HIV. Who wants to pay to see that?'

Our last meeting was at a doctor's appointment, where Steve received the devastating news that the virus in his body had mutated and the protease inhibitor he was taking was no longer working. The doctor recommended an alternative which Steve had tried once before and wasn't keen to try again as it made him nauseous. The doctor told him that things weren't looking good and persuaded him to give the drug another shot. He wrote out a complicated prescription and Steve asked the receptionist to fax it over to the local pharmacy.

As we waited, a painfully thin man struck up a conversation with Steve, telling him he'd tried all the drugs available and none of them worked. 'I'm really jealous of you,' he said with a grin. 'Honestly, I wish I could walk out of here with a prescription like the one you're holding.'

Steve left the doctor's surgery close to tears. 'Everyone is latching on to the protease as if it's some kind of magic cure,' he told me as we climbed into his car. 'Evidently it's not.'

We drove to the pharmacy in silence. Steve collected his drugs and we jumped back in the car.

'Do you know what?' he said as we drove off. 'It was really very important that I met that guy back there. I was about ready to burst into tears, thinking, "Oh God, I'm dying!" Then I go out and I think, "Nothing's working for him, so what the hell am I complaining about?"'

So would he continue making jokes about AIDS, I asked. Would he still get up on stage and tell people, 'Life is good, folks'? Or was he starting to feel a little bitter?

Steve Moore, the Happy AIDS Guy, took his eye off the road ahead, turned to me with his perkiest smile and said, 'I'm trying hard not to be! I'm still fighting it!'

When I wasn't busy hanging out with Steve, I spent time with Tim, who'd flown in from New York for a few days. Together we went to see a different kind of comedian – and one who also had a connection to the sitcom *Roseanne*. Sandra Bernhard was in town with a new show. I'd been a fan of hers since Tyler Brûlé first played me a cassette recording of *Without You I'm Nothing* a decade earlier. Tim was also a fan. So off we went to see Sandra in her new show, *I'm Still Here . . . Damn It!*

It was just the tonic I needed. Bernhard was on top form, making caustic comments about Mariah Carey, talking about the deaths of Gianni Versace and Princess Diana, and casting aspersions about Elton John's new recording of 'Candle In The Wind'. 'The reworked lyrics are genius! The candle burned out long before the royalties ever did!'

She also took a swipe at people who stereotyped LA as a city full of airheads where nobody could really be creative. This hadn't been my experience at all. I'd met a lot of creative people in LA. I found their enthusiasm inspiring.

Also in the audience that night was Marianne Faithfull, who Bernhard praised for being a true rock survivor and a far cry from the wispy, wailing women singers who were currently dominating the charts. 'I don't know how much more of these waifish, alternative singers I can take,' she said. 'The Alanis Morissette, Fiona Apple-esque, "I'm fed up, I'm rich, I'm fucked over, I'm bitter, I'm confused." Honey, just get out of that dirty bathtub for starters and work your way forward!'

I'd been a fan of Faithfull for many years. She was such an icon of cool – dating Mick Jagger in the late '60s and duetting with Bowie on 'I Got You Babe' in his Orwell-referencing 1974 television special *The 1980 Floor Show*, where she wore a nun's habit with her knickers showing. It was often said that anything Mick had, Bowie wanted a piece of, such was the rivalry between them.

But Faithfull was far more than a mere rock god's plaything. She had hit singles of her own and made several film appearances before battling anorexia, heroin addiction and homelessness. Then, in 1979 she made a critically acclaimed comeback with her landmark post-punk album *Broken English*. The discordant rhythms and jagged guitars don't sound so dissimilar to those on Bowie's *Scary Monsters* album, which was released a year later.

I was dying to meet her and hoped that Tim could swing an introduction, but it wasn't to be.

I flew back from LA the following day, sad to say goodbye to the people I'd met, happy that I had my first big feature for the *Sunday Times* under my belt, hopeful that this would be the first of many similar assignments.

Chapter 23:
When The Going Gets Tough

No sooner was I back from LA than I started work on *Tony's Fairy Tales*. My fourth and final documentary for Channel 4, the film was produced by Just Television and billed as an 'authored polemic' about the Blair government's failure to deliver on their manifesto promise and repeal Section 28.

I was far more relaxed than on previous shoots, and even enjoyed the pieces to camera – one of which involved an early morning call on Clapham Common, where Ron Davies MP had recently experienced the 'moment of madness' that led to his resignation as Secretary of State for Wales. Commenting on how the Blair government appeared to be dragging its heels over gay law reform, I said pointedly, 'And how ironic that this should be happening at a time when MPs are falling out of the closet, left, right and centre left.'

At the start of 1999, Labour had been in power for the best part of two years. There were a number of out lesbian and gay Labour MPs. Stephen Twigg had recently appeared on the cover of *Gay Times*, having won Michael Portillo's seat in the general election. Angela Eagle was out and proud, as was Ben Bradshaw. None of them were willing to talk to me.

We did manage to grab a few words with Chris Smith MP at the unveiling of Maggi Hambling's statue of Oscar Wilde, where Stephen Fry was also happy to talk to us. We also spoke to Matthew Parris, who had recently caused a stir by alluding to Peter Mandelson's sexuality live on *Newsnight*, and to author Will Self, who was contemptuous of the government's failure to deliver on its manifesto promise to gay voters. But the silence from Labour's great, gay and good was deafening.

One scene in the film showed me making phone calls to MPs' offices and being told that nobody was available or had any comment to make. In another, I was filmed outside the House of Lords, having just been shown evidence that Labour had been given several opportunities to repeal Section 28 but had failed to take them. Furious, I fumed that, while the government continued dragging its heels, young lesbians and gay men were feeling isolated and driven to suicide. Some accused me of hyperbole, but this was the exact same argument put forward by Chris Smith MP in the House of Commons when Section 28 was first introduced.

There were rumours, neither confirmed nor denied by Channel 4, that the government was putting pressure on the channel to rein me in. Certainly, elements of the script that had been agreed previously were suddenly called into question. Sometimes revisions were phoned through at the last minute, just as we were about to start filming. At one point, I was informed that the programme we were making wasn't really an authored polemic after all, but 'more of a rhetoric' – whatever that means in TV talk.

As challenging as it was to make, I was immensely proud of *Tony's Fairy Tales*. When the going got tough, the tough got creative. The director, Mark Soldinger, was a kindred spirit in many ways – as bloody-minded as I was often accused of being, equally passionate about the project and determined to hold those in power to account, however many obstacles were thrown in our way. Producer Nina Davies was equally formidable, though more diplomatic in her approach. Together we made a great team. We challenged politicians, highlighted hypocrisy and even found a novel way of getting our message across.

At midnight on the final day of filming, the production team assembled on Westminster Bridge – the same bridge where I'd been arrested with ACT UP a decade earlier. Again, there was a van. But this van didn't contain a group of AIDS activists about to jump out and chain themselves to the bridge. It contained a giant projector. Standing close by was journalist Deborah Orr, who was reporting on the programme for the *Independent*. As the camera rolled, I called on the government to stop making excuses and deliver on its promises to gay voters. Behind me, the Houses of Parliament were suddenly lit with a hundred-foot-high projection asking 'Why 28?'

Not only was this my finest moment in front of the camera. In many ways, it felt like a return to my activist days. ACT UP would have been proud. And so, I dare say, would my old friend Vaughan.

Tony's Fairy Tales was broadcast on Saturday, 13 March 1999. The commissioning editor Jacquie Lawrence hosted a viewing party at her house in Camberwell. The celebrations continued well into the early hours. A great many bottles of champagne were consumed. We had a lot to celebrate. The reviews were the best I'd ever had.

In her *Independent* column, Deborah Orr explained why the programme was so necessary, citing studies showing that as many as one in five gay teenagers had attempted suicide, and that under Section 28 it was difficult for teachers to discuss such feelings or develop strategies to combat anti-gay bullying. 'This is what "promoting homosexuality", the inflammatory words of Section 28, mean in reality,' she wrote.

Did it bother me that the column was headlined 'Of queers, poofs and politics' – or that I was referred to as 'a big poof' in the opening sentence? Yes, it did. Some might argue that the choice of words was, shall we say, disrespectful in the context of a piece about gay rights and homophobia. And this was in the left-leaning *Independent*, not some right-wing tabloid – a sign, perhaps, of how gay men were viewed by the liberal establishment as recently as 1999.

Still, the piece as a whole was supportive. Orr thought it was safe to assume that the documentary would be pretty embarrassing for the government. She stressed that none of the New Labour ministers invited to take part in *Tony's Fairy Tales* took me up on my offer. She noted that Chris Smith was perfectly charming when he was button-holed while making a speech at the inauguration of Maggi Hambling's statue of Oscar Wilde. She reminded her readers that Wilde had been dead for almost a hundred years and was jailed for 'gross indecency', a charge that still existed under the Sexual Offences Act of 1956 as a specifically gay crime. 'If Wilde were with us now,' she wrote, 'this homophobic law could be invoked to ensure that his whole sad and destructive story was played out again in much the same way. How little we learn in a century.'

I couldn't have put it better myself – and there was a more shocking reminder just around the corner.

Six weeks later, on Friday 30 April, I was in a pub in Soho with some colleagues from *Time Out*. It was the start of the bank holiday weekend. I was supposed to meet a friend for drinks at the Admiral Duncan on Old Compton Street, only he texted to say he'd been delayed at work and was running an hour late. Shortly after 6.30 p.m., we heard an almighty bang. People's phones started pinging as text messages came through. There'd been an explosion on Old

Compton Street. Details were still emerging but it appeared to be an act of terrorism.

Heading up Wardour Street, I heard the chaos before I saw it. People were screaming. Sirens screeched. The corner of Old Compton Street looked like a war zone. There were people running in all directions, many of them cut and bleeding. Glass littered the street, and smoke billowed from what was left of the frontage of the Admiral Duncan.

Quickly it became apparent that a nail bomb had exploded inside the pub. Two similar attacks had taken place on the previous two weekends – one at the heart of the black community in Brixton Market; the other in Brick Lane, which is home to a large number of Bangladeshis. The homemade bombs contained up to 1,500 four-inch nails, designed to cause as much carnage as possible. Forty-eight people were injured in Brixton and thirteen in Brick Lane.

MI5 had predicted that a gay venue would be the next target. This information had been leaked to the *Pink Paper* and appeared as a front-page news story the day before the explosion. The national press picked up on it, and pressure was put on the police to hit the streets and warn Soho's gay venues – all to no avail. Of the three nail-bomb attacks, the one on the Admiral Duncan was the most devastating and the only one that led to loss of life.

Three people were killed that day, including a pregnant woman named Andrea Dykes and her friends, Nik Moore and John Light. Andrea's husband, Julian, was seriously injured. Much of the subsequent media coverage focused on the fact that two of those killed and injured were heterosexual. There was a distinct whiff of the good victim/bad victim mentality we saw during the AIDS epidemic, where some lives were deemed more worthy than others.

Four of the survivors were so badly wounded they needed to have limbs amputated. A total of seventy-nine people were injured in all – including barman David Morley, who suffered burns but bravely helped to rescue wounded customers and later went to visit the worst-affected in hospital. Others were seen returning to the smouldering building in search of missing friends. Several media commentators expressed surprise that gay men could display such courage – as if we hadn't already done so by living through an epidemic and fighting for our rights in the face of such hostility. We could be heroes, too. We'd shown it time and time again. I wrote a letter of complaint to one left-leaning newspaper. They chose not to print it.

The attack on the Admiral Duncan was the worst act of anti-gay violence ever recorded in the UK. It served as a stark reminder, if any were needed, that homophobia was still alive and kicking in modern Britain – and I don't just mean the homophobia that drove a man to detonate a nail bomb in a crowded gay pub. Five years later, on 30 October 2004, David Morley was beaten to death by a gang of youths near Waterloo station. He survived an act of terrorism only to have his life taken by group of teenagers whose idea of a fun night out was attacking innocent people and filming it on their phones. The pathologist said Morley's injuries were consistent with those suffered by someone involved in a car accident or who'd fallen from a great height. He was thirty-seven years old.

A few days after the bombing at the Admiral Duncan, the *Sunday Times* published an article by Tony Blair expressing his sincere belief that it was the nail bomber and not the victims of the attack who were 'the true outsiders' in our society. He was confident, he said, that the vast majority of people in Britain were appalled by homophobic violence and wished to see 'a society where there is opportunity for all, where the barriers of prejudice are dismantled'.

Still, he wasn't confident enough to introduce tougher penalties for homophobic hate crimes, which would have served as a fitting tribute to those killed or maimed by the attack on the Admiral Duncan. Nor was he confident enough to act on recommendations from the Home Office and amend the Sexual Offences Act to remove the specifically gay crime of gross indecency – the same crime Deborah Orr had highlighted in her column and for which Oscar Wilde was imprisoned over a century earlier. The Home Office report concluded that there was 'no justification for retaining an offence that deals solely with same-sex behaviour between consenting adults'.

The prime minister didn't agree. Same old Tony, yet more fairy tales. The reason given for failing to act on the findings of the report was the fear of backlash. But from whom, exactly? The vast majority of people in Britain who were appalled by homophobic violence and wished to see 'a society where there is opportunity for all, where the barriers of prejudice are dismantled'? Weren't those the prime minister's own words? And what of the famous leaked memo, in which he wrote about the need to rebrand New Labour as the 'party of the family' and introduce 'eye-catching initiatives that are entirely conventional in terms of their attitude to the family'. This was Tony Blair talking, but it could just as easily have been John Major or even Margaret Thatcher.

In the end, it was the European Court of Human Rights that forced Blair's hand, ruling a year later that a gay man arrested in Yorkshire and charged with gross indecency was entitled to damages and costs amounting to £33,000. This came shortly after another European Court ruling over lesbians and gay men expelled from the armed forces. In that case, the government was ordered to pay compensation to eighty defendants, to the tune of £20,000 each.

In light of the gay law reform that came later, during Blair's second term in office, some people thought I was too tough on the government in *Tony's Fairy Tales*. Frankly, I don't think I was tough enough.

Fighting for your rights is important, but sometimes you just need to party. I welcomed in the new millennium at Crash in Vauxhall, off my face on a cocktail of vodka and Red Bull, cocaine, Ecstasy and ketamine, dancing with Javier and hundreds of other shirtless men. So far, so familiar. There was just one difference. I no longer smoked.

Earlier that month, *Time Out* had asked for volunteers for their annual 'New Year, New You' issue. Stopping smoking was high on the list of readers' resolutions. December is a tough time to quit the nicotine, so I volunteered on the understanding that the method on offer would need to be something I hadn't tried before. No patches. No gum. I wanted serious help. What I got was hypnotherapy. Much to my amazement, it worked. I knew after the first session that I wouldn't smoke – and I didn't, even when I was off my face at Crash and a friend offered me a cigarette. But I mustn't sound too pleased with myself. At my second hypnotherapy session I was asked to visualise all the money I'd saved and what I'd spend it on. I visualised a gram of coke.

Before arriving at Crash, we watched the firework display from Vauxhall Bridge, together with gay men in full leather on their way to The Hoist and a gathering of nuns from the local convent. It was one of those nights when London felt like one big community.

An hour later, the only fireworks were the ones exploding inside my head. On the dance floor, someone grabbed my arm and said, 'Whatever you're on, I wish I was on it!'

I remember grinning at him and raising my hands up towards the ceiling. 'I feel fabulous!' I said – and at that precise moment, I did. I was as high as a kite. I was happy in my chemically altered state. I'd finally stopped smoking and the DJ was playing all the big gay dance hits of the year. What more could I possibly ask for?

Chapter 24:
White Lines

Research for the novel continued in earnest – cocaine during the week, Ecstasy at the weekends. There were long drinking sessions at the Groucho Club, where I became friendly with Caroline Aherne and spent a very memorable evening hanging out with her, Craig Cash and Amanda Donohoe. Knowing what a lesbian icon Amanda was, I phoned a friend and invited her to join us. Amanda gamely fed her cocktail sausages in a suitably suggestive manner.

Caroline was every bit as entertaining in real life as she was on TV. At one point, Courtney Love showed up. Nobody paid her any attention. There were two kinds of people at the Groucho – celebrities and those, like me, who valued our membership and knew better than to make a fuss.

Clearly, Courtney was used to turning heads and found this level of nonchalance hard to comprehend. After a few minutes of being ignored, she started playing frisbee with her friend's beret, spinning it over people's heads in a desperate bid to draw attention to herself.

She succeeded. 'Is that Courtney Love?' Caroline asked.

I confirmed that, yes, it was.

'It's a funny name, Courtney Love,' Caroline mused. 'It's like, "Courtney, luv, can you come here?" Or, "Thanks, Courtney, luv!"'

She found this terribly amusing and began shouting out 'Courtney, LUV!' in a Mancunian accent, with one hand covering her mouth.

Courtney heard, and kept swivelling her head to see where the voice was coming from. Caroline pulled a straight face and then cackled with laughter.

Later, I returned from the toilet to find that Michael Barrymore had taken my seat. He refused to move. Having just snorted a line, I was in no mood to be messed with and tipped the chair over, sending him sprawling to the floor.

Another night I ran into Jude Law. I'd recently interviewed him for the *Sunday Times Magazine*. It was after he played Bosie in *Wilde* and before his career really took off in Hollywood. Law was at the height of his beauty then and totally charming with it. He was at the Groucho with Ewan McGregor, who insisted on buying me a drink and chatted about our mutual friend Todd Haynes, who'd recently directed him in the glam rock musical drama *Velvet Goldmine*.

In those days, the popular image of the Groucho Club was one of coke-snorting celebrities. The *Evening Standard* once ran an undercover report on the growing use of cocaine in the capital's bars and clubs. The reporter had a device that tested surfaces for traces of the drug. He began his investigation in the toilets at the Groucho, reasoning that if no traces were detected there, the device clearly wasn't working.

Scoring cocaine wasn't a problem for me. At one point I had the numbers of three drug dealers stored on my phone. One would come to the *Time Out* office and sell me Ecstasy pills, coke, ketamine and MDMA – the active ingredient in Ecstasy, sold in powdered form. Another would deliver cocaine to me at home. A third could usually be found at The Box in Seven Dials, where I often went for lunch. Long boozy work lunches became lunches where little food was eaten and multiple lines of coke were consumed. In the mainly gay social circles I moved in, this was considered perfectly normal.

No dinner party was complete without little white lines for dessert. One night, my sister Jac was visiting from South Wales. I had a few friends over for dinner – people who, like me, were regular cocaine users. No sooner had I cleared the plates away than I was racking up lines of coke.

'I don't know why you do that stuff, Paul,' my sister said. 'You don't need it to be interesting.'

I was never interesting on coke. I only thought I was. That's what cocaine does to you. It turns you into an egocentric, mono-maniacal bore. It hollows you out until all that's left is a shadow of a human being. I of all people should have known this. Hadn't I grown up worshipping David Bowie? How many interviews had I read where he talked about the damaging effects of cocaine – how it very nearly destroyed him and how he struggled to free himself from its grip? Isn't that what 'Ashes To Ashes' was about? Wasn't that the subtext to the patterns of addictive, self-destructive behaviour he describes on 'Always Crashing In The Same Car'?

If it was, I didn't want to know. I was still at the earlier stage of denial, cheerfully singing along as I chopped yet more lines on the cover of my *Station To Station* CD. It wasn't the side effects of the cocaine, I told myself, thinking that I was somehow special and wouldn't succumb to addiction like so many before me. But it was already too late. I rarely let a day pass without finding some excuse to enjoy my favourite drug.

Javier and I had always had a tempestuous relationship. But as my cocaine use escalated, things became more emotionally vola-tile. There were lots of heated arguments and a lot of passionate make-up sex. We went on a press trip to Miami and the Florida Keys, then returned to South Beach for the White Party – which was even more aptly named than I'd thought. I'd never seen so many handsome men dressed all in white – or so many drugs. An entire week was spent at warm-up parties, pre-parties and what were laughingly referred to as 'recovery parties'. Not a single day went by without some drug or other passing my lips or burning my nasal passages. The morning we were due to fly home, I lay on our hotel bed having the mother of all comedowns. I don't know how we got on the plane.

I kept telling myself that it was all material. This is what writers tell themselves when life throws them a curveball or shit happens. It's also what drug addicts tell themselves when they're still in denial. My social calendar revolved around scoring drugs, taking drugs and recovering from having taken drugs. There were a lot of blue Mondays and even bluer Tuesdays. By Wednesday I was usually feeling back to normal, and as the weekend approached I was ready to start all over again – Fridays at Coco Latté in Mayfair, Saturdays at Crash in Vauxhall or Love Muscle in Brixton, Sundays at DTPM or Salvation in the West End.

These long drug-fuelled weekends weren't without incident. One night at Love Muscle a friend collapsed after taking too much coke and Ecstasy and was carried off the dance floor by paramedics. Still coming up on the pill I'd taken half an hour earlier, I went in search of him. The door to the recovery room was closed. A DJ whose face I recognised suddenly appeared from behind the door. I asked him if my friend was okay. 'Sorry,' he said, pulling a sad face and making a throat-slitting gesture with his finger.

I felt sick. Our friend had died of an overdose and it was all my fault. I was the one who'd given him his first line of cocaine. I was the one who'd introduced him to Ecstasy. I'd even given him the number of a dealer.

It turned out the DJ was lying. He obviously found it funny to pretend that someone had died. I didn't. The ambulance came and Javier and I escorted our friend to the hospital, where we were told he'd be okay but they were keeping him in for observation. We went home for a few hours and returned to collect him in the morning.

Javier was often away on business trips or visiting friends and family. Rather than stay home alone, I'd go out clubbing with friends. One night a friend came over, parked his car outside and had dinner, washed down with two bottles of wine followed by a few lines of coke. Afterwards, we climbed into his car to drive down to Brixton. As he pulled out, another car sped up from behind us and slammed into the driver's door. Everything went into slow motion. I remember turning to my friend and saying, 'This isn't funny!' I think it was the shock talking. The driver's door was crushed against the dashboard. It's a wonder nobody was hurt.

Another weekend, I went clubbing in Vauxhall with three friends. I could easily walk to Vauxhall but it was the middle of November, it was bitterly cold out and my friend insisted on collecting me in his car. Earlier that day he'd gone to his ex-boyfriend's house and removed all the gay porn and sex toys in anticipation of an elderly relative visiting. These were all loaded into the boot of the car.

As soon as we arrived at the club, I went off in search of drugs for everyone. This wasn't unusual. I was the Gay Editor at *Time Out*. Club promoters knew me and wanted me to have a good time. Introductions to in-house dealers were one of the perks of the job. Introduction made, the dealer and I went into the disabled toilet where I purchased several wraps of coke, a dozen Es, some MDMA and four bags of ketamine. The dealer left. I waited a few minutes to avoid suspicion and was just about to follow him out when I spotted a neatly chopped line of white powder next to the wash basin. 'Oh look,' I thought. 'Free drugs!'

You'd think my recent, similar experience in New York would have taught me a lesson. But you'd be wrong. Assuming it was coke, I snorted it. Seconds later I realised my mistake. It wasn't coke but ketamine. I'd only ever taken ketamine in small bumps, never a whole line. Too much ketamine can send you into a K-hole, where you become disoriented and lose control of your limbs. Which is exactly what happened.

I don't know how long I stayed in the disabled loo, but when I finally managed to pull myself together and unlock the door I had no idea where I was, where my friends were or where I'd concealed the copious amounts of Class A drugs I'd just purchased. I was wearing designer combat trousers with multiple pockets and carrying enough drugs to be charged with dealing.

One of my friends appeared and led me back to the group. Everyone was desperate to get high but I couldn't remember where I'd put the drugs. I panicked. I'd been so eager to ensure that everyone had a good night, and now I'd screwed up. What the fuck had I done with the drugs? Were they in my pockets or stuffed inside my socks? Had I left them in the loo?

Someone suggested we go outside for some fresh air. It was the early hours of the morning, I was shirtless and oblivious to the freezing cold. We climbed into my friend's car, where I finally remembered which pockets the drugs were in and handed them round. People eagerly opened their plastic baggies and wraps of paper and began chopping lines. Suddenly there were lights outside the window, and a voice through a loudspeaker instructing us to step out of the car and 'keep your hands where we can see them'.

There were six police officers in all – one to question each of us and two to search the car.

'What's your name?' the young officer asked me.

'Paul,' I mumbled. The ketamine was still having an effect. My tongue felt too big for my mouth.

'Have you taken any drugs tonight, Paul?'

'No, officer,' I replied, barely able to form the words.

'Have you seen anyone else taking any drugs tonight?'

'No, officer. I'm a law-abiding citizen.'

God knows why I said that. I probably thought it sounded convincing. Never mind that it was 2 a.m. and I was standing outside without my shirt on, sweating profusely and gurning like an idiot.

'I'm going to have to search you now,' the officer said. It was at this point that the gravity of the situation began to sink in. I had visions of myself locked in a police cell and dying of dehydration.

'Go ahead,' I replied, putting on a brave face. 'I've got nothing to hide.' Well, not unless you counted the bag of ketamine, wrap of coke, Ecstasy pills and bottle of poppers.

I don't know how I got away with it. Maybe he was confused by the ridiculous trousers I was wearing and lost track of which pockets he'd searched and which he hadn't. Maybe he felt sorry for me. Maybe they'd mistaken us for dealers, realised we were just a bunch of messy gay clubbers and decided to give us a fright. Or maybe it just wasn't worth the paperwork.

Whatever the reason, no drugs were found on my person. Nor were any drugs found on any of the others, or any comment made about the stash of porn and sex toys in the boot of the car. Ten years earlier, I'm sure we'd have been arrested for less. Instead, the police told us we were free to go, and we returned to the club high on adrenaline and feeling pretty pleased with ourselves.

The following evening I was supposed to go to Deborah Orr's house for dinner. She was then married to Will Self and lived close to me in Stockwell. That morning she rang to say that Will's American publisher was in town and was taking them out for dinner at Sheekey's. I was also invited as the publisher's guest. There was just one condition: 'You have to play it cool.'

The reason for this was that the other dinner guest was none other than Marianne Faithfull. Deborah knew I was a fan and didn't want me to say anything that might make her uneasy. She also reminded me that Marianne was in recovery so I shouldn't drink alcohol or take coke or do anything that might otherwise embarrass her. I promised to be on my best behaviour.

Marianne was already seated at the table when we arrived, along with her manager François and Will's American agent. She sensed that I was nervous and insisted that I sit opposite her so we could get to know one another. She kindly asked me questions to help put me at ease. I was dumbstruck. This was the woman who'd once performed with Bowie – the same woman who'd survived years of drug addiction and released an album, *Broken English*, which contained the snarling, sexually explicit song 'Why D'Ya Do It?' And here she was, encouraging me to order the lobster and then showing me how to tackle it with a cracker and a lobster fork.

Other people at the table were drinking wine, so after a while I decided that I would, too. One glass led to another and pretty soon I was downstairs in the toilet, snorting a quick line of coke to help sober myself up. Returning to the table emboldened by booze and buzzing from the cocaine, I decided that now would be the perfect time to tell Marianne about my close encounter with the police. This was Marianne Faithfull after all – '60s survivor, former heroin addict and queen of cool. Surely she of all people would understand?

I recounted the story in painstaking detail. By the time I'd finished, her face was aghast. Pale blue eyes filled with concern, she reached across the table and cupped my face in her hands.

'Now, Paul,' she said in that famously husky voice. 'Listen to your Auntie Marianne. You must never, ever take ketamine again!'

'I won't,' I promised.

But I did.

Chapter 25:
Shameless

Despite my spiralling drug use and brushes with the police, I managed to complete the novel and deliver it to my publisher. My former editor Andrew Wille had moved on and I was now in the capable hands of his replacement, Antonia Hodgson. Though our lifestyles were very different, she understood me completely. Like me, she was born north of Watford and came from a working-class background. Like me, she adored *Valley Of The Dolls*. We were bound to get along.

Antonia loved the novel, though I was still struggling to come up with a better title and still doing copious amounts of 'research'. One night at Crash I climbed the stairs to the VIP Bar and there, dressed in a white kaftan with an industrial fan blowing her hair around her face, was Kirsty MacColl. It was a bit like that scene in *Absolutely Fabulous* where Edina dreams that she's dead and Marianne Faithfull is God. Only I wasn't dreaming and I'd already met Marianne. Despite owning most of her albums, I'd never met Kirsty before.

After a few years in the wilderness, she'd recently released her critically acclaimed *Tropical Brainstorm* album, with the hit single

'In These Shoes?' Walking up to her, I grinned and said, 'In these shoes?'

She smiled politely.

Convinced that I was the only person ever to have cracked this joke, I tried again. 'Hey, Kirsty! I said, in these shoes?'

She continued smiling. Either she was a really good sport or simply too intent on enjoying herself to let an irritating E-head like me spoil her evening.

Eventually we got chatting and she invited me to a gig and after-show party at the Shepherd's Bush Empire. A few weeks later, I attended a more intimate gathering at her house. Some members of The Pogues were there, as well as Crash promoter Wayne Shires and a small group of gay men and women. After the meal, Kirsty took me out into the garden, where we stood on the bridge over-looking the fish pond and fed the koi carp.

Returning to the house, the enormous dining table had been cleared away and people were dancing. After a while, someone put on 'In These Shoes?'

Kirsty grabbed me by the arm. 'C'mon,' she said. 'You've waited months for this. Now's your chance.'

And so I danced with Kirsty MacColl, in her house, to 'In These Shoes?'

It was the last time I saw her. A few weeks later, I was in the waiting room at the dentist, waiting for the anaesthetic to kick in, when the news came on the radio. She'd been killed in Mexico, in a speedboat accident. The dentist knew I wasn't the most relaxed patient and thought I was shaken because of the root canal treatment she was about to perform. I didn't tell her otherwise.

'Shameless' was the title of a song by Pet Shop Boys – first released as the B-side to 'Go West' and later redeployed for their hit musical with playwright Jonathan Harvey, *Closer to Heaven*. It's a song about the pitfalls of celebrity – rather like Kirsty's single 'Fifteen Minutes' – but one day it struck me that it also applied to the novel I'd written. Most gay men's life stories involve a journey from gay shame to gay pride, and in the case of me and my protagonist there was a fair amount of shameless behaviour thrown in for good measure. What would be a more fitting title? My editor agreed. *Shameless* it was.

With my publication date still many months away, Little, Brown hosted a dinner at the Groucho Club for Candace Bushnell and David Sedaris, to which I was also invited. I liked David a lot. He had an easy charm and wasn't nearly as famous then as he became later. Candace was already a star thanks to the success of *Sex And The City* and she made sure everyone knew it. She also knew how to work a room. I warmed to her, though I had the distinct impression that she was a tough cookie who preferred the company of men to women.

Her new book *Four Blondes* was due out soon, and samplers were being made available to journalists and fellow authors. She signed my copy, 'To Paul, a cool guy in London', which made me feel ridiculously proud. Candace Bushnell – the woman one reviewer described as 'Jane Austen with a martini' – thought I was cool! And yes, I may have imbibed a cocktail or two myself that night.

If my publisher was secretly hoping for an endorsement from Bushnell, we didn't get one. But being told I was cool was something – even if she was only being polite.

Shameless was published in the summer of 2001, during Pride month. The irony of this wasn't lost on me. The novel held a coke mirror up to the London gay scene at the time. Most reviewers saw it for what it was – a gay social satire, with a hapless protagonist who goes looking for love in all the wrong places (nothing remotely autobiographical there, obviously!). Russell T. Davies said it was 'fast, wild, sexy and outrageously funny'. Jonathan Harvey called it 'a glorious, high-energy read, both entertaining and thought-provoking'. Will Self wrote: 'Paul Burston has penned the sharp truth about gay London, cleverly coated with sweet and sour wisecracks.'

Maybe my wisecracks left a bitter aftertaste, but a few – mainly gay – critics took exception to some of the characters and situations described. There were several reviews of the 'this doesn't represent ME!' variety. Personally, I don't think it's the job of any novelist to be 'representative' – whatever that means. Besides, very little in *Shameless* was entirely fictional. My protagonist was based on someone I knew. I'd interviewed people who'd been in social situations similar to those described in the novel. There were even cameos by real-life characters familiar to anyone who'd spent any time on the London gay scene.

What I hadn't realised, at least not until publication, was just how much of myself I'd put into the book. I remember an early conversation with my publicist, Alison Menzies, who asked me how I was feeling about the novel being read by people outside my immediate circle. Was I worried that I'd revealed too much?

I told her I felt fine. I'd written elements of autobiography before. I was used to writing confessional journalism. For me, writing fiction felt like a different exercise entirely. This wasn't nearly as personal. This was about fictional characters, partly inspired by other people. Somehow, I'd forgotten that old Oscar Wilde quote that had made such a big impression on me at college. Wilde was right. Give a man a mask and he will tell you the truth. *Shameless* was my mask – and through it I revealed myself in ways I never imagined.

The book was divided into three themed parts – 'Pride', 'Muscle' and 'Crash'. These mapped the trajectory of my protagonist's physical and emotional journey – from attending Pride, to developing the kind of muscular physique so desirable on the gay scene, to watching his world come crashing down around him. What I failed to see at the time was that this was also the trajectory my own life was taking.

To draw on another quote from Wilde, 'Life imitates art far more than art imitates life'. What I regarded as an observational comedy about other people actually said a lot more about me and where I was heading. Soon the truth of this would be brought home to me with a bump. But for now I remained wilfully oblivious, determined to enjoy the pre-publication buzz around my debut novel and silencing any self-doubts I may have had with whatever substances came readily to hand.

My first choice of venue for the launch party for *Shameless* was a male lap-dancing club in Soho called the Adonis Lounge. I'd recently reviewed it for *Time Out* and thought it would be the perfect setting. My editor agreed. But then the club suddenly closed. It later reopened as the Shadow Lounge, which would have made a great setting for a scene in the book.

Instead, the launch party was held at a venue in Leicester Square, arranged with the help of Wayne Shires and partly sponsored by Crash. Many of the people featured in the book were in attendance, along with one of my drug dealers and various friends and family members. After the speeches and wine, there was more of a clubby atmosphere, complete with go-go boys dancing in jockstraps and very little else. My favourite photo from the night is of my mother and sister perched on the edge of a podium, grinning at the camera as two go-go boys rest their bare backsides on their shoulders. It was that kind of book launch.

My mum read the novel and enjoyed it, but clearly needed reassurance that this wasn't my own life I was describing. 'That scene when he takes drugs and . . .'

'Totally fictional,' I assured her.

'And that scene with the amputee . . .'

'Totally fictional.'

I lied. Just about every incident and sexual mishap described in *Shameless* happened in real life – either to me or to someone I knew. One such incident involved my publicist, Alison. While I was writing the book, it struck me that a story she'd once told me would make a really good plot point. I rang her to ask if it would be okay to use the story.

'Hang on,' she said. 'Let's ask Gore.'

At that precise moment, she was in a car with Gore Vidal, who was also published by Little, Brown and in the midst of an author tour.

Moments later she was back. 'Gore says go for it!'

So I did.

I met the great Gore some months later at a party thrown for him at the Polish Embassy in London. The old rogue was every bit as grand and acerbic as his reputation suggested.

'So you're the author who stole Alison's story and used it in your scandalous novel,' he said, aghast. 'How could you?'

He was winding me up, of course. Had he not done, I'd have been bitterly disappointed.

Early indications suggested that *Shameless* would be a hit. There was a full window display in Foyles on Charing Cross Road and table placements in several other bookshops. I'd never seen a book of mine displayed so prominently before. I still get a rush each time I see a book I wrote in a bookshop, library or someone's hand. In bookshops, I'm usually found snuggled up between Candace Bushnell and William Burroughs, which feels strangely appropriate. But nothing beats the thrill of seeing your first novel out in the wild.

Unless, of course, it's the thrill of being talked about. Marc Almond warned me that the novelty of being recognised would wear thin pretty quickly. But for now I was enjoying every moment. In the weeks immediately following publication, I was accosted in gay clubs by total strangers insisting that they were the inspiration for the characters in the novel. I took this as the ultimate accolade. People identified with my characters. The book had obviously struck a chord.

This was reflected in sales. Early reports showed *Shameless* hovering just outside the *Sunday Times* Top 20, which wasn't bad for such an explicitly gay novel with little or no advertising or marketing spend. Foreign rights were sold. The book was published in France, where the title was changed to *Sexe, amour et amitié* – or *Sex, Love and Friendship*. As one friend joked, 'It sounds like the title of every French film I've ever seen'. But I took comfort in the fact that the publisher was Belfond, who also published Jacqueline Susann.

In Germany, the title was changed to *Schöne Männer muss man küssen* – or *Beautiful Men You Have To Kiss*. The cover featured a very straight-looking, shirtless man with a bucket hat on his head and a lipstick kiss on his shoulder. What this had to do with the book's shamelessly gay contents, I haven't the faintest idea.

Only the American publisher, Warner Books, retained the original title. It was this edition that earned me the best book review of my career so far. Writing in the *New York Times Review of Books*, Liesl Schillinger said, 'If Bridget Jones's gay brother were to write a diary of his own, with a little help from the Farrelly brothers, the result might read something like Paul Burston's rueful and raunchy *Shameless*, a hootingly funny yet strangely tender first novel about the post-break-up sexcapades of a hapless gay Londoner named Martin and his (usually) luckier friends.'

Describing some of the more outrageous, drug-fuelled episodes in the novel, Schillinger added: 'It would be hard to pull this off on-screen, but on paper Burston makes the gay singles scene "cute". His hero stands at the end of a long line of fictional protagonists – from the weight-and-youth-obsessed, pill-popping stars of Jacqueline Susann's *Valley Of The Dolls* to their shoe-shopping sisters in *Sex And The City* – and his buoyant zeitgeist vehicle scuds gaily along the familiar peaks and valleys already mapped by chick lit.'

It's hard to say who was happier – me or my editor. Antonia took me out for a celebratory lunch at Joe Allen. As the waiter took our order, an explosion of flashbulbs greeted the arrival of Joan Collins. For a couple of working-class kids who grew up watching *Dynasty*, it didn't get much glitzier than that.

People kept telling me that *Shameless* would make a great film or TV series. I had high hopes for a while. But it wasn't to be. It was so soon after *Queer As Folk*, and it wasn't in the nature of terrestrial TV companies to indulge gay viewers with an over-abundance of queer content. One gay drama series a decade was pretty much the best one could expect in those days. Channel 4 did express an interest in optioning the book and requested multiple copies for consideration, but nothing ever came of it.

A few years later, they launched a new TV drama by Paul Abbott. The title? *Shameless*.

Most people remember where they were when the planes flew into the twin towers on 11 September 2001. I was exiting the Tube station at Tottenham Court Road on my way into the *Time Out* office when my mobile phone rang. For once, the harbinger of bad news wasn't my friend Tim, though my thoughts quickly turned to him. It was my friend Elaine Finkletaub.

'Have you seen the news?' she asked.

I hadn't, but by the time I arrived at the office there was an air of stunned silence as events unfolded on TVs and computer screens. My colleagues sat transfixed as the first plane appeared out of a clear blue sky and the moment of impact was replayed time and time again. Then the second plane appeared and people looked to one another in horror and disbelief. The staff at *Time Out* had close ties with New York via our sister publication. At the same time, it all looked so unreal, more like a scene from a disaster movie than an actual news broadcast.

It took days for it to sink in, by which time the conspiracy theories had already begun.

The following week, I interviewed Diamanda Galás over the phone. Best known for her *Plague Mass* for the AIDS-ravaged community of New York, the classically trained singer with an astonishing three-and-a-half-octave range was due to appear at the Royal Festival Hall with a new show, *La serpenta canta*. I'd interviewed Diamanda several times before. We'd even hung out together the last time I visited the city.

Ever uncompromising, she refused to join in the chorus of knee-jerk patriotism that followed 9/11, describing it instead as the inevitable outcome of American foreign policy in the Middle East. 'The chickens have come home to roost,' she said, adding that this was the latest in a series of attacks and counter-attacks and there'd be more to come. She wasn't wrong about that.

Chapter 26:
The Drugs Don't Work

The day the twin towers fell, David Bowie was in a recording studio overlooking the Catskills, working on a new album. An early riser, he heard the news and immediately phoned his wife, Iman, who was at home in New York. He talked about this in interviews to promote the album, *Heathen*, which marked his return to working with producer Tony Visconti. Some critics detected references to the twin towers on the title track, with its mentions of steel and sky and glass.

Heathen was released in June 2002 and was widely acclaimed as Bowie's best album since *Scary Monsters*, the benchmark by which his output had been measured for the past twenty years. That same month, he was the guest curator of the Meltdown music festival at London's Southbank Centre. On the closing night, he performed his influential *Low* album in its entirety, followed by his latest release. I managed to blag tickets through *Time Out* and took Javier along. He wasn't a huge Bowie fan but he was working as a music journalist and was well acquainted with the great man's work after living with me for the past seven years. During the interval, we ran into a couple of friends of ours, writers Karen Krizanovich and David Quantick, who informed us that there was an after-party and kindly offered to help us get in – a decision they probably regret to this day.

In my defence, I'd had a few lines of cocaine and rather a lot to drink. Bowie took a long time to arrive at the party, and there was a free bar. The thought of finally meeting the man who'd meant so much to me for so long turned me into a star-struck teenager – so much so that when he entered the room, I literally charged at him.

'Hello David,' I said. 'My name's Paul. You don't know me, but when I was fourteen you saved my life!'

He must have been used to this kind of thing because he smiled, cocked an eyebrow and said, 'Really?'

'Yes, really,' I gushed. 'And you still rock! You're still the man!'

No, I don't know why I said that, either. He must have thought I was a total idiot, but he continued smiling gamely as the crowd gathered round.

I remember thinking he looked shorter and more delicate in the flesh than I'd expected. His bone structure was exquisite. On his feet he wore little Japanese slippers. Realising that I hadn't made the best impression and my time with him was rapidly running out, I struggled to think of something intelligent to say. Then it dawned on me. Javier was about to go to the Montreux Jazz Festival, where Bowie would be performing.

'David,' I said. 'I know you're going to Montreux. Will you be playing a similar set?'

At this point, Bowie visibly relaxed and explained that he and the band had rehearsed dozens of songs, so the set list was very flexible. Then he turned to talk to one of the many other journalists clamouring for his attention.

Weaving his way through the crowd, Javier appeared at my side. He hadn't heard any of my conversation with Bowie. We waited until he'd finished talking to someone and turned to face our way again.

'David,' I said. 'This is my boyfriend, Javier.'

'You again!' Bowie replied, rolling his eyes theatrically.

'Hello David,' Javier said. 'I'm going to Montreux. Will you be playing a similar set?'

Pausing slightly, Bowie gave me a knowing smile, then answered the question as though he were hearing it for the first time.

People say you should never meet your heroes. But I'm glad I met mine. Call it charisma or the power to charm – Bowie had it in spades. He made you feel like you were the only person in the room.

A recovering alcoholic and former drug addict, he'd been clean and sober for years by then. My only regret is that I wasn't.

Celebrity encounters were the theme of my second novel. *Star People* was my stab at a Hollywood bonkbuster with a gay twist. It was partly inspired by *Valley Of The Dolls*. I even named one of the characters in honour of beautiful, blonde, doomed Jennifer North – played so perfectly by beautiful, blonde, doomed Sharon Tate in the film adaptation.

Jamie West is a gorgeous blond boy who survives an abusive childhood, comes to Hollywood, changes his name to Billy and works as a male escort, servicing the closeted men who occupy the entertainment industry. I christened him Billy after my teen-age crush and the gay porn star Billy Brandt, who was extremely popular at the time. At the start of the book, Billy meets and falls in love with a famous movie star whose career is founded on the lie that he's rampantly heterosexual and whose management will do anything to protect him from a potentially damaging relationship with a male escort. What could possibly go wrong?

Quite a lot, actually. The book took me four years to write, which is a long time by commercial fiction standards. I was suffering from second novel syndrome and had a bad case of writer's block – something I'd never believed in until it hit me. I'd been working as a journalist for the best part of fifteen years. I was used to writing to order and meeting a deadline. But all those years of experience deserted me, along with my self-confidence. Each morning I'd sit at my desk, staring blankly at my computer screen. If I managed to write a few hundred words, I'd reward myself with a line of cocaine. Then, when the initial rush was over, the anxiety and crippling self-doubt would set in and I'd end up deleting everything I'd just written. As a popular song of the time warned, the drugs didn't work. They just made it worse.

There were other warning signs, too. I'd often had trouble sleeping. The slightest sound would disturb me and I'd lie awake for hours, worrying about how tired I'd feel and how rough I'd look the next day. I'd never really thought about why this might be the case. I just took it for granted that I was a light sleeper and often suffered from insomnia.

One day a friend told me he sometimes took a bump of ketamine to help him fall asleep. So I tried that – and soon became as dependent on ketamine at night as I was on cocaine in the morning. If cocaine turns you into an egocentric bore, ketamine makes you a catatonic mess. God, I must have been such fun to live with!

Only I was no longer living with anyone. Javier and I broke up at the start of 2003, though in all honesty the end was a long time coming. I'm not going to apportion blame. We both said and did things we regret. With the benefit of hindsight, I'm sure we'd have handled things differently. But at the time it was a pretty acrimonious split. He moved out and I was left feeling lower than I'd felt in years. I reverted back to my old ways, desperately seeking a suitable replacement instead of learning to be independent. Only this time it was worse. I had a serious drug habit, and was living on the edge of the Vauxhall gay village and the edge of my nerves.

I started seeking out people who were as messy and as miserable as I was. They weren't hard to find. Misery loves company, after all.

I recently played one of those silly games on Twitter where you type in a few words and let your smartphone predict the rest. The prompt was 'I'm gay but . . .' My result was: 'I'm gay but you don't have to worry about it because you don't have any drugs.' It sounds funny now. It wasn't so funny at the time. I carried drugs with me everywhere I went – a wrap of coke in my wallet, a bag of ketamine in a pocket. On one occasion I went to visit friends in Finsbury Park, carrying enough cocaine for the six or seven people who were expected. As I left the ticket hall, a group of police with sniffer dogs came charging down one of the tunnels and my heart stopped. I was certain I was about to be busted.

On the rare occasion that I wasn't already carrying my own supply, I made sure that there'd be someone dealing drugs when I reached my destination. Why? Because I needed them to ensure that I had a good time. Without them, I might have had to face the fact that I was deeply unhappy, and I wasn't prepared for that. I was afraid that if I stopped and gazed long enough into the abyss, the abyss wouldn't just gaze back at me. It would swallow me up.

Drug addiction was rarely talked about on the gay scene. If it was mentioned, it was usually in the form of a joke. There was a popular gay T-shirt that read 'My Drug Shame'. Another announced 'Will Suck Cock for Coke'. The more I think about it, there's nothing particularly funny about this, but at the time I thought it was hilarious.

I spent the summer of 2003 sleeping around, kidding myself I was having fun when really I was still grieving for the eight-year relationship I'd lost. It hadn't been perfect. For a long time, it was very far from perfect. But there was still an overwhelming sense of bereavement – and I'd experienced so much of that already. I numbed myself with drugs and alcohol. One night I even ran into

Javier and practically begged him to come home and sleep with me – which he did. But deep down I knew it was just a pity fuck. There was no hope of us getting back together. It was over.

One night, at a gay sauna in Waterloo, I met a sweet Brazilian guy called Sylvio and we started dating. All my friends commented on the fact that he bore a striking physical resemblance to my ex. I couldn't see it myself. But then I couldn't see very much of anything. My perception was skewed, to say the least. Photographs from the time attest to the fact that everyone was right. They could have been twins.

One night we went out clubbing and a friend of Sylvio's offered me GHB. Sometimes marketed as 'liquid Ecstasy', gamma-hydroxybutyrate or G bears no relationship to Ecstasy. It's usually taken in liquid form and is known as both a club drug and one commonly used in cases of date rape. A little G will make you high and horny as hell. A little too much and you could pass out, suffer respiratory failure or end up in a coma. Assuming you survive, amnesia isn't uncommon – hence the use of G as a date rape drug. It's especially dangerous if mixed with other drugs and alcohol. That's why it's sometimes referred to as 'GBH'.

G was already big on the gay scene in 2003. I'd seen people lying unconscious on the dance floor while their friends danced around them as if this were perfectly normal behaviour. 'Oh, he's taken too much G,' they'd say casually. 'He'll come round.'

Maybe he would – and maybe he wouldn't. A man I knew had a heart attack and died after taking G. My gay GP had warned me of the dangers of it. He'd had several patients die after taking the drug at a club, going home with someone for sex, taking another hit to intensify their pleasure and then overdosing. The taste was described as salty or soapy, though when mixed with alcohol this was often hard to detect – making it easy to spike someone's drink without them knowing. The effects were euphoric – and sometimes fatal. No way was I ever going to take this drug.

Sylvio and I left the club shortly afterwards, high on good old-fashioned Ecstasy. That was the night he told me he loved me. I told him I loved him too, but I didn't really. It was the drug talking.

A few days later he revealed that he'd been for a routine check-up and had tested positive for syphilis. I freaked out, which wasn't really fair. To be honest, I think I was looking for an excuse to break up with him and an STI was the perfect opportunity. I took myself off to the clap clinic, where tests revealed that I'd been exposed to syphilis and a friendly Irish nurse stabbed me in the buttock with what felt like a knitting needle.

I told her it hurt like hell.

'You're lucky you've a fair bit of meat on your backside,' she replied. 'Some of you lads come here and there's no arse on them at all. It's like poking a needle into bone.'

I returned a few weeks later, was given the all-clear and immediately started dating someone else. I'd first met Michael with my ex a year or so earlier, at the Kazbar in Clapham. He looked like a pint-sized version of Sylvester Stallone, when Stallone was young and cute. One groggy morning, the entryphone rang and there he was – Michael, not Stallone. He told me he was just passing and thought he'd check to see if I was at home. He didn't ask after Javier and it didn't strike me as remotely odd that he knew where I lived. One thing led to another and soon we were in bed.

Our relationship lasted a few weeks. It was only afterwards that I discovered the truth. Michael had bumped into my ex a month or so earlier and was told that we'd broken up. A mutual friend had given him my address and he'd dropped by, knowing full well that I was now living alone and potentially available. I suppose I should have been flattered. In fact, it creeped me out. I felt as if I was starring in my own yuppie-in-peril movie – and the worst was yet to come.

In August 2003, almost twenty years to the day since the time I almost drowned, I had my second near-death experience. This time it was largely my own fault.

Six months after we'd officially broken up, I received the news that a close friend of Javier's was seriously ill in hospital. It was someone I'd known for eight years and also regarded as a friend, so there was never any question of me not visiting. He had a tumour on his heart and they were going to have to operate. He was also HIV+ and on various medications, which complicated matters. The operation was invasive and risky and nobody knew for sure if he'd pull through.

The day before the operation, I went to visit him in hospital. Javier was also there. Seeing him again, and being in a hospital ward at another gay man's bedside, brought back so many traumatic memories that it all became too much. I went out afterwards and got completely hammered. Drinks, cocaine, Ecstasy – anything I could lay my hands on. It was Saturday night and Vauxhall was buzzing. I buzzed with the worst of them, lurching from bar to club. I cruised at Barcode, danced at Duckie and scored more drugs at Action. I ran into people I knew, then moved on, constantly in pursuit of the next high or the next hot guy.

Eventually I ended up at an after-hours club. By now I'd been caning it for the best part of twelve hours. I could barely stand up, let alone dance. But there on the dance floor was a guy I recognised from my gym. We'd cruised each other a few times before. I knew he was interested and I desperately didn't want to sleep alone tonight. I thought he'd do.

I joined him and his friend and we started making out on the dance floor. At one point he pulled out a small bottle and held it to my face. I thought it was poppers and went to sniff it. He laughed and tipped the liquid into my open mouth. It tasted soapy and salty. I dimly recall thinking, 'This isn't good.' Then I blacked out.

I woke up several hours later in a hospital bed with a drip in my arm and a man I vaguely recognised sitting next to me. My first words were 'What are you doing here?'

The answer, it turned out, was 'saving your life'. The man's name was Richard and he worked as a barman at the club where I'd collapsed. He'd taken me to hospital in a taxi because the management didn't want to call an ambulance and risk a police report. It was lucky for me he had. The male nurse informed me that, shortly after I arrived, I'd flatlined. That explained the burning sensation in my chest. They'd had to shock me back to life with a defibrillator.

I felt sick at the thought and had a sudden, desperate urge for the toilet. The nurse told me I should stay put but I insisted that he let me go.

'If I don't, I'll shit the bed.'

He gave me a disapproving look.

People often say, 'I could have died.' But in this case, I really could have.

I was discharged from King's College Hospital that afternoon. Richard escorted me back to the club to collect my jacket with my house keys and wallet. Some faces I knew were still there, drinking at the bar. When they saw me, they fell about laughing.

'Nice one, girl!' someone said.

I forced a grin but deep down I felt humiliated – and scared.

As soon as I got home, I rang a friend – the same friend I'd called that night at the Groucho Club with Caroline Aherne and Amanda Donohoe, the one who'd got such a kick out of being fed sausages by Amanda. When I told her what had happened, she was furious. I'd supported her through the break-up of her last long-term relationship and had barely seen her since my own break-up six months earlier. Now here I was crying down the phone, and her first response was to scold me about my behaviour and the company I was keeping. That was the beginning of the end of that friendship.

I then rang my ex, who wasn't exactly brimming with sympathy either. To be fair, one of his best friends was undergoing major heart surgery. He had enough on his plate. Still, a little kindness wouldn't have gone amiss. I couldn't phone my family. It was late Sunday afternoon and they'd be preparing tea or settling down to watch the telly. My parents had no idea about the lifestyle I was leading and would only worry.

I listened to Bowie's *Low* album, telling myself that if he could live through the drug-induced breakdown and emotional purging that produced songs like 'Breaking Glass' and 'Be My Wife', I could live through this. Finally I went to bed and cried. I was terrified of falling asleep in case I didn't wake up again. For the first time in my life, insomnia felt like a blessing. I watched the sun set and the sun rise. That particular Monday morning will remain etched in my memory forever. It was the morning I decided that today really was the first day of the rest of my life. Some serious changes were in order, and it was up to me to make them.

Chapter 27:
All The Love

There's a song on the Kate Bush album *The Dreaming* called 'All The Love'. In it, she imagines herself dying and pictures all the false friends who haven't been near her for years weeping as they come to pay their respects. Reborn, she becomes fearful and mistrustful, hiding herself away and refusing to even answer the phone.

Life after my second near-death experience wasn't nearly as dramatic as that. To be fair, few things in life are as dramatic as *The Dreaming* by Kate Bush. But I did emotionally distance myself from a few people. Chief among these was my ex. I'd spent far too many months grieving over a love affair that was long dead. Against all odds and despite my own stupidity, I'd been given another lease on life. I owed it to myself to put the past behind me and move on.

Ending my relationship with substances more addictive than a former lover proved to be rather more difficult. Coming off drugs isn't nearly as straightforward as some people think. Contrary to popular belief, David Bowie didn't suddenly quit cocaine when he famously moved to Berlin to clean up his act in the late '70s. The drugs were still calling to him in 1980 on 'Ashes To Ashes', where he describes his alter ego Major Tom as a junky. As many biographies testify, he was still indulging in the odd line a decade later. By his own admission, 1987's *Never Let Me Down* was 'a drug album'.

Much as I would love to say that nearly dying as a result of an overdose was enough to make me take stock and turn my back on the druggy lifestyle, the truth is more complicated. I still went for long, boozy lunches at The Box, still spent far too much money on cocaine. It was at The Box that I was introduced to a very charming but very unavailable dancer called Paulo, who took a ballet class with one of the crowd I hung out with. He was tall, dark and handsome – just my type. He was also clean-living, non-scene and in a long-term relationship – my polar opposite. They say that opposites attract, and I was certainly attracted to Paulo from the start, but I didn't think for one moment that the feeling was mutual. The first time we met, he had no idea that everyone else around the table was taking drugs. He thought the reason we kept going to the toilet was because we all had really small bladders. Returning from one of many trips to powder my nose, I was emboldened enough to tell him he had a lovely smile. There was just one thing that would improve it, I said, and referred him to part of my anatomy. Hardly my proudest moment, but one that made a greater impression than one might think.

I still went out looking for sex. I went to a gay sauna – and had a steamy encounter with Marcus D'Amico, who played Michael 'Mouse' Tolliver in the early '90s TV production of *Tales Of The City* and was famously outed by author Armistead Maupin when he suddenly acquired a girlfriend and pretended to be a gay ally rather than a gay man. Despite his denials, D'Amico still tended to be typecast in gay roles and was nominated for a Laurence Olivier Award for his portrayal of Louis in *Angels In America*. He'd recently starred in *The Lisbon Traviata* at the King's Head and was currently appearing in *Mamma Mia!* in the West End.

A decade after I first lusted over him dancing in his underwear in *Tales Of The City*, D'Amico was still cheekily handsome and not exactly backward at coming forward. I left the sauna feeling like the cat that got the cream – and indeed the mouse.

I still went out clubbing – and kept bumping into Javier. Despite everything, I still had feelings for him. Seeing him brought back painful memories and I'd find myself studiously avoiding him all night, or leaving and going to another club instead. For a city with a gay population as large as London's, my world felt uncomfortably small.

To make matters even more complicated, sparks were beginning to fly between Paulo the dancer and me. It started off as playful banter but soon developed into something far more flirtatious.

'He's coming on to you,' my editor and friend Antonia told me one night at The Box.

'Of course he's not,' I replied – and I meant it. He was in a long-term relationship, strikingly handsome and four years my junior. What could he possibly see in me? I think it's safe to say that my self-esteem during this period was at an all-time low.

In any case, I wasn't looking for a relationship. I certainly didn't want to risk getting hurt again. I was barely over my latest breakup. But it turned out that Antonia was right. He was coming on to me – and soon we were having an affair. It all happened really quickly. Before I knew it, I could feel myself falling for him.

I needed to get away. I needed time to think – and to see just how much he missed me. As luck would have it, my good friend William Gibbon was now living in Cape Town and invited me to visit. I booked two weeks off work and packed my suitcase.

As it turned out, Paulo missed me rather a lot. Barely a day went by without him calling to see how I was.

'That young man's on the phone for you again,' William's boy-friend, Elliott, would say. 'He has a voice like cappuccino!'

When I wasn't flirting with Paulo long-distance or lounging by the pool, William and I would make plans. 'What would you most like to do while you're here?' he asked me one morning over breakfast.

It took me a split second to decide. 'Go shark diving.'

Having narrowly escaped the jaws of death only weeks previously, it seemed only natural to go cage diving with the man-eaters that inspired the original summer blockbuster. I was ten years old when *Jaws* was first released in the UK and had been fascinated with Great White Sharks ever since.

William joked that I had a death wish.

I joked that he was thinking of a different '70s film altogether.

Calls were made, and before I knew it a plan was in place.

Shark Alley is a thin stretch of water between the islands of Geyser Rock and Dyer Island, just off the coast of the sleepy town of Gansbaai, otherwise known as the Great White Shark capital of the world. Dyer Island is home to a large population of Cape fur seals, and it's this plentiful food source that attracts the sharks in record numbers.

The drive from Cape Town to Gansbaai takes a little over two hours and the boats generally leave at dawn, so by the time we boarded I was feeling equal parts sleep-deprived and overexcited. I'm also prone to sea sickness, especially on smaller boats – and our boat was small. More than once I thought of that famous line from *Jaws,* when Police Chief Brody says, 'You're gonna need a bigger boat!'

When I first saw the cage, I also thought, 'We're gonna need a bigger cage!' It was nothing like the shark cage shown in the film, which appeared to have solid iron bars like those found in a prison cell. This looked more like a shopping trolley, albeit one big enough to contain four people at a time.

You know those wildlife documentaries where Great Whites are shown leaping clean out of the water with a seal caught between their jaws? The chances are, that footage was shot in Shark Alley. As the fur seals swim between the two small islands, the sharks hunt them from directly below, reaching speeds of up to sixteen miles per hour and fully breaching the water before crashing back down again. By the time we arrived at our destination, there were already a dozen or more boats in position and the big fish were jumping. I still recall the thrill at seeing an enormous Great White Shark breach metres from our boat. It was awe-inspiring – and more than a little nerve-wracking.

There were twelve passengers on our boat, including a young German woman who laughed loudly each time someone threw up overboard, wolfed down a large bag of gummy bears and spent the latter half of the trip being violently sick herself. I think the correct word for how I felt at that precise moment is 'schadenfreude'. There was also a very macho American guy who made no attempt to disguise the contempt he felt for the three rather conspicuously gay men sitting opposite.

With the crew regularly chumming the water with fish parts, bone and blood, it wasn't long before the sharks were lured towards us and began circling the boat. I climbed up to the crow's nest to get a better look and counted at least half a dozen. Soon it was time for the first four divers to pull on their wetsuits, adjust their masks and snorkels, climb into the cage and be lowered a few metres down into the water. Visibility in this part of the Atlantic Ocean isn't great. At worst, you can see half a metre in front of you. On a good day you might see up to five metres. Today was an average day. The first four divers didn't see a thing. Neither did the second four. I was part of the third group, together with Elliott and the macho American. We didn't see any sharks, either.

As we were hauled back up, the American guy demanded a second dive. He'd paid to see a Great White Shark up close and he refused to climb out of the cage until he'd damn well seen one. There were murmurings of discontent among the crew. But the guy was adamant.

I wasn't about to let some macho homophobe get the better of me. 'If he's going down again, so am I!' I said. I hoped the double entendre wasn't lost on him.

Finally, the captain agreed. Taking a bloody tuna head from a bucket, he jammed it on to a hook welded to the outside of the cage. Then they lowered us back down for a second dive. We were barely below the surface when I heard whopping and hollering from the deck above. And that's when I saw it – a face familiar from so many films and wildlife documentaries, emerging from the gloom and heading straight towards me.

It's hard to describe exactly how I felt at that moment. Exhilarated. Cold. A little nervous. As the shark approached, it grabbed the fish head from the hook and I felt the power of the animal as it shook its head from side to side, displaying red gums and rows of gleaming white teeth. I knew those teeth had serrated edges and could tear through practically anything.

My heart pounded. I was out of my natural habitat, face-to-face with an apex predator, with only a few flimsy strips of metal between us. In the film *Jaws*, the Great White Shark rams the cage in an attempt to make a meal of Richard Dreyfuss. Who was to say that this shark didn't have similar intentions?

At the same time, I felt more alive than I'd felt in years. As it swam past the cage, the shark was so close I could have reached out and touched it. (It's just as well I didn't. A year later, a man did exactly that and had his arm ripped off.) When they lifted us out of the water, I was so excited I could barely catch my breath. A photo taken as I climbed back on to the boat shows me grinning manically with my tongue out.

As soon as we reached dry land, I rang Paulo to tell him what I'd done.

'You crazy creature,' he said.

'Crazy in love,' I replied.

Later, when we arrived back in Cape Town, I phoned my mother and told her.

'But you were terrified when I took you to see *Jaws*,' she said.

I reminded her that I was only ten years old at the time. A lot of things scared me when I was ten – *Jaws*, communal showers, *The Naked Civil Servant*.

She didn't laugh.

Even with thousands of miles between us, my feelings for Paulo grew stronger. I found myself missing him more and more. One day, William, Elliott and I attended an open-air concert in honour of Nelson Mandela. Beyoncé was on the bill. When she sang 'Crazy in Love', I called Paulo, held up my mobile phone and sang along. To hell with data roaming charges. This love was bigger than any phone bill. I hadn't felt this way in a very long time.

I spent that Christmas with my family. This was nothing new. My ex and I had rarely spent Christmas together. He'd visit his mother in Switzerland and I'd visit mine in South Wales. As usual, I was only home for four days but I remember it as a tortuously long Christmas. Nothing seemed to distract me – not books, films, TV or vodka. I was waiting for a call from Paulo to tell me he was breaking up with his partner.

The call came on Boxing Day. Later, the friend who first introduced us would nickname me Sheila Tequila Husband Stealer. I laughed it off, but not without a sense of guilt.

Paulo and I got together as soon as I returned to London. We agreed to take things slowly to begin with. Two days later, he moved in. On New Year's Eve we went out clubbing in Vauxhall. As 2004 dawned, it marked not only the start of a new year but a new life. That summer, 'Lola's Theme' by The Shapeshifters became our song. Paulo would sing along, changing the lyrics to 'I'm a different Burston' – and I was.

Over the next few years, he showed me all the love I'd been missing for so long. I'd never felt so secure. He showered me with gifts and demonstrated his affection in a million different ways – planning surprises, encouraging me with my work, transforming our tiny garden, turning our house into a home. My friends and family had never seen me so happy.

Some of my scene friends were less than happy for me, but this hardly mattered. My lifestyle had changed dramatically. I no longer had the numbers of various drug dealers stored on my phone. I no longer needed them. Everything I needed, I had at home. In a few short years, I'd gone from nearly dying of a drug overdose to a life of domestic bliss. I didn't know what I'd done to deserve it, but I felt like the luckiest man alive.

Chapter 28:
DJ

Just as I was once labelled an 'accidental gay maverick', so I became an accidental gay DJ. In 2007, I published my third novel, *Lovers & Losers*. The closest I'd come to seriously addressing the emotional impact of AIDS on my circle of friends and the wider gay community, the book tells the story of a fictional '80s pop duo – an amalgam of Yazoo and Eurythmics with a bit of Soft Cell thrown in for good measure – set against the shifting sexual and socio-political landscape of the time. Looking back now, it also tells the story of where I was emotionally at that point – trying to reconcile myself to my past, but not yet ready to face it head on.

As the title suggests, it's a book about love and loss. The story is told from the points of view of its two protagonists, whose biggest hit is a song called 'Lovers & Losers'. The duo is named A Boy and His Diva, after the production company credited on Sandra Bernhard's *Without You I'm Nothing*. The boy is called Tony and is partly based on fellow Bridgend boy Steve Strange and partly on my younger self, had I run away to London at eighteen and become a pop star. Like Steve, Tony enjoys a brief window of success before succumbing to drug addiction. Like me, he is an obsessive Bowie fan and a cokehead who sometimes says and does things he lives to regret. The diva is called Katrina and was my personal tribute to all the women who'd supported me over the years, from my first school friend Caroline to more recent female friendships. One reviewer called the book 'the longest love letter to the fag hag ever written'.

The story is told via a dual timeline – one set during the '80s and one in the present, where Tony is desperately trying to resurrect his career by appearing on a celebrity reality TV show called *The Clink*. It is a book about the decade of excess but also about the fleeting and corrupting nature of fame – something I witnessed many times and heard about from many of the celebrities I interviewed over the years.

Fame was a subject I knew a thing or two about. Not that I considered myself famous. I was merely a (not so) humble hack. But I certainly recognised certain characteristics I shared with famous people I'd met – in particular, the desire to reinvent oneself in order to escape a traumatic or unhappy past, and a history of dependency issues. Listed among the acknowledgements in *Lovers & Losers* are Marc Almond, Pete Burns and Steve Strange. Of these three, only Marc is still with us – and if you read his brutally honest autobiography *Tainted Life* you'll appreciate how narrowly he escaped death on more than one occasion.

I first met Pete Burns in 1995, at the launch of Jayne County's autobiography *Man Enough To Be A Woman*, at the Gardening Club in Covent Garden. Pete climbed on stage and made a speech dressed in a suit jacket, thigh-high boots and very little else. He looked otherworldly and slightly terrifying – but behind the outrageous image was a sensitive and very intelligent man. I subsequently spent several enjoyable evenings with Pete and his wife Lynne. This was before his infamous appearance on *Celebrity Big Brother*, when most people still knew him as the freakiest and most ferocious of the so-called gender-benders.

Pete could certainly be acerbic. He didn't suffer fools gladly and gave me a good tongue-lashing on more than one occasion. But he was also witty and incredibly kind. The first time he invited me to his house in Notting Hill, he answered the door with a face full of thick pan-stick foundation, crying, 'Don't look at me, it's hideous!' He then cackled with laughter and claimed that the make-up he was wearing had been stolen by a friend from Cher's dressing room. I still don't know if he was making this up or not. Later he joked with me about his plastic surgery. 'I don't make my face with powder and paint any more,' he said. 'I make my face with knives!' But for all his eccentricities, he was a charming host and fed me a delicious slice of chocolate cake – quickly followed by a plate of sushi.

I'd seen Steve Strange around for many years, but the first and only time I interviewed him was in 2002, when he published his autobiography, *Blitzed!* In the book, he writes at length about how he overcame his heroin addiction. For the interview, we met at a café of his choosing on the King's Road, where Steve insisted on sitting outside despite the fact that it was mid-February and freezing cold. I wore a padded Schott bomber jacket, scarf and gloves. He wore a short-sleeved shirt and kept disappearing inside to use the toilet, then reappearing with a sweaty face and pupils like pinpricks, telling me how pleased he was to finally be clean. I felt sorry for him. I knew from personal experience how drugs and denial go hand in hand.

I attended Steve's book launch with Pete and Lynne, who I happened to bump into on the way. The party was at a club called Sin on Charing Cross Road. Steve was clearly in an altered state and Pete wasn't very impressed. He had an aversion to people under the influence of drugs. Ignoring Steve, he pushed his way to the bar.

'Fame does strange things to people, Paul,' Lynne offered by way of explanation. 'Either they turn to drugs or . . .' She nodded knowingly in Pete's direction and smiled affectionately.

Later, someone approached Pete and asked if they could interview him for a book about gender identity. He refused point-blank and told them to leave him alone. 'I won't be someone else's idea of me,' he said afterwards. 'People always ask me, are you gay? Are you bi? Are you trans? Fuck that! Why do I have to be any of those labels? I'm just Pete.'

His marriage to Lynne was a constant source of media fascination and speculation. All I ever saw were two people who went back a long way and clearly loved each other very much. Pete died in 2016 of a cardiac arrest. I know Lynne still misses him terribly. They may have divorced in 2006. Pete may have entered a civil partnership with Michael Simpson a year later. But he and Lynne remained soulmates right up until the end. Theirs truly was a tale of love and loss.

The launch party for *Lovers & Losers* was held at Trash Palace in Wardour Street, which embodied the spirit of the story. Images of '80s icons adorned the walls. The late, great Simon Hobart had died two years earlier but his spirit lived on in the venue he'd created, which was now run by his partner, Tommy Moss.

Like Simon, Tommy is no longer with us. Sadly, he took his own life in September 2020 – one of many people in the hospitality industry driven to financial ruin and despair by the impact of the pandemic. I was heartbroken when the news broke on Facebook. He was such a sweet, kind soul, and the London club scene is a lot worse off without him.

Back in 2007, Tommy was a force of nature, busy running Soho's most successful alternative full-time venue, as well as Popstarz at the Scala in King's Cross. I asked him if I could hold my book launch at Trash Palace and he immediately said yes.

Duckie DJs the Readers Wifes kindly offered to spin the discs for the night, and Tommy insisted that I play a guest DJ set. I'd never played a DJ set before in my life. But as my friend William Gibbon always used to joke, every time he came to my place for dinner the evening usually ended with me DJing in a manner of speaking, by excitedly playing him my favourite tracks. How hard could it be? A bit harder than it looked, actually – but after a few technical hitches I soon got the hang of it.

My old friend Caroline was there – the one who'd illustrated my adventures stories about Jim when we were both at junior school. Marc Almond popped in briefly, adding some iconic '80s pop-star glamour. My parents also came. If my mum was disappointed by the lack of go-go boys in jockstraps, she didn't say anything.

The book was well received and even earned me a nomination at the Stonewall Awards for Writer of the Year. The ceremony was held at the Victoria and Albert Museum, and never has my sense of imposter syndrome felt so strong. Even in my dinner jacket, I felt like a fraud. Among my fellow nominees were Val McDermid and Victoria Wood, who was shortlisted for her TV drama *Housewife, 49*. McDermid was the queen of crime fiction. Wood was nothing short of a national treasure. Like many of her gay fans, I could quote most of her sketches word for word, and frequently did. Hovering awkwardly at the drinks reception beforehand, I knocked back a few glasses of champagne and practised my gracious loser face. What was I doing here? I wasn't in the same league as these people!

Needless to say, I didn't win. The award went to Val McDermid, who gave a stirring acceptance speech about lesbian visibility and growing up at a time when the only lesbian novel she'd heard of was

The Well Of Loneliness. Like me, she'd spent her early years hunting high and low for positive representations of people like her.

Later, I found myself standing next to Wood at the post-award drinks. I offered her my commiserations and told her how much I'd enjoyed *Housewife, 49.* She was polite but seemed ill at ease, or perhaps a little put out at not having won.

Years later, I took part in a charity pub quiz at the Groucho Club with her, Helen Lederer and Harriet Thorpe. 'Vic' was far friendlier on this occasion, but very serious about winning. We came second. Runners up, once again.

The launch party for *Lovers & Losers* led to a club night of the same name, which opened on May Bank Holiday. 'Paul Burston's sizzling novel comes to life in a debauched '80s night,' read the poster. Much to my amazement, there were queues around the block. I shared the DJ duties with Tommy himself and clubland legend Princess Julia, playing everything from '80s synth-pop to Bowie, Blondie, Hi-NRG, electro, rap and disco. It was exhausting and exhilarating.

By the time the second club night came around in August, I'd taught myself how to use GarageBand on my iMac and started making my own mash-ups – a hugely popular genre at the time. Basically, a DJ or producer took one song and mixed it with another, creating a whole new hybrid track containing elements of both, often isolating the vocal from one song and adding it to the instrumental from the second. Famous mash-ups included 'Can't Get Blue Monday Out Of My Head', which mixed Kylie Minogue with New Order, and 'Rapture Riders', which mixed Blondie with The Doors.

Joining me on the decks for the second club night was DJ Dom Agius, who was in an electro-pop band and far more technically proficient than I could ever hope to be. He created my favourite track of the time and a guaranteed floor-filler – a mash-up of 'Just Can't Get Enough' by Depeche Mode and 'Music' by Madonna. He and his band Furiku also recorded a track called 'Lovers & Losers', incorporating lyrics from the fictional song in the novel, with yours truly on backing vocals. It was all very meta, as the kids say.

Following the success of A Club for Lovers & Losers, there were invitations to DJ at DTPM, Popstarz, the RVT and the Shadow Lounge, where I warmed up for the late, great Tallulah. Dom and I ran a short-lived night called Electrosexual at Freedom Bar in Soho and became residents at a far busier night called Kill Your Pets at The Ghetto in Shoreditch. I took this as an opportunity to relive my Buffalo Boy days, wearing a bowler hat with the word 'Killer' emblazoned across the front.

Then, in September 2007, I did something unthinkable – I got married. Two decades earlier, in *Queens' Country*, I wrote, 'I wouldn't get married if you dragged me to the altar in a wedding dress with the offer of a world cruise as a wedding present.' Reader, I changed my mind. Strictly speaking, it was a civil partnership – but everyone referred to it as our 'wedding'. We had a wedding reception and a wedding photographer and my mother bought herself a new hat. Our wedding song was 'Amazing' by George Michael.

So far, so traditional. The ceremony took place on Tower Bridge. The photographer knew about my activist past, and afterwards we literally stopped traffic. The entire wedding party blocked the road, just as I'd done over twenty-five years earlier with ACT UP. Had you told me then that gay weddings would happen in my lifetime, or that I'd be sitting here writing that sentence, I wouldn't have believed you.

Shortly after getting hitched, I was offered a DJ gig at the Green Carnation on Greek Street. The music producer Tris Penna had his own Friday-nighter there called Wilde Ones and asked me to fill in for him, playing everything from lounge music to chart pop. It was a long set – starting at 8 p.m. and ending as late as 2 a.m. – so I offered to split it with Dom and we worked alternate shifts, warming up one week and doing the late slot the following week.

It was at the Green Carnation that I was asked to DJ for Sandie Shaw's sixtieth birthday. She came with her daughter, who was an absolute delight, and they were treated to a bottle of champagne on the house. It was all going swimmingly until I put on 'Express Yourself' by Madonna. Sandie didn't want to hear Madonna expressing herself. She didn't want to hear Madonna at all. Storming up to the DJ booth, she demanded that I change the record.

Tempting as it was to play 'Puppet On A String', I put on 'Survivor' by Destiny's Child and hoped that this would do.

Wilde Ones was such a success that eventually the Green Carnation offered me my own regular night. I came home full of excitement and broke the news to Paulo.

'Are you mad?' he replied. 'You're at *Time Out* three days a week. You spend days planning your DJ sets and another day recovering. When will you find time to write? People will start to think you're a DJ and not an author!'

I felt deflated but deep down I knew he had a point. I slept on it and by the morning I had a plan. Polari was about to be born.

Chapter 29:
Speak My Language

Bowie once said that ageing is the process by which you become the person you were always meant to be. He also said the key to ageing happily was learning to accommodate your past selves within your current persona. This was the man famous for adopting and discarding various guises. Now here he was, learning to live with them.

In 2007 I turned forty-two and launched my own literary salon. Polari was the culmination of everything I'd ever done. It was me accommodating my pasts within my persona – drama student, theatre practitioner, activist, journalist, author and shameless exhibitionist.

I was a man on a mission. For me, Polari was never only about providing a platform for LGBTQ+ authors, poets and performers. It was also about reshaping the narrative and making it about our lives, our experiences, our stories. In the books people read from at Polari, we weren't just the gay best friend or the lesbian next door or the trans woman up the road. We weren't secondary characters or plot devices. Here we could be the stars of our own stories. We could be heroes.

Despite publishing three novels and several non-fiction titles, I'd never once been invited to speak at a book festival. Twelve years after it was first published, *A Queer Romance* was widely recognised as a classic of queer studies in the UK and was a set text on many university courses. Still, those invitations failed to materialise. Despite being shortlisted for a Stonewall Award, I had very few opportunities to promote *Lovers & Losers*. So I figured I could either bitch and complain or I could get off my backside and do something about it. Maybe it's the activist in me, or maybe it's just bloody-mindedness. But if an opportunity doesn't exist, I'll create one.

Polari began life in November 2007 in the upstairs bar at the Green Carnation in Soho. It was billed as 'an evening of words and music', with guest writers and me as DJ and host. The owner of the venue had a few reservations. He was convinced that as soon as the music stopped, people would run out into the street rather than be exposed to the spoken word.

In fact, the opposite was true. The first event was a small affair – just me and a dozen friends. But word spread and soon we were packed. Neil Bartlett read and the audience grew. Stella Duffy performed and it grew even further. The night Will Self came to read from his reworking of Wilde's *Dorian Gray*, it was standing-room only, with a queue halfway down the street.

Why the name Polari? Sometimes described as 'the lost language of gay men', Polari – sometimes spelt Palare – was a form of slang also used by travellers and other communities, and employed by gay men at a time when male homosexuality was against the law and speaking freely could easily land a man in prison. In the 1960s, it was popularised by Hugh Paddick and Kenneth Williams's camp characters Julian and Sandy on *Round The Horne*. As the laws around gay sexuality became more relaxed, so the need for speaking in code became less of an issue.

When I first came out in the mid-1980s, I would sometimes hear older gay men speaking in Polari. This is rarely the case nowadays – though some words have found their way into common usage. The word 'naff' comes from Polari and originally meant straight or 'not available for fucking' (ironically, by the Noughties, the word 'gay' had become another word for naff – as in, 'That's so gay!').

To me, Polari literally means 'gay words' – and what could be a more appropriate name for a spoken-word night dedicated to LGBTQ+ writing?

After six months, Polari outgrew the Green Carnation and moved to Trash Palace. We relaunched with a night dedicated to Gay Dandies. Sebastian Horsley headed the bill with a reading from his memoir, *Dandy In The Underworld*. I liked Sebastian. He was arch and often acidic. His emails to me usually opened with 'Paul, you big poof . . .' But he was also incredibly witty and hugely entertaining. With his towering stovepipe top hat, bright velvet suits and painted, powdered face, he was about as queer as a vigorously heterosexual man could be. In fact, you could say he was his own special creation – much like Quentin Crisp or indeed Pete Burns.

Sadly, like them, he's no longer with us. He died of an overdose of cocaine and heroin on 17 June 2010 – hours after Tim Fountain's one-man play about his life opened at the Soho Theatre. Horsley's friend Toby Young firmly believed that his death was an accident – 'If it had been suicide, Sebastian would not have passed up the opportunity to leave a note.'

Back in September 2008, he was still very much alive and very much Sebastian – arriving at Trash Palace in a bright red sequinned suit with a heavily made-up face and telltale rings of white powder around his nostrils. A photograph of us both taken that night shows the vulnerability behind the mask – what his friend Stephen Fry later described as his 'essential sweetness', and his brown eyes that stopped 'just short of pleading'.

Among the audience at Polari that night were Marc Almond and Bette Bourne and Stuart Feather of Bloolips. I'd first met Bette twenty years previously, when I interviewed him for *Capital Gay*. Bloolips were performing a spoof of *Ben Hur* called *Get Hur*. Partly inspired by the American theatre troupe Hot Peaches, and drawing heavily on the politics of the Gay Liberation Front, Bloolips helped put the radical into drag. They weren't drag queens in the traditional sense, but rather gay performers who used cross-dressing to deconstruct and explore the meaning of gender in shows that combined elements of agitprop, cabaret, music hall and pantomime.

Long before queer theorists like Judith Butler began writing about 'queer performativity', Bloolips were doing it live on stage in shows that were accessible, entertaining and thought-provoking. Together with the lesbian theatre company Split Britches, they once produced a gender-swapping remake of *A Streetcar Named Desire*, with Bette as Blanche DuBois and Peggy Shaw as Stanley Kowalski. The night I saw the play at London's Drill Hall theatre, I swear there wasn't a gay man in the audience who wasn't at least a little bit turned on by Peggy Shaw's swaggering channelling of Marlon Brando. Bette also performed with Neil Bartlett in *Sarrasine* and a number of plays by Tim Fountain – including *Resident Alien*, where he played his old friend Quentin Crisp.

Bloolips once performed a show called *Living Leg-Ends*. To me, Bette is nothing short of a living legend. He's been to Polari many times since, and it's always an honour to have him among us.

Polari at Trash Palace lasted for six months, after which the venue closed down. We moved to Freedom Bar in 2009, where I launched my fourth novel for Little, Brown. *The Gay Divorcee* was another comedy of manners, this time on the subject of gay marriage, which was a hot topic at the time and something I knew about first-hand. I went on my first real author tour, organised largely by myself. The tour began with a stag night at The Ghetto in Shoreditch and included talks and book signings in Birmingham, Bradford, Brighton, Cardiff, Hereford, Manchester and Margate. The marketing strategy for the book seemed to be: 'Paul has lots of media contacts and runs his own literary salon, so let's just leave him to get on with it.'

The Gay Divorcee got great reviews and was subsequently optioned for television with Jonathan Harvey attached as screen-writer, though nothing ever came of it. I was disappointed, but after my earlier experience with *Shameless*, hardly surprised. I resigned myself to the fact that books with gay protagonists and explicitly gay content still faced an uphill struggle. After all, that's why I created Polari in the first place.

Polari at Freedom continued to grow steadily. The basement space had more of a nightclub feel than previous venues, complete with mirrorballs. It was glitzy in a slightly shabby way and gave us room to grow. Susie Boyt read from her moving memoir *My Judy Garland Life* and even brought some of her prized Garland memorabilia for people to inspect for themselves. VG Lee made her first of many crowd-pleasing Polari appearances, as did Karen McLeod. Christopher Fowler read for us, along with Adam Mars-Jones. Things were often quite riotous. Many were the times I ended up dancing on a podium, dressed in a fake fur coat and denim shorts or channelling Grace Jones in black swimming trunks with the word 'Grace' printed across the crotch. I think she would have approved.

One night Polari was attended by Rachel Holmes, who I knew from way back in my activist days and who was now Head of Literature and Spoken Word at the Southbank Centre. At the end of the evening, she told me, 'You should really bring this to us.'

So I did. Polari opened at the Southbank in September 2009. It was quite a step up from the Soho gay bar scene to the UK's largest arts centre. But the celebrations were short-lived. Shortly after we moved to the Southbank, I was dropped by my publisher. The mass market edition of *The Gay Divorcee* hadn't even been published yet and already it was decided that the book hadn't been the success everyone hoped for. I was gutted.

A lot of authors I know were dropped in 2009, as the fallout from the banking crisis impacted on the publishing world and the industry as a whole became more risk-averse. I'd had a good run with Little, Brown, who'd published five of my books in total. Still it's hard not to take these things personally. I have an author friend who says, 'It's my job to write the bloody book and their job to sell it.' If only it were that simple. Increasingly, authors are expected to write, market and publicise their books in any way possible. Create a website. Build a mailing list. Engage with readers on social media. Give talks at bookshops and local libraries. Really put yourself out there.

I don't mind doing any of those things. I accept that they're part of the job, despite the fact that most of this work is unpaid labour. But it's hard to compete in an increasingly overcrowded market-place, and easy to feel as if any failure is yours and yours alone. If a book fails to sell in sufficient numbers, an author becomes tarnished with what's known as 'bad track' – making it harder to find a publisher for their next book. Few people stop to consider the many other factors that help determine whether a book becomes a hit or not – marketing, advertising, sales and distribution networks.

Being dropped threw me into a tailspin. My agent at the time suggested I change my name and refrain from writing gay characters. I refused. I know lots of authors who write under various pen names. I understand their reasons for doing so, but it wasn't what I wanted. And as for writing gay characters, that was non-negotiable.

I've written books where the main protagonist isn't gay. I may well write more. But to create an entire world in which no gay character exists would feel somehow dishonest to me. It would feel like going back in the closet. And those doors were kicked off their hinges a long time ago.

Polari didn't take long to establish itself at the Southbank Centre. Audiences grew and the event evolved into something far more ambitious than I'd originally envisaged. Of course it helped that I was no longer working alone. I had an event manager, technical support and the publicity department of the UK's biggest arts centre behind me. Soon I didn't need to go in search of authors to read at Polari. They came to me. Book publicists would contact me about potential headliners. Where once there'd have been one or two writers on the bill, now there'd be four or five. I'd confirm the bigger names first, then fill the bill with writers and spoken-word performers at various stages of their careers, some of whom had never read their work in public before. Having created a successful platform for LGBTQ+ writers to showcase their work, here was an opportunity to encourage new talent, just as I'd been encouraged by those who came before me.

When it comes to finalising each line-up, my motto has always been 'the more diverse, the better'. I don't say this out of some desire to be seen as 'politically correct', 'woke' or whatever term people are currently using to describe the efforts of those trying to be more inclusive. I say it because it makes sense. There's little point in creating an event in the name of diversity if you don't use it to celebrate the diversity within the community it's supposed to represent. I've been to far too many literary events where the line-up consists of authors all drawn from the same narrow demographic – usually white, male, heterosexual and predominantly middle-class.

Quite frankly, they're often boring. Diversity isn't about ticking boxes. It's about different perspectives and a variety of stories and voices. Surely that can only be a good thing?

The audience at Southbank certainly seemed to think so. Numbers grew month on month. Events sold out weeks or even months in advance. Polari's reputation spread far and wide, with the *New York Times* hailing us as 'London's most theatrical salon'. Everything was going so well.

And yet. As Polari continued to go from strength to strength, my own writing was a struggle. In 2010 I began work on a book that would take my career off in a whole new direction. Having started out as a writer of comedies, I was about to go over to the dark side and become a writer of crime fiction – and my personal life was about to take an even darker turn.

Chapter 30:
Glittering Prize

But first I became a work of art. Many is the time I've made an exhibition of myself. This was the first time someone made an exhibition of me – or should I say, an exhibition featuring me. In the autumn of 2010, I was approached by Mark Wardel, the artist otherwise known as TradeMark. I'd been an admirer of his work for years. One of the original Blitz Kids who counted Steve Strange and David Sylvian among his friends, he'd since made his name as a pop artist.

In 1986, Wardel met his idol Andy Warhol. Mark was making his own hand-printed T-shirts at the time, and Andy bought one. It was just the encouragement the aspiring young artist needed. Adopting the name TradeMark, he first found fame with his iconic flyers for clubs including Trade and Heaven. Since then, his work has graced magazine and record covers and ad campaigns for the likes of Absolut Vodka.

Working from photographs, he produces sharp-focus, ultra-glam portraits in acrylic and oils. Often compared to Warhol, with whom he shares a fascination with celebrity, sexuality and the relationship between art and commerce, his subjects include gay bikers, muscle boys and pop-cultural icons as diverse as Divine, Grace Jones and Kylie Minogue.

Instantly recognisable, his paintings have been exhibited to great acclaim in museums and galleries internationally. In 2013, he was commissioned by the V&A in London to create a limited-edition David Bowie life-mask sculpture in conjunction with the museum's blockbusting 'David Bowie Is' exhibition. The 300 'Silver Duke' masks soon sold out. Mark later produced variations on the masks, two of which were purchased by Bowie himself for inclusion in his official archive.

I knew Mark to say hello to and was hugely flattered when he asked me to sit for him. He was working on an exhibition of new paintings called 'Scene – A-Listers, Heroes & Heroines', to be displayed at La Galleria Pall Mall. Among his other subjects were Boy George and my ultimate hero, David Bowie. How could I refuse?

These days, Mark has his own artist's studio in Limehouse, but back then he was working from a studio belonging to fashion, music and portrait photographer Simon Harris, which was located in the middle of a go-kart track complex off Burdett Road in Mile End. One afternoon in July I met Mark there and sat for a series of photos, dressed in a white short-sleeved shirt and skinny black tie with a white lightning-bolt insignia, topped with a black leather flat cap.

The shoot was over before I knew it. Mark selected the photo he'd chosen to work from and showed it to me on the viewfinder. I approved it and waited with characteristic impatience to see the finished portrait. It was four months until that moment finally arrived, but it was well worth the wait. To say I was blown away by the result would be putting it mildly. Arriving at La Galleria for the private view with Paulo, my parents and Jac in tow, I could hardly believe that was my portrait staring back at me. The painting was almost a metre square and very flattering. But what clinched it for me wasn't the firm jaw or flawless skin. Knowing I shared his love of Bowie, and picking up the detail from the tie I wore for the shoot, Mark had painted me with a glittering silver lightning bolt over my shoulder. Not only was I part of an exhibition featuring my hero – I'd also been Bowie-fied!

Mark's painting of the great man hung on another wall, next to a portrait of Grace Jones. It depicted Bowie during his Thin White Duke phase, with the words 'Hero/Heroin' splashed across the top in powdery blue, post-punk graphics. My mother wanted to know what it all meant. I told her it was probably best not to think about it too much.

Among the crowd at the private view were actor Mark Gatiss, singer Holly Johnson, artist Molly Parkin and fashion designer Antony Price – as well as scene celebrities Fat Tony, Princess Julia and Tasty Tim, whose portraits were also featured. As the evening wore on, little red stickers started to appear next to several paintings, indicating that they'd been sold. Before the night was out, mine was one of them. The buyer? Me, of course.

I'm under no illusions that anyone else would have paid to have a painting of me hanging on their wall. My 'celebrity' is limited, to say the least. No, the demand for such a portrait was most likely limited to one customer and one alone. And why wouldn't I want to own it? It seemed doubtful that a similar opportunity would arise ever again – and I'd never looked better. Though, as one reviewer noted at the time, one striking feature of the painting is that, despite the high-gloss finish, the artist succeeded in capturing a certain vulnerability in my eyes.

Soon this vulnerability would be tested to the limit.

But for now, my eye was firmly on the prize. As 2010 drew to a close, I decided it was time for Polari to launch its own book prize. We'd been running in London for three years and had a loyal following online and at the Southbank Centre, where events frequently sold out. It was abundantly clear to me that there were lots of emerging LGBTQ+ writers out there, some published by major publishers or smaller independents, others self-published. Often these books received little or no press coverage, flying under the radar and relying on word of mouth and live events like Polari to help reach potential readers. It seemed to me that a book prize dedicated to new LGBTQ+ writing would help shine a light on these books and offer further encouragement to the people who wrote them.

I spoke to Rachel Holmes at Southbank, who was equally keen on the idea and put me in touch with Fiona McMorrough of FMcM Associates, an award-winning communications consultancy specialising in literature and the arts. An early supporter was Joe Storey-Scott, book buyer for the gay lifestyle store Prowler. Another was Suzi Feay, a former colleague from *Time Out*, then Literary Editor at the *Independent On Sunday*. Together we formed a judging panel, and in February 2011 the Polari First Book Prize was launched. The prize was open to writers born or based in the UK and Ireland whose first book explored LGBTQ+ themes and characters. All kinds of books were eligible – fiction and non-fiction, prose and poetry. The only requirement was that the work spoke to and about the LGBTQ+ experience.

The decision was taken early on to accept self-published work, largely because of the uphill struggle faced by many queer writers to find a publisher willing to take a chance on books regarded as too niche to be profitable. Previously dismissed as 'vanity publishing', self-publishing had really come into its own since the advent of the e-book and was now seen as a legitimate way for writers outside the mainstream to own the means of production and get their stories out there. Often these books would have benefited from having an editor. Some should probably never have been published at all. But among the dross there were some real gems to be found.

That first year, it felt as if every self-published gay writer in the UK entered their book for the prize – and I use the word 'gay' advisedly. The vast majority of submissions came from gay men. Relatively few came from women. Most writers were white and there were very few entries from trans authors. Over time, this would change. In recent years, prize winners have included a diverse array of writers from a wide range of cultural backgrounds. But for now we were mainly judging books written by gay men.

Not that this in any way detracted from the overall quality of submissions. The standard was extremely high and included a wide variety of genres. Clearly, the books were out there. Now we were faced with the challenge of drawing up a longlist, whittling it down to a shortlist and deciding on a winner.

Never having judged a book prize before, it was very much a case of learning as I went along. Luckily for me, Suzi Feay brought a fair amount of experience to the table, as did Rachel Holmes and Fiona McMorrough. I listened and learned from all of them.

Our first-ever shortlist included two women and three men. The five books included three novels and one book of poetry. Two of the shortlisted books were self-published, including the winning entry. It's only in retrospect that I can fully appreciate the signifi-cance of that decision. Our first winner was literally the hero of his own story. In November 2011, the inaugural Polari First Book Prize was won by singer James Maker for his memorable memoir *Autofellatio*.

Described by journalist Mark Simpson as 'a glam-rock Naked Civil Servant in court shoes', *Autofellatio* charts Maker's personal journey from the mean streets of Bermondsey to Manchester and beyond. It also recounts his friendship with one Steven Patrick Morrissey. In the early days of The Smiths, Maker sometimes appeared as a guest performer and was mistakenly referred to as the Fifth Smith. As he says himself, 'I am far too Susan Hayward to share the spotlight with anybody else' – and so he pursued his own musical ambitions in rock bands including RPLA and Raymonde. The original book cover featured the author with a towering quiff and matching high heels, pointing a gun directly at the camera. It's a pistol-sharp book, loaded with witty one-liners and peppered with Maker's scattergun observations on life, love and the music industry.

The judges agreed that Maker's memoir stood out, with its humour, honesty and heartfelt exploration of British queer life over the past thirty years, recounting the often harsh reality of growing up gay with wit, wisdom and tenacity. The winner was announced at a special ceremony at the Southbank Centre. Shortly afterwards, the book was picked up and republished by an independent publisher. Our prize had arrived.

A month later, in December 2011, I received the heartbreaking news that Paulo's brother-in-law in Toronto had died of cancer. His name was Hercules Brasil and I was very fond of him – so much so that, four years earlier, I'd named a character in *Lovers & Losers* after him. The fact that the fictional Hercules was a young, muscular, heavily tattooed gay porn star who looked nothing like his heterosexual namesake amused Paulo's rather short, somewhat squat, grey-haired and bespectacled brother-in-law greatly.

The last time I saw Hercules was the previous year, at his son's wedding in Toronto. He was no longer squat but had slimmed down through a combination of diet and exercise. He'd given up alcohol and quit smoking. Sadly, he'd also been diagnosed with lung cancer.

When he died, I posted a tribute on Facebook. Shortly afterwards, an email arrived. It was from someone whose name was vaguely familiar. Months earlier, she'd contacted me at *Time Out* about a mutual friend's book. The email began pleasantly enough. She told me she'd seen my Facebook post and expressed her condolences. Then came the sting in the tale. She ended by saying it made her 'snarky comments' on Twitter seem petty and ill-timed. I knew, of course, that this was her way of alerting me to what she'd actually said on Twitter.

As a gay journalist, I'd had more than my fair share of online abuse. I wondered what this person's idea of 'snarky comments' amounted to. My stomach tightening, I logged on to discover that it was mostly the usual trolling one finds on the most anti-social of social networks – barbed comments about me and my work, in which I'd been tagged to ensure that I saw them. There was also a link to a blog post titled '101 Wankers', where my name was listed alongside those of various feminist newspaper columnists and LGBTQ+ authors and journalists. The entire post reeked of professional envy. Clearly the writer was seething with resentment that, despite studying for a PhD in Gender Studies, her own talents had largely gone unnoticed. This was her way of drawing attention to herself.

I blocked her email address and Twitter account and hoped that this would be the end of it. But she was just getting started.

Chapter 31:
I'm Deranged

Like many writers, I spend a fair amount of time on Twitter. It's part of the job. And like any public person who happens to be gay, I'm used to receiving a certain amount of homophobic abuse. Learning to ignore the trolls comes with the territory. But as I soon discovered, this particular troll refused to be ignored. The snarky comments gave way to homophobic insults. I was called names like 'pansy', 'fag', 'queer' and 'gaylord'. As LGBT Editor at *Time Out*, I was running both my own personal Twitter account and a second professional account on behalf of the magazine.

The tweets kept coming. Some days there'd be one or two. Other days there'd be dozens. Mostly they were playground insults, but when you're someone who was bullied a lot in the playground, those words still have the power to hurt. When the *Guardian Weekend* magazine ran a dedicated gay issue, I shared the link on Twitter and headed off to the gym. By the time I arrived, my mentions were mostly from this person. 'GAY, GAY, GAY, GAY, GAY!' read one. Another described me as one of 'the AIDS generation' and said I was lucky to be alive. I lost a lot of friends to AIDS. I knew I was lucky to be alive. I didn't need a random stranger on the internet to remind me of the fact.

I'd already blocked the account sending the tweets, thinking this would be the end of it. But I hadn't counted on how determined my cyber-stalker was to make their presence felt. Because I use Twitter largely for work, both my accounts were public. So they simply logged off Twitter, opened their internet browser and checked to see who I was interacting with, then continued to tag me and several others in their tweets. If one person responded, the mention would appear in my notifications and I'd be alerted to what was being said.

I posted a tweet asking them to stop harassing me and threatened legal action if they continued. I asked my Twitter followers to not respond to their tweets. None of it made a blind bit of difference. If anything, the situation escalated. There were comments on the *Time Out* website and on various other sites where my work was published. They posted blogs describing me as a 'middle-class wanker' and a 'gay Yuppie' – a term I hadn't heard in decades, not since I was young enough and just about professional enough to qualify. They accused me of 'gayism'. They doctored my Wikipedia page, deleting large parts of my bibliography and other professional achievements.

I use the word 'they' advisedly. For a long time, I hardly knew anything about the person harassing me at all. I didn't even know for certain that it was a woman. A troll who went by the name of Quiet Riot Girl or Notorious QRG, they used female pronouns but also shared views often expressed by men's rights activists – leading some to question whether the person hiding behind the girlish screen name and stock photos on Twitter was in fact a man.

The harassment wasn't confined to Twitter. For months they continued to send me emails from various accounts, cc-ing friends and work associates to ensure that I got the message. No sooner had I blocked one email address than they'd create another. It was relentless. One day I received dozens of malicious communications in the space of a few hours. I became so anxious, I could no longer focus and had to stop work for the day.

To understand the emotional and psychological impact of online harassment you need to bear in mind the amount of time many of us spend in front of our computers or glued to our phones. In my line of work, email is the main method of communication. Authors and journalists are expected to have a strong online presence, which means a considerable amount of time is spent on Facebook and Twitter. And that's not counting the hours you might choose to spend on social media for personal reasons. Online harassment affects you in the workplace, on the move and at home. Abusive tweets and emails are often the first thing you see in the morning and the last thing you see before switching off your devices. Soon it reached the point where I dreaded logging on to my computer or checking my phone.

Foolishly, rather than report all this to the police immediately, I thought I could handle it myself. I spent hours seeking advice in online chatrooms and forums and was told that the best way to stop an internet troll was to expose them. As soon as they're identified, most anonymous trolls back down.

In the spring of 2012, the person who'd been subjecting me to homophobic abuse for the past four months attempted to enter their self-published book for the Polari First Book Prize. Yes, you read that correctly. Someone engaged in a campaign of homophobic harassment entered their book for a prize dedicated to LGBTQ+ writing and founded by the person they'd been calling 'pansy', 'fag', 'queer' and 'gaylord' all over the internet. I'd blocked their email address but they'd found the contact details for another of the judges and sent it to them instead. I asked the judge to reply saying we'd accept the submission but pseudonyms weren't allowed.

This was a first book prize, and for all we knew the writer could be an established author. We needed them to confirm their true identity. They replied immediately with their full name and address.

I now knew that the person who'd caused me so much distress was a woman called Elly Tams. She was in her early forties and lived in North London. Armed with this information, I was able to find out a bit more about her – though for someone who spent so much of their time online, it struck me as odd and rather disturbing that there wasn't a single photograph of her to be found anywhere on the internet. I knew where she'd studied and a little of her employment history, though these days she hardly appeared to work at all but spent most of her days on Twitter, attacking strangers. I wasn't her only target – though I seemed to bear the brunt of most of her anger.

Sick of being bullied, and going on the advice given to me in the chat rooms, I decided to fight back by posting a blog revealing the identity of the person hiding behind the screen names and avatars. This proved to be a really big mistake. The blog didn't silence her. It made her a hundred times worse. There were more blog posts, more emails and even more tweets. She gave interviews to other bloggers, confirming her identity and raging at me for 'outing' her. She painted herself as the victim, a champion of free speech who was being unfairly punished for daring to speak the truth. Her behaviour escalated to the point where she started making thinly veiled threats, booking tickets for my events and posting pictures of the booking confirmation on Twitter, saying she couldn't wait to come and sort me out in person.

By now, I was seriously alarmed. I still had no idea what this person looked like. She could have been anyone sitting in the audience. She might be harmless. Or, for all I knew, she might be planning to rush at me with a knife. I informed staff at the Southbank Centre of the situation and was given added security. I spoke to friends, who were becoming increasingly concerned about the impact the harassment was having on my mental health. I was drinking heavily, sleeping badly and in a state of constant anxiety. Paulo advised me to cut down on my drinking and reduce the amount of time I spent online. My mother doesn't really understand the internet but she's known me all my life and was convinced that I was on the verge of a nervous breakdown. My friend VG Lee was so worried about my fragile emotional state and personal safety, she urged me to take action before things got any worse. 'This woman could be dangerous,' she said. So I finally did what I should have done months before and contacted the police.

What took you so long, the female detective asked. The truth is, I was embarrassed to admit that I was being bullied by a woman. I was bullied a lot as a child – usually by other boys, always on the basis that I was a 'poof' – and the shame still lingered. I've also been on the receiving end of homophobic abuse as an adult – but that was either verbal or physical and therefore seemed more 'real'. Waiting to give a statement at Brixton police station, my eyes were drawn to a poster urging people to report domestic violence. The stark image of a woman's battered, bruised face made my complaint seem petty in comparison. The online nature of the harassment made me question whether the police would take me seriously. Thankfully, they did.

But it took several months before an arrest was made and the accused charged. For weeks I had personal security whenever I appeared at public events. For months I had to keep a record of every unsolicited email and unwanted social media contact, in order to help the police build a case and persuade the CPS to prosecute. Naively, I'd assumed that once I reported the crime, someone else would monitor the accused's online behaviour. But the police simply don't have the resources. The detective stressed that a case like mine all depended on the volume of evidence. So I had to keep

copies of every email and take screenshots of every abusive, homophobic tweet, print them out, and then give further police state-
ments where I had to relive the abuse and its impact all over again.

The police referred me to Victim Support but I didn't contact
them. Why? I think that word 'victim' had a lot to do with it. To
my mind, *Victim* was the title of a 1961 film starring Dirk Bogarde,
about a closeted gay barrister who's threatened with blackmail. It
was Quentin Crisp in *The Naked Civil Servant*, apologising to his
attackers for having offended them in some way. It wasn't me. I'd
been a gay rights activist since the 1980s and had lived through a
period of enormous social change. During my ACT UP years, we
campaigned against the use of terms like 'AIDS victims', which we
regarded as disempowering and dehumanising. This was the language of the tabloids. We preferred the term 'people with AIDS',
which conveyed a sense of personal agency and dignity.

Calling Victim Support would have meant thinking of myself
as a victim. It would have felt like a step backwards. In a very real
sense, my gay pride got in the way. But I was certainly in need of
support. I was hardly sleeping at all, barely managing a few hours a
night, drifting through the day in a state of high anxiety. I began to
wonder if my mother was right. Maybe I was already having some
kind of nervous breakdown.

David Bowie often spoke about mental health and the fear that
he might one day 'go mad'. It's there in the song titles – 'All The
Madmen,' 'Aladdin Sane,' 'I'm Deranged'. My dictionary defines
'derangement' as 'the state of being completely unable to think
clearly or behave in a controlled way, especially because of mental
illness'. This pretty much describes my state of mind in the summer
of 2012, when I went to see my GP and practically begged him to

prescribe me sleeping tablets. When he asked me why I was having trouble sleeping, I broke down crying in his surgery.

For the past six months, the harassment had been relentless. Even talking about it triggered a mixture of panic and shame. When I told my GP what was happening and how I was feeling, he immediately prescribed antidepressants. I think he was concerned that, without them, I'd crack up before the case got to court. I'd never been on antidepressants in my life and hated the way they made me feel. I became unfocused and found it difficult to write. I lost my libido. I still had trouble sleeping.

The case was one of the first Twitter trials and seemed to take forever to reach court. Had I known just how long it would take, I might never have gone to the police in the first place. At the first hearing, the prosecutor wasn't properly prepared. He hadn't even read the bundle. Had he done so, he'd have seen the email where Elly Tams confirmed that she was the author of the book entered for the Polari First Book Prize and that she wrote under the pseudonym linked to the Twitter account responsible for all the homophobic tweets. Because he hadn't seen the email, the defence was able to argue that there was no proof that she was the person behind the account. The judge came close to throwing the case out. Instead, a new date was set and a new prosecutor found – one who understood social media and was meticulous in her preparations. The date was moved back – and then back again. I suspect that the defence was hoping to keep it dragging on for so long, I'd give up. But I'd come too far to turn back now.

It was the best part of eighteen months from the day the accused was first arrested until the day she finally stood trial. A few weeks before the trial began, I was having dinner with two friends, one of whom comes from an East End family with criminal connections. She told me that if things didn't go my way in court, there were other ways of ensuring that the woman responsible never harassed me or anyone else ever again. Looking back, I'm pretty sure she was joking in an attempt to lighten the mood. But it's a measure of my state of mind at the time that for a brief moment I took her seriously.

I first saw the accused long before taking the witness stand. Approaching the court building on the morning of the first hearing, I spotted a slightly dishevelled, skittish-looking woman, accompanied by an older man I took to be her father. Something in my gut immediately told me it was her. She looked rather pathetic and more likely to be afraid of me than I of her. Sure enough, as soon as she saw me, the look on her face turned to one of panic and she scuttled off.

Two things crossed my mind. One, that she was a typical keyboard warrior – brave behind a screen, but not so courageous in real life. Two, that something about her wasn't quite right. Her appearance and body language suggested that this was someone with problems. I might have felt sorry for her, had she not caused me so much distress.

Testifying in court is a nerve-wracking business. However much the police and prosecution tell you otherwise, it's hard not to feel that you're the one on trial. The defence made light of the homophobic nature of the harassment, dismissing it as 'playful banter' and suggesting that I was oversensitive. They argued that I was a public figure on a social media platform and should therefore be open to healthy debate. I insisted that healthy debate did not include the right to harass and abuse someone, and that the defendant's behaviour towards me was homophobic and relentless. The district judge agreed and found her guilty of harassment without violence. Unlike racially or faith-motivated offences, there is no 'aggravated offence' legislation in UK law for crimes motivated by homophobia. But in her summing-up, the judge stressed the homophobic nature of the case. Elly Tams was given a two-year suspended sentence and issued with a restraining order.

Having finally seen my tormentor in the flesh, I assumed that the anxiety she provoked in me would quickly dissipate. My biggest fear had been not knowing who I was dealing with. Now I'd seen her – and a pretty sad figure she'd turned out to be. I thought that, now it was all over, I'd simply put the whole thing behind me. But the impact of the harassment lingered. I still had trouble sleeping, waking in the night with feelings of anxiety. I found it hard to concentrate and was easily startled. Sometimes I'd see random women on the Tube and my heart would pound, convinced for a split second that it was her.

On the advice of my GP, I continued taking antidepressants for several months. I also did what I should have done far earlier and sought help from Victim Support. It wasn't my first experience of counselling. In my mid-twenties, someone I dated survived a suicide attempt and I went to see the Samaritans for advice on how best to support them. I was taken aback when the woman I spoke to asked me how I was feeling. It wasn't long after Vaughan was first hospitalised and, to be honest, my feelings were rather complicated. But calling Victim Support was the first time I'd made an appointment on my own behalf – and I was every bit as shaken as I had been on that earlier occasion.

The offices were close to the old Elephant and Castle shopping centre. I arrived ten minutes early and sat waiting nervously on a grey plastic chair. The counsellor was a man around my age, who ushered me into a tiny room and asked me why I hadn't contacted them sooner. I told him I'd been too busy with work. He asked about the impact of the harassment and I described it to him – the sleepless nights, the pangs of anxiety. He told me this wasn't uncommon with victims of crime. There was that word again. I think I might have bristled. Finally, he told me I was suffering from a form of PTSD. Talking about trauma was a vital part of the recovery process, he said. There was no shame in feeling like a victim, but in order to move forward, first I had to face up to my emotions and put them into words. I felt a flicker of recognition at this but was unable to put a name to it. After a few sessions, I stopped going.

What nobody tells you is that around 40 per cent of people issued with a restraining order breach it within a few months. I read this online and worried about what would happen if the harassment continued. I was already at my wit's end. Had Tams continued to harass me, what would I have done? I now knew exactly who I was dealing with and where she lived. Might I have been tempted to take the law into my own hands? I'd have liked to think not. But given my state of mind at the time, I couldn't say for certain. That scared me.

I needn't have worried. I neither saw nor heard from her ever again. But for a long time afterwards, I kept a photo of her taken by a *Court News* photographer on both my phone and laptop. I knew how much she hated having her picture taken, how she hid behind stock photos to avoid being identifiable online. If she bothered me again, I'd respond by posting her photo.

Looking back, there are many things I wish I'd done differently. I wish I'd listened to the well-worn advice to 'keep calm and don't feed the troll'. I wish I'd sought professional help sooner, instead of letting my pride get in the way.

But one positive thing came out of my experience. It gave me the seed of an idea for a novel.

Chapter 32:
Station To Station

A month after my court case, in December 2013, I was made redundant. I'd been at *Time Out* for twenty years. A lot had changed in that time. What had once felt like a family business now felt increasingly corporate. In twenty years, I'd rarely taken a day off as sick leave. If I was ill, I swapped my days around so I could still meet my deadlines. Yet when I asked the new HR director for two days' leave to testify in court against the woman who'd been homophobically harassing me for the past eighteen months – and even using the *Time Out* website to do so – I was told I'd have to deduct it from my holiday allowance.

The redundancy was handled with an equal degree of sensitivity. One day the editors of all the smaller sections were summoned to a meeting and told how important we were. The phrase 'heart and soul of the magazine' was used. Three days later we received our redundancy notices. Christmas was just a few weeks away. Work had already started on the annual Christmas double issue. There was a time when *Time Out* rewarded staff with a Christmas bonus. Now they marked the season of goodwill by handing out redundancy notices.

Still struggling after the stresses of the trial, I can't say I was sorry to leave. My only regret was that, after twenty years of loyal service, I wasn't shown a little more courtesy. Few senior staff attended my leaving drinks. My former editor Dominic Wells turned up and later wrote a piece for the *Guardian*, expressing his dismay at the direction the magazine was taking. 'It seems to me extraordinarily short-sighted to axe the LGBT section,' he wrote. 'In the words of Oscar Wilde, it's the act of people who "know the price of everything and the value of nothing". For decades its recommendations have guided people, perhaps unsure of their sexuality or new to London, to safe spaces in the capital. More than that, it has reassured them that they are as normal and as numerous as lovers of music, dance or grainy subtitled films.'

During my long tenure at *Time Out*, we won a Stonewall Award for our LGBT coverage. I was also shortlisted for Journalist of the Year at the European Diversity Awards and again by Stonewall. My name regularly appeared in the *Independent*'s annual Rainbow List of LGBT influencers where I'd recently graduated to the dizzy heights of 'national treasure'. When the news broke that *Time Out* was axing my section, I received many messages of support. Among them were emails from singer David McAlmont and screenwriter Russell T. Davies.

People kept telling me I had a lot to feel proud about. But to be honest, I wasn't feeling very much of anything. Still weaning myself off antidepressants, I was exhausted, demoralised and drinking heavily. Self-medication was second nature to me. It never crossed my mind that binge-drinking might be adding to my problems – or that the urge to numb myself with alcohol might be a sign that something was seriously amiss.

As 2014 dawned, my career prospects were looking grim. For the first time in over twenty years, I had no day job and no publisher. For me, writing is as essential as breathing. It's how I function in the world. And while I know that writing and publishing are two very different things, they'd gone hand in hand for as long as I could remember. I was paid to write. It's what I did for a living – or used to.

Suddenly it felt as if I had no reason to get up in the morning. I was an author without a publisher, a journalist without a deadline. By 2014, we were well into the age of free content. Opportunities for freelance journalism were far fewer and further between. During my last few years at *Time Out*, section editors were often referred to as 'content providers' – which felt like an insult to our professionalism. We were experienced journalists, experts in our field. People who left comments on our website could be classed as 'content providers' – people like the internet troll I'd recently taken to court.

Now that my two main sources of income had dried up, I had a crisis of confidence. How was I supposed to earn a living when so few media outlets offered regular freelance work and so many younger journalists were willing to write for free? One editor approached me with the offer of unpaid work, insisting that it would be 'great exposure'. I'd been a professional journalist for twenty-five years. I'd published ten books and written thousands of magazine and newspaper articles. I'd even written and presented television documentaries. I didn't need exposure. I needed to pay my bills. What if I was never commissioned to write another piece? What if I never published another book? If I wasn't a professional writer, who was I? It felt as if a vital part of my identity had been stripped away.

Thankfully, I had the support of my husband, who'd been a tower of strength throughout the court case and whose belief in me never faltered. And I had Polari. The salon was the one thing I'd created that nobody else could take away. Events at the Southbank Centre continued to sell out and featured some of the biggest names in LGBTQ+ literature – Paul Bailey, Patrick Gale, Jackie

Kay, Ali Smith. The Polari First Book Prize was attracting a growing number of submissions and garnering more media attention. About to enter its fourth year, the prize had previously been awarded to three very different but equally worthy winners – memoirist James Maker, poet John McCullough and crime writer Mari Hannah. We'd attracted a sponsor in the shape of Société Générale and hosted a huge prize-giving event at the Purcell Room, with Sarah Waters heading the bill.

We'd even won a few prizes of our own, including the Co-op Respect Award for Best LGBT Cultural Event of the Year. We'd been reviewed in the *New York Times* and named one of the world's top LGBTQ+ events by Art Info. The *Huffington Post* described Polari as 'the most exciting literary movement in London'. People raved about us wherever we went. Only we hadn't gone very far. We'd appeared at literature festivals in Soho and Stoke Newington. We'd popped up at the Metropolitan Archives and the Museum of London. But so far, we hadn't been north of Watford.

2014 was the year this all changed. If there's a Bowie song for every occasion – and after years of extensive research, I can confirm that there is – in this case the song would be 'Station To Station'. The track opens with the sound of a train leaving a station. And just as it marked a change in direction for the singer, from the 'plastic soul' of *Young Americans* towards the European experimentalism of *Low*, I was also in the process of reinventing myself. To invoke the work of one of Bowie's own heroes, Christopher Isherwood, it was a case of Mr Burston Changes Trains – and changes careers. No longer employed part-time as a journalist, I began to carve out a new career for myself as a producer.

Despite running Polari for the past seven years, I'd never really thought of myself as a producer before. It was only when I met with the Arts Council and was encouraged to broaden my ambitions that the idea took hold. In reality, I'd been producing live literary events for quite some time. But when Polari began, I was employed first and foremost as a DJ. Since moving to the Southbank Centre in 2009, I'd worked with an events manager and thought of myself primarily as a host. In fact, my job entailed far more than this. I selected the line-ups, sourced the publicity materials, liaised with writers and booksellers and promoted the events. In short, I was doing everything a producer might be expected to do, only without the job title. It was time to take my role more seriously.

In March, Polari took up an invitation to appear at Huddersfield Literature Festival. It was our first major event far beyond London and featured our most recent Polari Prize winner, Mari Hannah, together with poet Keith Jarrett, writer Adam Lowe and author and comedian VG Lee. Polari Up North was a huge success and has since become an annual fixture, largely thanks to the support of festival director Michelle Hodgson. It also inspired me to take Polari on the road. I met with Sarah Sanders at Arts Council England, submitted an application for funding and was soon busy planning the first-ever Polari national tour.

The tour kicked off in September and ended in November. It took in eight destinations including Birmingham, Brighton, Liverpool, Manchester and Newcastle, and showcased a variety of local authors, poets and spoken-word performers, together with travelling artists. Among those featured were Neil Bartlett, Sophia Blackwell, Rosie Garland and Jonathan Harvey. We performed in theatres, libraries and arts centres. We ran creative-writing workshops during the day and invited one participant from each workshop to share their work at the evening event. Attendance was high and the feedback from audiences and workshop participants was overwhelmingly positive.

I was never very confident as a performer, especially when faced with new and unknowable – potentially hostile – audiences. I once did an author event with Stella Duffy for LGBT History Month and the first question came from a man who asked, 'Why do you have to go on about being gay all the time?' The question threw me, but Stella handled it with aplomb. Another time I took part in an event at a library in Manchester. Sitting in the front row were a group of teenagers who sensed my nervousness and sniggered loudly as soon as I opened my mouth. My fight-or-flight response kicked in. Suddenly I was back in the playground, being publicly humiliated by the school bullies. The stammer I had as a child returned with a vengeance and I gabbled my way through my reading, desperate to get it over and done with as quickly as possible.

Going on tour with Polari was exciting but it also filled me with trepidation. I'd pop a Valium before the show or have a glass of something alcoholic to help steady my nerves. Sometimes I did both, which really isn't advisable. Gradually my confidence grew, though for a long time I still suffered from stage fright and relied on the Valium. Mixing it with alcohol after the show meant that I often ended the night the worse for wear.

Despite my performance anxiety, I took to touring like a duck to water. I enjoyed the planning, the travelling and checking into strange hotels – even when the old imposter syndrome surfaced and I half expected to be summoned to the linen room and scolded for abandoning my duties. I loved discovering new towns and cities and meeting new writers. Even in places with a small LGBTQ+ community, the quality of local writing talent was often astounding. Sometimes it was too difficult to choose just one person to take part in the evening event and we'd extend the offer to two or more.

In fact, that first tour was such a resounding success, we've toured every year since, taking in more towns and cities across the UK and beyond. We've been to Belfast, Cardiff, Dublin,

Edinburgh, Glasgow, Hastings and sunny Mallorca. In 2020, our plans for a twenty-two-date tour marking the tenth annual Polari First Book Prize had to be adapted in response to the pandemic. Some events were postponed. Others took place online, hosted live on Zoom and later shared on our YouTube channel. We included writers nominated for the 2020 awards, as well as previous winners and those shortlisted during the prize's ten-year history.

We made a virtue of being online by featuring writers from various corners of the country and other parts of the world. Our 2017 winner, Saleem Haddad, joined us live from Lisbon. Shortlisted authors Alison Child and Juno Roche logged in from the island of Lesbos and the mountains of northern Spain. Audiences were slow to respond at first but interest soon grew. By the time tickets for our fourth virtual event went on sale, we were attracting numbers similar to those we'd expect at many of our touring events. Some people had never attended a Polari event before. Suddenly we were accessible to anyone with a Wi-Fi connection, wherever they lived and whatever their personal circumstances.

Taking Polari online enabled us to reach new audiences in a way few could have envisaged but one man might have foreseen. Speaking to Jeremy Paxman on *Newsnight* way back in 1999, David Bowie predicted a future where the internet would change the relationship between artists and audiences beyond all recognition. Dismissing a bemused Paxman's suggestion that it was just a new delivery system, Bowie argued that the internet offered a whole new means of interaction between the user and the provider, one that would revolutionise our ideas of what communication systems or mediums are all about.

He could have been describing a Zoom meeting.

For me, taking Polari online was simply the next logical step for an event that is constantly growing and ever evolving – year on year, venue by venue, station to station.

Chapter 33:
Criminal World

I didn't mean to turn to crime. But I've always had a taste for it. As a teenager, I devoured crime fiction – everything from the detective novels of Agatha Christie and Sir Arthur Conan Doyle to the spy fiction of Ian Fleming and John le Carré. I grew up watching detective shows – *Columbo*, *Police Woman*, *The Rockford Files*, *The Streets Of San Francisco*. Later I became obsessed with *Cagney & Lacey* and developed a major crush on Magnum PI. I still hold firm in my belief that men's shorts should always be worn as short as those sported by Tom Selleck. Anything longer is an anti-gay hate crime.

I was also drawn to horror. One of my all-time favourite novels is *Carrie* by Stephen King. I've read it dozens of times. The first time I was eleven and found myself identifying strongly with the central character. Unlike Carrie, I wasn't a teenage girl and I didn't have the power of telekinesis – though for a while I wished I did. But like her I was bullied at school and felt like a stranger in my own home. I think this is a feeling many young LGBTQ+ people are all too familiar with.

Later I discovered the suspense novels of Patricia Highsmith and her queer anti-hero Tom Ripley. Crime fiction has long been a haven for queer representation. I suppose this is only to be expected. For a long time, gay men in particular were classed as sex criminals. In the '80s I was a sex criminal simply by virtue of being sexually active below the gay age of consent. Between the ages of nineteen and twenty-one, I broke the law many times. I also broke the law as an AIDS activist and worked for a police monitoring project at a time when large numbers of gay and bisexual men faced prosecution for consenting sexual offences no heterosexual would be charged with. It wasn't until 2014 and the introduction of same-sex marriage that I enjoyed full legal equality. Naturally, I have a vested interest in the criminal justice system. Inevitably, this is reflected in the books I read.

My own journey to the dark side began with a short story called 'The Gift', which I wrote for an anthology called *Bloody Vampires*, published by Limehouse Books in 2011. The story was about vampirism as a metaphor for HIV. The move towards crime fiction was more gradual. Partly it was to do with being dropped by my publisher and needing to reinvent myself by finding a new authorial voice. Partly it was influenced by my personal circumstances. I'd recently been the victim of a crime, the impact of which I was still processing. It was only natural that this would feed into my writing.

It wasn't a total change in direction. My first four novels are usually classed as comedies, but there is a darker edge to them. Crimes are committed in those books. People die. Men are queer-bashed, stabbed and hospitalised. Some overdose on drugs or are abducted and forced to withdraw money from their bank accounts. One is murdered. There is no shortage of grit between those glittery covers. But it's certainly true that my fifth novel marked a departure in many ways. There are very few jokes – and for the first time my protagonist isn't a gay man but a heterosexual woman.

By the time the first Polari national tour drew to a close in November 2014, I had the first draft of a new novel. It had the working title of *The Soldier's Wife* and would eventually become *The Black Path* – my first crime novel, and one that mined elements of my childhood in South Wales. As the working title suggests, *The Black Path* is about a woman who's married to a soldier. But it's also about a childhood shaped by trauma. The protagonist, Helen, has fond memories of her father, who was killed in a brutal attack when she was small. She has a strained relationship with her mother and stepfather, and a husband who is thousands of miles away, serving in Afghanistan. One night she meets a young woman who takes her well outside her comfort zone and forces her to rethink many of the things she takes for granted.

The Black Path is both a real, physical place and a metaphor for the personal journey Helen must take in order to face her fears and come to terms with some uncomfortable truths. I didn't know it yet, but my subconscious was trying to tell me something.

Working on the novel, I took the train back to Bridgend often and spent weeks re-familiarising myself with the places I was writing about, many of which I hadn't visited in decades. Central to the story is the Black Path. The remnant of an early nineteenth-century horse-drawn tram road, the path runs alongside the Ogmore River and was originally built in order to transport coal and iron ore from the Maesteg area to Bridgend. I have fond memories of playing on the Black Path as a child. The fields beside it were often filled with dairy cows and I was always drawn to the river. My friends and I would catch eels, minnows and other small fish, or make rafts from old inner tubes and pieces of scrap wood and let the current carry us all the way to Newbridge Fields on the other side of town. It was all very Tom Sawyer.

Then there are the less sunny memories. The path runs close to Glanrhyd, where my mother and Auntie Alma both worked at various times – back in the days when it was commonly referred to as 'the mental hospital'. Further up there was an abattoir. As a child, the thought of what happened within those walls gave me nightmares. As an adult, I scoured local news websites for stories connected to the Black Path. I discovered that a woman was raped there. A man killed himself. All of this went into the novel, together with some of my childhood reminiscences.

These days, the north end of the footpath opens near the McArthurGlen shopping outlet. The south end leads directly onto St Christopher's Road – one of a cluster of streets in Wildmill sometimes referred to as the Saints, mainly by the people who live there, who like to distinguish themselves from the sprawling housing estate locals tend to picture when they think of Wildmill. It was here that I spent my early childhood, in a house on St Nicholas Road.

I hadn't been back to the Saints in years. Everything was so much smaller than I remembered, including the house. A semi-detached dormer bungalow with gardens at the front and back, it sits near the top end of the road, just a short walk from the entrance to the Black Path. Seeing it again gave me quite a jolt. The large goldfish pond that had once dominated the front garden had been paved over. The decorative concrete blocks my father made from a rubber mould still lined the walls. I remembered the cement mixer on the driveway and him red-faced and soaked with sweat, shovelling sand and cement as the garden hose lay coiled and dribbling at his feet and the machine turned and churned.

Behind the house is the garden where we once had a swing. I have a photo of me aged six or seven, sitting on the swing with a look of abject fear on my face, hands gripping the ropes. Each time I see it, I'm reminded of how anxious I was as a child – 'a nervous wreck', as my mum used to say.

I couldn't see the back garden from the street, but as I stood in front of the house a rush of memories came flooding back. I recalled the time I drained my father's precious goldfish pond and rehoused the fish in a makeshift pond of my own, hidden behind the garage – one of the few times I went out of my way to annoy him, and was punished for it. I remembered the guinea pigs we kept in a hutch in the garage, out of reach of my father's boxer dog, Kim, who was all bark and no bite but whose bark was enough to give a small mammal a heart attack.

I knew this because my Auntie Alma was once entrusted with looking after a neighbour's pet guinea pig while they were away on holiday. One day she was filling the guinea pig's food bowl when my mum happened to walk by with Kim. Recognising Alma, the dog bounded over to say hello, jumping up and barking with excitement. The guinea pig died of fright on the spot.

Nothing if not resourceful, Alma popped the dead guinea pig in her handbag and went to every pet shop in town, looking for a suitable replacement. With my mother's help, she eventually found one. She and Mum congratulated themselves on having averted a diplomatic incident. A week later, the neighbours returned from their holiday and were surprised to discover that their guinea pig's eyes had mysteriously changed colour.

The house where Alma still lives is two doors down from the one where I spent my formative years. I remember running to her house for help, the day my father left. There'd been signs that my parents' marriage was on the rocks for months. There was a family holiday in Benidorm – the one time we went abroad – my mother drunk on Bacardi, holding my hand and leading me away from my father, telling me we'd be fine on our own. I think this was when she discovered he was having an affair. Things were never the same after that. My father would disappear and I'd hear my mother crying quietly behind closed doors.

There was nothing quiet about the way he left. My mum, sister and I were in the kitchen. The steam kettle was whistling on the hob as my mother opened the biscuit tin. My father entered the room and a row erupted. Minutes later, he stormed out. My mum cried. 'Fetch Auntie Alma! Paul, go and get Auntie Alma!'

I was eight years old.

It wasn't for nothing that I chose to set the prologue to *The Black Path* on the street where I grew up – or that the book opens with an act of violence inflicted upon the protagonist's father.

The Black Path was the first novel I wrote out of contract – without a publisher or the certain knowledge that the book would see the light of day. In this respect, I've been very fortunate. Even my first novel was commissioned on the basis of a synopsis and a few sample chapters. Still, we each have our own obstacles to overcome, and facing such uncertainty at this late stage felt daunting, to say the least.

It was also strangely liberating. It allowed me to go to places I hadn't been before. For a long time, I'd written books populated by openly gay characters facing the kinds of challenges I'd experienced personally or observed in my capacity as a journalist. I'd written about the gay scene, gay celebrities and even gay marriage – and to be honest, I felt I had nothing left to say on the subject. For the first time, I wasn't following the age-old advice and writing about what I know. I was largely writing about what I don't know – people I have little in common with, places I've never been. Large parts of *The Black Path* are set in a world far removed from the one I inhabit – a world of military training and toxic masculinity, domestic violence and compulsory heterosexuality. But those gay characters wouldn't leave me alone. There's a subplot involving Helen's husband, Owen, and a rumoured relationship with a young gay soldier.

Whether this had anything to do with the difficulty my agent had in selling the book, I really can't say. Publishing is still over-whelmingly heterosexist, despite recent attempts to be more diverse and inclusive. Eventually the book was bought by Rebecca Lloyd at Accent Press. It was published in 2016 and went to the top of the WHSmith Travel chart. The reviews were overwhelmingly positive and the crime writing world welcomed me with open arms. I went to the Harrogate crime festival knowing virtually nobody, and came away feeling like one of the gang.

In all my years as an author, I've never known such a friendly, generous, supportive community of writers. Maybe it's because crime writers channel all their dark thoughts into their work. Maybe it's the sense of solidarity often found among people who've been on the receiving end of class snobbery or some other form of prejudice. Crime fiction may be fashionable now, but for a long time it was regarded as the poor relation to literary fiction – a bit dubious, a bit questionable, not quite right. In the minds of some people, it still is. It's no wonder I feel so totally at home.

Chapter 34:
I Can't Give Everything Away

The morning the news broke that David Bowie had died, I was in bed, sleeping off a hangover. Paulo was away, visiting his mother in Rio. Left to my own devices, I'd worked my way through half a bottle of vodka, and woke with a pounding headache and chronic heartburn. I felt sick to my stomach and my anxiety levels were through the roof.

But there was worse to come. As soon as I switched on my phone, I knew something was wrong. There were missed calls, texts and voicemails. My first thought was that someone close to me had died. In a way, they had.

I'd spent the previous day listening to Bowie's latest album, *Blackstar* – poring over the lyrics, wondering what on earth it all meant. Of course, I should have known. There are references to death all over the album. It's there on the title track, where he sings about 'the day he died'. It's there again on 'Lazarus', where he's up in heaven, looking back on his life. It's there on the final song, 'I Can't Give Everything Away', where he wants to set the record straight. This is the sound of a man putting his affairs in order.

I've never really been one for looking back. 'Look forward' has always been my motto. Walk tall. Act fine. Even when your legs are giving way beneath you.

I learned this from my mother, who has always preferred not to dwell on the past, sometimes to the point of avoiding it altogether. Some family secrets remained buried until only a few years ago. I don't blame her. This was how she coped. It was the only way she knew how.

Looking back now has been an emotional experience. I've discovered things about myself I didn't really know before – some of which make me proud, others that make me squirm with embarrassment. I've recognised patterns of behaviour that were ingrained in childhood and have remained with me all my life. The child truly is the father of the man, as Wordsworth famously wrote. I studied the Romantic poets at college but was too young then to appreciate how wise those words were. Maybe if I'd known this sooner, I could have spared myself from making quite so many mistakes.

But this isn't the first time I've turned myself to face me. No, that happened in January 2016 – when David Bowie died. Something in me changed. I don't just mean the grief I felt for a man I had the pleasure of meeting only once but whose music has been the soundtrack to my life for over forty years. I don't mean the pilgrimage to Brixton to lay flowers at the mural. I'm talking about something else – something buried so deep I'd managed to ignore it for most of my life.

A few months earlier, I'd turned fifty. In the weeks leading up to my birthday party, I'd suddenly find myself short of breath for no apparent reason. Sometimes I'd wake up with a great weight on my chest and my stomach in knots. Typical midlife crisis, I thought. Get over yourself. So many men I knew didn't have the luxury of turning fifty. How insulting to their memory would it be for me to have a meltdown at my age?

Then, for my party, Paulo and Jac filled the flat with old photographs, some of which I hadn't seen in over forty years. And there was this one black-and-white photograph – a picture of me aged five or six, gazing directly at the camera. I saw it and I knew

285

immediately what was happening to that little boy at the time that photograph was taken. I could see it in his eyes.

Suddenly it all made sense. The way I'd freeze whenever I was bullied, willing myself to be somewhere else, somehow present but removed from the situation at the same time. The fact that I was never able to picture my childhood bedroom. The passivity that occasionally gave way to a rage so violent, it scared me. One of the few times I fought back as a teenager, I nearly cracked a lad's head open, straddling him and bashing his head repeatedly against the ground. My friends had to haul me off. I remember their shocked faces and the feeling of triumph quickly giving way to one of shame and panic.

Finally, I began to understand where the urge to drink myself to oblivion or get out of my head on drugs came from. There's a poem by Yung Pueblo where the writer describes addiction as filling a void within yourself with something other than your own love. I was never simply drinking to forget. I was trying to fill a void within myself – a gaping black hole that could never be filled, no matter how many drugs I took or how much alcohol I poured into it. Now I'd looked into the void – and what I saw scared the hell out of me.

That childhood photograph was the trigger. That was the point when the nightmares began. I say 'nightmares' – I should really say 'repressed memories'. They came slowly at first – once a week, sometimes twice. For months I didn't breathe a word about them to anyone. Not even my husband, who I love dearly and who makes me feel safer and more secure than I've ever felt in my life.

Then Bowie died and my whole world seemed to tip on its axis. The bad dreams came thick and fast. Some nights I was afraid to fall asleep. There were days when I was able to carry on as normal and others when I could barely drag myself out of bed. I started having flashbacks and what I now recognise as panic attacks. One long, grey afternoon, I sat at my desk and wept for hours.

My husband was still in Rio and had no idea what I was going through. The day he arrived home we talked about everything except the one thing that was filling my thoughts. Then the following night as we were falling asleep, I turned to him and said, 'I think I was abused.'

There are some things I can't say, some people I can't name. Like Bowie, I can't give everything away. Not because I don't want to. Because I have to, for the sake of others. There are innocent people whose feelings I have to take into account – even if it means that the guilty party's crimes go unpunished. I suspect that many survivors find themselves in a similar position. It seems to come with the territory. We can't change what happened to us and we can't seek justice without hurting other people in the process. We have to make peace with it as best we can.

I wonder if one of the things Bowie couldn't give away is that he was also a survivor? In his book *David Bowie: A Life*, author Dylan Jones quotes Earl Slick, who played guitar on several Bowie albums, most famously *Station To Station*. His is the controlled feedback sound you hear at the opening of the epic title track. He also played live with Bowie many times. He was guitarist on the game-changing Serious Moonlight tour I saw when I was seventeen.

In the book, Slick claims that there was a part of Bowie few people knew, a personal problem he and the singer had in common, 'a certain thing' that had shadowed them their whole lives and which they only spoke about in private a couple of times.

What were those private conversations about, I wonder? What was the personal problem Slick and Bowie had in common, the 'certain thing' Slick won't name? During his lifetime, Bowie was extremely candid about his bisexuality and his struggles with alcohol and drug addiction. What topic could be so taboo that, even after his death, Slick is unable to 'go there'?

For a long time, I wasn't able to go there, either. For most of my life, I self-medicated – alcohol, mostly, but also recreational drugs, Valium and anything else I could lay my hands on. Anything to make the pain go away. Anything to stop me looking for the source. Whenever my mother reminded me of what a 'nervous wreck' I was as a child, I never stopped to ask why. I didn't want to know. I wasn't ready to face up to what had happened to me during those early years, so I buried it deep inside and hoped that it would go away.

Many of us know about gay shame – the internalised homophobia that can cause so much damage, leading to low self-esteem and self-destructive patterns of behaviour. It's why we invented Gay Pride. We rejected shame and replaced it with pride. But few people – gay or straight – talk about the shame of childhood abuse. It's something survivors carry with us, another kind of survivors' guilt, too shameful to even admit to another person. Why shameful? Because at some level, we blame ourselves for what happened. We can't help it. We think we brought it on ourselves. It's why so many abusers get away with it. They don't need to silence their victims. We silence ourselves.

But it doesn't go away. It has a way of making itself known. It festers and grows and comes through in our behaviour. In my case, it affected me in ways I'm still only beginning to understand. My twenties and thirties were a tumultuous time. I lost a lot of people I cared about. I made a lot of bad decisions. And like many survivors of abuse, I turned to drugs and alcohol as a means of escape. But you can't escape yourself. No amount of self-medication can do that. As soon as the inebriating, mind-altering effects wear off, you're right back where you started – just you and your thoughts, alone.

Bowie often sang about isolation. 'Space Oddity' is about a man cut adrift, floating out in space. 'Life On Mars' is about a mousey-haired girl, friendless and alone, seeking solace in the silver screen. 'Fame' is about the hollow, isolating nature of celebrity. 'Sound And Vision' is a deceptively catchy little tune about emotional withdrawal, pulling down the blinds and making the world go away. 'Rock 'n' Roll Suicide' is an anthem for alienated outsiders everywhere, complete with the assertion that we're not the only ones. As Bowie repeatedly assures us during the song's shamelessly melodramatic finale, we're not alone.

Those aren't just words, you know. Abusers make you feel alone. It's your dirty little secret, and even if you dare tell someone, nobody will believe you. This is what they tell you. This is the fear they instil in you. This is why, when a star of Bowie's magnitude tells you you're not alone, it matters. 'Rock 'n' Roll Suicide' saved me from becoming another gay teenage suicide – and the song still resonates with me all these years later, its meaning shifting and deepening over time.

One of the toughest challenges survivors of childhood abuse face is the fear of not being believed. All I'll say is that those who matter believe me – and those who don't no longer matter. The night I finally told my husband, it felt as if a huge weight had been lifted. The next day, I talked to a counsellor online and then to a therapist I know, and then to close friends and family. Telling my mum was the hardest. I knew she'd blame herself. But all I can do is assure her that she's no more guilty than I am – and yes, I do still have feelings of guilt and shame, as many of us do. I know, of course, that the shame isn't mine. It's my abuser's. But knowing this and feeling it are two very different things.

Therapy helped enormously. I grieved not only for the boy I was and the trauma he suffered but also for the young man I became, the horrors he witnessed and the friends he loved and lost. The journey from abused child to embattled AIDS activist wasn't such a long journey to make. I realise that now. Somewhere along the line, the loss of control I felt as a small boy and the multiple losses I experienced in my twenties became bound up together – hurt upon hurt, trauma upon trauma, all swallowed down and impacted. Drawing them out was part of the process.

It wasn't easy. I hadn't placed my trust in a mental health professional since my experience with Victim Support – and this felt far more daunting. Again, the thought of being seen as a victim rankled, though in this case the term was never used. But as I arrived for my first session, I recalled the previous counsellor's advice about trauma and recovery, and the flicker of recognition I'd felt at the time. Now I was finally facing the far deeper trauma I'd avoided for so long. No wonder I felt so exposed.

I don't remember much of that first session, though I do know there were tears and at some point something deeply affecting happened. I left in such a daze I took the wrong train and ended up travelling in the opposite direction. Realising my mistake, I changed trains and made the return journey, but was so lost in my thoughts I completely missed my stop. Eventually I arrived home feeling shaken and confused, curled up on the sofa and cried. I'd regressed back to that frightened child, helpless and in pain.

But over the course of the next six months I began to take back control. The therapist encouraged me to look at that childhood photo and tell the little boy that I loved him. I tried but I couldn't say the words. I was too self-conscious. With the therapist's help, I focused on bringing my abuser down to size, reminding myself what a weak man he really was. I managed to find some happy childhood memories among the years of fear and shame. I learned to let go of the rage inside me and come to terms with what happened and how it shaped who I am.

When I first sat down with my therapist, she asked me what I hoped to gain from the experience. 'To stop wanting to kill him,' I replied – and I'm pleased to say that I no longer have the urge to track him down and cause him severe physical pain. Some days I even feel sorry for him. What kind of man must he be, to do what he did? How does he live with himself?

I guess I'll never know. I did write to him, though. I told him what I'd been through, all the pain he'd caused, how he'd traumatised me as a child and how I refused to be a victim any more. I never heard back. I didn't expect to, or need to. It's enough for me to know that he received my letter – and I made sure of that by sending several copies by regular post and also recorded delivery. The rest is between him and his conscience – assuming he has one.

My therapist told me something very interesting about survivors of childhood trauma, something that rang so many bells it was like a cacophony of sound inside my head. In order to cope, we disassociate. This is a mental process by which we disconnect from our own thoughts, feelings, memories, or sense of who and where we are. It's that feeling of being there and somehow not being there at the same time – a feeling I know only too well. The mental health charity Mind has this to say about disassociation: 'If you dissociate for a long time, especially when you are young, you may develop a dissociative disorder. Instead of dissociation being something you experience for a short time it becomes a far more common experience, and is often the main way you deal with stressful experiences.'

It's estimated that one in six men have experienced sexual abuse, whether in childhood or as adults. Many experience what's known as 'dissociative amnesia' for much of their lives. Some men go to their graves never having told a single soul what happened to them. Others experience some kind of trigger or reminder of the past and seek help from specialist organisations like Survivors UK. Someone told me that, of those who do, the average age is fifty-five.

I was fifty when I made that call. Premature, yet again.

Sometimes I wish it had been earlier, but then maybe I wouldn't have been ready. The important thing is that I did it. I looked back. I'm still walking tall and I'm fine most of the time. The shame is (mostly) on the other side. I'm no hero but I'm proud to say that I'm a survivor. And I know I'm not alone.

Chapter 35:
Life's A Riot

Shortly after *The Naked Civil Servant* was shown on British television for the first time, self-styled 'stately homo' Quentin Crisp started referring to actor John Hurt as his representative on earth. Later, he claimed that Hurt had been playing victims like him ever since, telling one interviewer after another that Caligula was simply him in a sheet, while the Elephant Man was simply him with a paper bag over his head.

As I approach an age where I too might be considered a stately homo, I have a Hurt of my own. His name is Alexis Gregory and I'm proud to call him both a friend and the only actor ever to have played me onstage. The play is called *Riot Act* and it charts five decades of queer activism, from the Stonewall Riots to the present day. It's an ambitious undertaking and one that demonstrates the old maxim about how the personal is political. The story is told from the perspectives of three key witnesses. The first is Michael-Anthony Nozzi, who was at the Stonewall Inn the night the riots began. The second is radical drag queen Lavinia Co-op (aka Vin), who performed with Bloolips and was a member of the Gay Liberation Front. The third is me.

Each character is played by Alexis himself, with a range of accents and minimal costume changes – a checked shirt, a pair of stilettos, an ACT UP T-shirt. It's a one-man show in which he channels three very different men – none of whom are what you might call a professional activist. To the best of my knowledge, neither Michael, Vin nor I have ever harboured political ambitions. We just happened to be in a particular place at a certain time and did what we had to do. In our different ways, we were – and to some extent still are – outsiders.

Alexis first approached me in the spring of 2017 and asked if I'd be willing to be interviewed. Willing? I practically bit his arm off. I'd been a fan of his work for years and greatly admired his ver-batim play *Safe*, about LGBTQ+ youth at risk of homelessness. The play was developed in association with the Albert Kennedy Trust, a charity close to my heart. In 2010 I edited a short story collection called *Boys & Girls*, which included the true-life stories of young people helped by the trust. Politically speaking, I knew that Alexis and I were on the same page. Personally, I felt safe sharing my story with him. I knew he was someone I could trust.

So one night he came to dinner and interviewed me about the period of my life I'd hardly ever talked about – those dark days when friends were dying and I became an AIDS activist. He told me the interview would take roughly an hour. In fact, it took three. Once I started talking, I couldn't stop. I think it helped that I was still in therapy and was used to spilling my guts on a weekly basis. And spill them I did. Afterwards, Alexis commented that of the three interviews he conducted for the play, mine was the most overtly emotional.

I don't think it could have gone any other way. I was twenty-three when I joined ACT UP and twenty-four when I started bury-ing my friends. At fifty, I was only just beginning to process the trauma. A lot of it came out during that interview. In some ways, it felt like a therapy session. I came close to tears a number of times. Each time, Alexis asked me if I was okay to continue and each time I told him I was. The interview ended with me confirming that he could use anything I'd said and stating that I was willing for him to use my real name. Then I opened a bottle of wine and, shortly afterwards, dinner was served.

It was several months before I saw Alexis serving up a glimpse of *Riot Act*. We were at Hemel Hempstead Library as part of that year's Polari tour – myself, Alexis and authors Leon Craig, Sarah Day and VG Lee. It wasn't my story Alexis was telling that night but Michael's. A boy from small-town Pennsylvania, Michael arrived in New York the night the Stonewall Riots began. He was seventeen years old. It was the summer of 1969, a week after Judy Garland died, and the patrons of the Stonewall Inn were preparing to watch *A Star Is Born* on a makeshift screen fashioned from a bed sheet. Then the police raided the bar and the rest is history.

There are so many varying accounts of what happened that night – who was there, who urged the crowd to fight back, who threw the first brick. According to Michael, the crowd mainly consisted of hustlers, older gay men and drag queens. He recalls the police beating people with clubs, the blood on the walls and on the sidewalk. By his account, it was a drag queen who sparked the riot by whacking a cop over the head. Others have the instigator as butch lesbian Stormé DeLarverie, while some insist that it was Marsha P. Johnson – despite Marsha being on record as saying that she arrived much later, when the uprising was already in full swing.

What most people agree on is that the Stonewall Riots marked the start of Gay Liberation as we know it today. There'd been protests before, but nothing on the scale of what happened on that hot summer night in New York. Michael's personal testimony was the perfect opening to a play about the modern gay rights movement, and it went down extremely well with the audience that evening in Hemel Hempstead.

Each of the three monologues that make up *Riot Act* had its first public airing at Polari. Alexis first performed Lavinia Co-op's monologue as part of an event we held at Senate House Library in Bloomsbury. Vin's story was a little closer to home. Growing up in Hackney in the '50s and '60s, he always knew he was different. Aged nineteen, he begged his doctor for help, thinking he was suffering from some form of illness. He'd never heard of gay people. 'I hadn't a clue.' Then he discovered Gay Lib. Drag was the drug and he threw himself into it. He met Bette Bourne and became a member of Bloolips. They put on stage shows and went out in public in outrageous clothes and make-up, testing people's reactions.

Listening to Alexis channel the spirit of Lavinia, I was reminded of Quentin Crisp, who famously paraded the streets of London plastered in make-up and often paid the price. In *The Naked Civil Servant*, he describes exhibitionism as a drug. Hooked in adolescence, he was now taking doses so massive they would have killed a novice. There's so much to unpack here – not just the self-irony, which was as much a part of Crisp's armoury as the hair and make-up, but also the reminder that these personal decisions carried potentially life-threatening consequences.

Vin knows this, too. It's there in the play. He talks about the danger of being so visibly gay in public, how some spaces are never safe for people like him, how he's endured death threats and abuse all his life and is still fearful now, in his mid-sixties. Vin's testimony is a stark reminder that, for some LGBTQ+ people, liberation comes at a cost. For all the progress we've made, we're still not out of the woods yet.

In September 2017, a few days after my birthday, I saw Alexis perform my piece for the first time at The Printworks in Hastings. The audience for Polari in Hastings tends to be older. Many people are retired. Most are old enough to remember the '80s and the horrors we lived through. I was keen to see how they'd react.

It's a strange experience, hearing your own words and speech patterns coming from another man's mouth, especially when it's someone you know. In fact, it was such a strange experience that I forgot all about the audience. I was so focused on the words, I barely noticed the effect they were having. It was only afterwards, when people lined up to congratulate Alexis on his performance and thank me for my activism, that it began to sink in. This play was going to be something special. I could feel it.

In November, Polari turned ten and I invited Alexis to perform the piece again as part of our birthday celebrations at the Southbank Centre. This time, the audience was composed largely of younger men, many of whom had come to the Southbank for the weekend-long Being A Man festival and wandered into our event quite by chance. Alexis closed the first half, which was just as well as I found myself choked with emotion and could barely get the words out to thank him and announce the interval.

No sooner had we left the stage than we were approached by a group of younger guys with concerned faces and lots of questions. They were part of the generation I refer to in the play – the ones who came along after the epidemic, who didn't witness the horrors first-hand, who grew up under the shadow of Section 28 and have little sense of their own history. Their eyes were opened that night – and to a lesser extent, mine were, too. I'd often assumed that gay men of their generation weren't particularly interested in the struggles of those who came before them. Maybe that's true of some, but it wasn't true of the men I met that night. It wasn't that they weren't interested. They just didn't know how to broach the subject. Seeing Alexis perform that night gave them an opening and they took it. We talked at length, and I left the venue feeling a sense of connection I hadn't felt in a long time.

I first saw the play as a whole during a rehearsed reading at the Hospital Club in Covent Garden. I sat at a table with my cousin Elaine, who had accompanied me at many ACT UP demos, and my friend Angus Hamilton, who I first met when I worked for GALOP and who later followed in Derek Jarman's footsteps and was canonised by the Sisters of Perpetual Indulgence. Formerly a defence lawyer with a long history of defending gay and bisexual men charged with consensual sexual offences, now a judge, Angus had been recognised for his contribution to the fight against police discrimination and was henceforth known as St Angus of the Innocent Gaze. Both he and Elaine knew me during the period of my life described in the play. I couldn't have been watching in more fitting company.

Having seen each of the monologues in isolation, I assumed I was sufficiently prepared for the emotional impact the piece would have. I was wrong. As with all great theatre, the whole is far greater than the sum of the parts. The play packed a more powerful punch than I was anticipating. By the end of Michael's monologue, I could feel my throat tighten. By the end of Lavinia's sequence, tears were starting to prick my eyes. By the time I was hearing my own words, the tears were streaming down my face. I took a sip of my wine and tried to keep my emotions in check. I needn't have worried. When the performance ended and I looked around, there wasn't a dry eye in the house.

Riot Act opened at the King's Head Theatre in the summer of 2018 to glowing reviews. The *Evening Standard* described it as 'frank, warm and uninhibited. A forceful reminder of the importance of knowing your history'. *The Stage* hailed it as 'verbatim theatre at its best'. Others praised the skill with which Alexis switched between his three subjects. *Attitude* called it 'a career-defining performance' and audiences flocked to see it, despite the sweltering hot weather. Even at night, the temperature inside the King's Head was roasting. A sell-out performance at the Duchess Theatre in the West End followed on World AIDS Day. Sadly I was unable to make it as I was on tour with Polari. But friends who attended said I was certainly there in spirit.

Riot Act has gone on to enjoy great success. The play was published by Bloomsbury in 2018. In his foreword, Alexis writes that he considers the lives it celebrates 'to be vital parts of queer history spanning some of the community's landmark moments'. In the summer of 2019, the play toured to mark the fiftieth anniversary of the Stonewall Riots. In February 2020, it toured again in celebration of LGBT+ History Month. To date, *Riot Act* has been performed in Birmingham, Bolton, Bradford, Brighton, Bristol, Cheltenham, Crewe, Doncaster, Exeter, Guildford, Harrogate, Hull, Leicester, Manchester, Milford Haven, Newcastle, Oldham, and the place where I was born, York. Throughout the months of February and July 2022, a re-imagined digital version was streamed online. As I write, there are further tours and talk of a film adaptation in the pipeline.

I've attended several performances and taken part in post-show discussions. I've seen first-hand how strongly the play affects audiences. My section seems to really resonate with people, many of whom lived through the AIDS crisis or can relate to my personal experience in some way. Alexis believes it's the vulnerability on show. 'It's rare to see a man speak so openly,' he says in his foreword. 'Even today.'

I owe Alexis an enormous debt of gratitude. I don't personally know many people who've had the honour of seeing themselves portrayed onstage. My friend Susie Boyt is the only one who springs to mind. Moreover, if it weren't for Alexis asking me to participate in *Riot Act*, I probably wouldn't have sat down and finally started writing this memoir. It was something I'd been meaning to do for years but kept putting off, fearing that revisiting the past might be too painful. Sharing part of my story with him helped me to face my fears and opened the floodgates. Seeing the audience reaction to the play encouraged me to be as open and honest as possible.

It was also a reminder of the power of a good pop song. The original production of *Riot Act* incorporates gay anthems from Sylvester, Bronski Beat and more. My sequence opens with my fellow ACT UP activist Jimmy Somerville singing 'Smalltown Boy' and closes with my all-time musical hero David Bowie singing 'Heroes'. The message is clear. We're all heroes – Michael, Vin, me, and everyone in the audience who identifies with our struggles, whatever their sexuality.

Unlike Quentin Crisp, I don't consider myself a victim. Nor do I share many of the views he expressed during his lifetime. He once dismissed AIDS as a 'passing fad' and described homosexuality as 'a terrible disease' – comments that angered many in the community, and understandably so.

I think it's safe to say that Quentin wasn't a happy homosexual. But I'm happy to take a leaf out of his book and refer to Alexis Gregory as my 'representative on earth'. It's a tough job, but someone's gotta do it.

Epilogue:
Where Are We Now?

December 2021 and I'm in Heaven. In many ways, it's where my personal gay journey began – the first gay venue I ever visited, the club where I met the first man I ever slept with and, a few months later, my first proper boyfriend. I don't know how many nights I've spent underneath these railway arches, lost in music or cruising these corridors, looking for love or its nearest substitute. A lot of water has flowed under Hungerford Bridge since then. But tonight I'm back – not as a punter but as a performer.

The past two years have been a challenging time for those of us working in the live arts. Venues have closed. Some may never open again. A planned tour celebrating the tenth annual Polari First Book Prize had to be postponed. Some events moved online, where we've built up a loyal following. But it's not the same. I've missed the roar of the greasepaint, the smell of the crowd. Most of all, I've missed the sense of communion you only really feel when people are gathered together in the same physical space.

We still don't know where we are in relation to Covid – whether there'll be another variant, another wave, another lockdown. But for now restrictions have been lifted and some venues have reopened their doors. So here I am, onstage at Heaven, staring out across rows and rows of empty chairs and tables, waiting for the technicians to return from lunch so we can run through the sound and lighting cues. It's 3.30 p.m. Doors open in three hours.

Nightclubs are strange places during the day. By definition, these pleasure palaces are designed to be seen at night, when the lights are low and the magic happens. And none more so than Heaven, the gay super-club to rival all gay super-clubs. The first time I set foot inside these doors, I felt as if I'd been transported into another world. In a way, I had. It was a world of possibilities that hadn't existed until that moment. I cast my mind back to 1985 and the first time I descended that famous staircase and found my way to the dance floor. I remember how nervous I was and how alien and exciting and impossibly sexy it all seemed.

The stairs look very different today. Dazzling house lights reveal the wear and tear of all yesterday's parties. Cleaners clear away the debris left by last night's revellers, polishing floors and unblocking toilets. Little by little the atmosphere changes. Security staff and my fellow performers start to arrive. Bars are stocked and glasses polished. Preparations are made for tonight's show. Lights and sound are checked. Slowly the place springs into life.

This isn't my first time onstage in Heaven. Polari first appeared here in May 2019 and again in February 2020. Back then, it felt as if I was following in the footsteps of giants. This is the venue that once hosted performances by Cher, Divine, Grace Jones, Eartha Kitt, Madonna and so many more. But that was before Covid-19 forced the UK into lockdown. Like me, Heaven has survived two pandemics. It's changed a lot since the last time I was here. When restrictions were first lifted, the main dance floor was converted into an enormous bar area with tables and chairs, all properly socially distanced. People complained about the plastic partitions and table service, but it was a case of adapt or die. Now the layout has changed again. The partitions have gone. Later, the tables and chairs will be cleared away in preparation for the next club night.

I've changed, too. I'm eleven months sober. The decision to stop drinking was a long time coming. I drank heavily throughout the first lockdown and had the physical and mental health to show for it. I gained so much weight, my suit trousers no longer fitted. My anxiety levels were through the roof. Working on this memoir gave me plenty of time for reflection and I didn't like what I saw. I thought of all the previous times my drinking spiralled out of control, all the friendships tested and unnecessary risks taken. I remembered the night I fell down the escalator at Waterloo station, ripping the knees of my trousers and humiliating myself in the process. I thought of all the times I staggered home so drunk I could barely stand.

I listened to Bowie a lot during lockdown. In times of trouble, I always come back to Bowie. I wondered what he'd have made of it all, this man who sang so often about existential angst and self-isolation. I listened to 'Where Are We Now?' and thought about the power of memory. Released without warning in January 2013, it's a reflective song about a man revisiting his past, lost in time, walking with ghosts. I listened to 'Heroes' and an interview with producer Tony Visconti where he commented on the fact that, while the song is often played at celebratory events, it's actually a song about alcoholics. Bowie sings about drinking all the time – which was certainly true of him when 'Heroes' was first recorded. He was living next door to a gay bar in Berlin and developed a taste for the local König Pilsener beer.

It has also been true of me for most of my life. I've written about my two near-death experiences – the time I nearly drowned, the time I overdosed. I haven't written about all the times I was so drunk I could have been mugged, queer-bashed, or simply tripped and fallen over, cracked my head open and passed away on the pavement. I knew a man who died this way, yards from his own front door. What a sad way to go.

Misuse of alcohol currently accounts for over 5,000 deaths per year in the UK. That's more than the number of deaths resulting from drug abuse and AIDS-related illnesses combined. AIDS took the lives of far too many friends. Drugs very nearly killed me. Alcohol put me in more potentially deadly situations than I can remember. The fact that I can't remember half of them is worrying in itself.

So, on New Year's Eve 2020, I made myself a solemn promise. I toasted the end of one life and the beginning of another. Dry January gave way to booze-free February, and before I knew it I was six months sober, less anxious and more clear-headed than I'd felt in years. I prefer it like this. I prefer *me* like this. So I'm sticking to it. One day at a time. One month at a time. And who knows? Maybe forever and ever.

To mark my six-month anniversary, I did something I'd been meaning to do for years. On my inner forearm where I once pressed a razor blade, I now have a tattoo. It reads, 'We Can Be Heroes'. It's my first tattoo since my AIDS activist days, and both the choice of words and the process feel significant. After all, a tattoo is an open wound that gradually heals to form a permanent physical change to the body. Despite having gone through therapy, I know I still have a lot of healing to do.

Backstage at Heaven, the atmosphere is palpable. We're still socially distancing, still wearing face coverings. Mine has an image of Bowie with his finger pressed against his lips – a reminder that, in the age of Covid, careless talk can literally cost lives. I lift my mask to take a sip of water from one of the bottles provided. There's none of the

Dutch courage I've relied on for years, no Valium in my system. Tonight I'm running on pure adrenaline.

Our dressing room is enormous. It used to be known as the Star Bar, back in the days when I was a regular at Pyramid. It was here that I first mingled with Marc Almond, Boy George and all those magnificent '80s icons. Despite their own, very public battles with drugs and alcohol, Marc and George are both alive and well. But these walls contain ghosts, too. Freddie Mercury once partied here. So did Kenny Everett, Terrence Higgins and so many others lost to the big disease Prince sang about all those years ago. I remember the go-go boys who danced on podiums then disappeared, never to be seen again. I think of the casual acquaintances and one-night stands who went home to their families and never returned. I think of the song I first heard when I stepped foot inside these doors. So many men. So little time. How prophetic those words were. In the absence of an official memorial to commemorate our dead, their spirits can still be felt in places like this – those that have survived.

Tonight's event is in association with the National AIDS Trust. It's 1 December. World AIDS Day. Despite anxieties about the latest variant, it's our biggest audience since the arrival of Covid. The place is packed. There's plenty to celebrate. But the mood is solemn, too. Two days ago, it was reported that Stephen Sondheim had died. I've been thinking a lot about Vaughan, who first introduced me to Sondheim's work back in the late '80s. In honour of them both, I walk on stage to Eartha Kitt singing 'I'm Still Here' – a song of survival from *Follies*, covered by everyone from Shirley MacLaine to Barbra Streisand.

Survival is very much the theme of the evening. As I tell the audience, 'We got through all of last year – and we're here!' I open proceedings by displaying a photograph taken on World AIDS Day thirty years ago – a black-and-white image of me protesting with ACT UP on Westminster Bridge. The scene set, I read a short piece about AIDS activism, cumulative grief and survivors' guilt. I end by reciting the names of all the friends who died.

The last time Polari was in Heaven, Alexis Gregory performed a special multimedia extract of *Riot Act*, paying tribute to those tumultuous times. Also on the bill was Joelle Taylor, a fellow survivor whose performance poetry explores butch lesbian identity and the impact of physical and sexual abuse. Since then, she's been awarded the T. S. Eliot Prize for her book *C+nto and Othered Poems* – a landmark moment for her personally and for LGBTQ+ writers everywhere.

Tonight I'm joined by author Neil Bartlett, who reads from his short story collection *Address Book* and speaks movingly of all the people he lost to AIDS in the '80s and '90s. Trail-blazing historian Diana Souhami reads from her Polari Prize-winning book *No Modernism Without Lesbians*. Debut author Adam Zmith shares extracts from his book *Deep Sniff*, which tells the history of those little bottles of illicit pleasure we call poppers and which will forever be associated in my mind with my first visit to this very club. The show ends with Nigerian drag queen Son of a Tutu singing 'Something Inside So Strong' – a song about resilience in the face of adversity.

I manage to hold it together during Neil's reading and my own, but when Tutu sings, the floodgates finally open.

And now it's 2022. The worst of the pandemic appears to be over, at least in the UK. Polari has moved from the Southbank Centre to the British Library, where Polari Prizes were awarded to Joelle Taylor and Adam Zmith. We also have residencies in Hastings and Manchester and are busy touring again. We've appeared at Bradford Literature Festival and Capital Crime. I've also hosted events online, showcasing a wide variety of LGBTQ+ writers from all walks of life. Some are already the heroes of their own stories. Others have only just begun. As much as it's about me, this book is also for them and for all those whose tales were never told – the lost boys, fierce girls, friends, lovers and logical family who helped make me the man I am today. Activist. Journalist. Author. Producer. Survivor.

Since giving up in January 2021, I'm still not drinking. To be honest, I don't feel a huge sense of accomplishment. It's been far easier than I imagined. I don't feel that I'm denying myself anything. But I do feel better than I have in years, physically and mentally. I feel like the person I always should have been, had I not started numbing myself with alcohol from such an early age. I'm calmer, more focused and just as determined.

When I think of the bullied, shamed, silenced child I once was, I'm proud of the man I've become. A man who refuses to be silenced, because as ACT UP taught me, 'Silence = Death', and I still have a lot of living to do. I won't go quietly.

ACKNOWLEDGEMENTS

Writing and publishing a book is a collaborative process – even a book as deeply personal as this one.

Thanks to my agent David H. Headley for his early encouragement and boundless enthusiasm.

For their feedback and editorial suggestions, thanks to my dear friend and fellow author V.G. Lee and to editors Victoria Haslam, Sam Boyce and all at Little A. This is a far better book for your input.

For the cover design, thanks to photographer Gordon Rainsford and designer James Jones.

Special thanks to Alexis Gregory for interviewing me for his play *Riot Act* and setting the wheels in motion. 'Without you . . .' etc.

For their encouragement, love and support, I'm indebted as always to Paulo Kadow and my family, both biological and logical.

Thanks also to:
    Adèle Anderson
    Rebecca Barden
    Matt Bates
    Louise Beech

Sharmilla Beezmohun

Gerard Boynton

Susie Boyt

Marina Brasil

Elaine Burston

Angela Clarke

Paul Darling

Alma Evans

Bernardine Evaristo

Suzi Feay

Ché Feenie

Krystyna FitzGerald-Morris

Jonny Floyd

Jason Ford

William Gibbon

Chris Gribble

Antonia Hodgson

Matthew Hodson

Rachel Holmes

Jinan Hussain

Jeremy Joseph

Jacquie Lawrence

Laura Lee Davies

Lorna Lloyd

Andrew Loxton

Jo Mackie

Karen McLeod

Fiona McMorrough

Fiez Mughal

Tiffany Murray

Jacqui Niven

Sarah Sanders

Sam Taylor
Richard Thomas
Mark Wardel
Dominic Wells
Andrew Wille

Last but not least, thanks to Survivors UK, who helped me not only to survive but to thrive. I'm forever in their debt.

ABOUT THE AUTHOR

Photo © 2021 Krystyna Fitzgerald-Morris

Paul Burston is curator and host of award-winning LGBTQ+ literary salon Polari and founder of the Polari Prize book awards for LGBTQ+ writers, based at the British Library. In 2016, he featured in the British Council's Global List of '33 visionary people promoting freedom, equality and LGBT rights around the world'. A Rainbow List National Treasure and former AIDS activist with ACT UP London, he is one of the subjects of Alexis Gregory's critically acclaimed verbatim play *Riot Act*.

Paul's writing has appeared in the *Guardian*, the *Sunday Times* and many other publications. He has also written and presented documentaries for Channel 4 and is a regular contributor to TV and radio. Paul Burston is the author of six novels and five non-fiction books and the editor of two short-story collections.